CHARITY IN THE NHS: POLICY AND PRACTICE

CHARITY IN THE NHS: POLICY AND PRACTICE

Robert Meakin
Simmons & Simmons

JORDANS
1998

Published by
Jordan Publishing Limited
21 St Thomas Street
Bristol BS1 6JS

British Cataloguing-in-Publication Data

A catalogue record for this book is available from the British Library.

ISBN 0 85308 492 0

Photoset by Mendip Communications Ltd, Frome, Somerset
Printed by MPG Books Ltd, Bodmin, Cornwall

DEDICATION

This book is dedicated to my wife,
Mary Ambrose.

ACKNOWLEDGEMENTS

The publishers and the author are grateful to the following for giving their kind permission to reproduce materials set out in Appendix 2 of this book:

the Charity Law Association in respect of the model deed of trust for a charitable trust and the model memorandum and articles of association for a charitable company; and the Institute of Charity Fundraising Managers and Bates, Wells & Braithwaite in respect of the standard form of agreement between a charity and a fundraising consultant.

FOREWORD

It is entirely appropriate that, in the year that marks the 50th anniversary of the foundation of the National Health Service, a book should be published re-examining the National Health Service's charitable roots.

Robert Meakin takes a fresh look at the role of charity in the National Health Service today and provides a practical insight into the opportunities available to health service bodies, not only in terms of generating funds, but also in terms of community involvement.

As a trustee of two charities operating in the mixed health care economy, I welcome this book.

Sir Michael Richardson
President of the British
Home and Hospital for Incurables
and Trustee of the
Hospital Management Trust
June 1998

PREFACE

Growing up in a family mainly employed by the NHS, I was privy to many debates over dinner about the NHS which, on reflection, boiled down to funding and resources. It is therefore unsurprising that I should write a book like this.

I would especially like to take this opportunity to express my appreciation to Hilary Phillips. When I joined the Charity Commission as a legal officer, I was fortunate enough to be trained by Hilary in charity law practice and on how the Charity Commission operated. Hilary's creative approach to legal problems is, in my experience, unsurpassed and working with her was not only the best training that one could wish for in charity law but also included numerous seminars on the liberal arts! When I wrote this book, it seemed only natural to ask Hilary to comment, which she did and this book is a better book as a result.

More recently, I have given a number of lectures with David Poppitt, formerly the Appeals Director at the Christie Hospital in Manchester, on the interrelationship between health service bodies, charity law, tax and fund-raising. David's knowledge and enthusiasm about the health sector and fund-raising has been invaluable to me when writing this book.

Other people have helped me and should be thanked. They include Professor Robert Lee, University College of Wales, Cardiff, who is an expert on the NHS and funding and who supervised me during post-graduate studies at the University College of Wales, Cardiff, which included research into charity and the NHS; and Gary Barnett of Simmons & Simmons who commented on the VAT aspects. Thanks are also due to the library staff at Simmons & Simmons for their friendly and efficient service.

Finally, no one has helped me more with this book than my wife, Mary Ambrose, to whom this book is dedicated.

I am entirely responsible for any errors or omissions.

Robert Meakin
June 1998

CONTENTS

TABLE OF CASES

References in the right-hand column are to paragraph numbers.

TABLE OF STATUTES

References in the right-hand column are to paragraph numbers or roman page numbers.

TABLE OF STATUTORY INSTRUMENTS AND CIRCULARS

References in the right-hand column are to paragraph numbers.

INTRODUCTION

This book explores the development of the role of charity in providing health care in England and Wales from the medieval period to the late 20th century and presents opportunities for the expansion of that role over the coming decade. From being a preserve of the medieval Church, charity came under the aegis of the modern State through the creation of the National Health Service in 1948. In recent years, as the State has withdrawn from the responsibilities that it assumed in 1948, charity has rediscovered the role that it has traditionally played. A fundamental point of this book is that because it is charitable to relieve sickness regardless of whether the relief is funded privately or publicly, the role of charity will inevitably increase as State funding for health care diminishes.

With diminishing resources available, the National Health Service is increasingly looking at various options to generate further funds. The Private Finance Initiative has provided one opportunity and, in addition, there has been an intensified focus on the role that charity can play. This book examines the implications of the role of charity in the provision of health care in England and Wales. Although charity can provide a solution to the shortage of funding in the National Health Service, the use of charitable funds carries with it a range of important legal implications which are also explored. Perhaps the most important of these questions is whether it is right for the National Health Service to evolve with backing by a mixture of public, private and charitable funding in an ad hoc fashion or whether it should be centrally planned to ensure that it caters for all those with needs rather than just those with needs which command public sympathy.

Perhaps it is no coincidence that, as charity has played an increasingly important part in providing health care and welfare services, so the government has given a higher priority to increasing the efficiency and accountability of the charity sector. Concerns in the 1980s about the effectiveness of the Charity Commission's supervisory role led to the Woodfield Report in 1988.[1] Many of the report's recommendations have been adopted and are now contained in the Charities Acts 1992 and 1993.

1 *Efficiency Scrutiny of the Supervision of Charities* (HMSO, 1988) under the Chairmanship of Sir Philip Woodfield, KCB, CBE.

In particular, more resources have been directed to the Charity Commissioners' monitoring and investigatory divisions and their powers to deal with misconduct and mismanagement have been strengthened.

There has also been a tightening in the regulation of charities operating in the National Health Service. The Charity Commission has established an NHS Review Section to deal with applications for registration of the estimated 25,000 National Health Service charities.[1] Before the Charities Acts 1992 and 1993, the Charity Commissioners' practice was to register all NHS charities under the control of each Health Authority under one registration with one registered charity number. However, after 1993, in recognition of their duty to register every charity which meets the registration requirements set out in the Charities Act 1993[2] and which is neither exempt nor excepted from registration, the Commissioners reviewed their position through the NHS Charity Review Section. The only relaxation from the statutory requirements had been that a charity established for any special purpose of a registered charity or in connection with another registered charity could be treated as forming part of that charity for registration purposes as a subsidiary charity. Health Authorities and NHS Trusts are not charities and therefore cannot constitute the main charity to which other National Health Service charitable funds could be treated as subsidiary for the purpose of registration. As a result, each NHS charitable fund was liable for registration unless it could be classified as a subsidiary of another charity or was exempt or excepted from registration under the Charities Act 1993. The administrative inconvenience of organising multiple registration and accounts was the subject of strong protest. In response, Parliament has passed the Charities (Amendments) Act 1995 empowering the Charity Commissioners to treat a group of charitable trusts as one charity for the purposes of the Charities Act 1993 including registration. With more government funds being placed in the hands of charity trustees, the government naturally wants to ensure that the charity sector is efficient and properly regulated.

In the second part of the book, practical charity law issues such as charitable status, the duties and responsibilities of charity trustees, amalgamation of charitable funds, investment and commercial opportunities are covered. The book should enable health service officers to

---

1 Charity Commission Report 7, 1994.

2 See s 3 of the Charities Act 1993 for the registration requirements. In a nutshell, a charity, having permanent endowment or the use and occupation of land, or whose income from all sources does not in aggregate amount to more than £1,000 a year and is neither exempt nor excepted from registration, fails to be registered as a charity.

understand the issues facing them in respect of existing charitable funds and show them how charities can be established to the benefit of their respective health service bodies.

PART I

POLICY

Chapter 1

THE DEVELOPMENT OF CHARITY IN THE PROVISION OF HEALTH CARE IN ENGLAND AND WALES

1.1 FROM THE MIDDLE AGES TO THE EIGHTEENTH CENTURY

Charity in the late medieval period was mainly organised and funded through the medieval institutions, including the feudal system in the countryside, the merchant and craft guilds in the towns, and, in particular, the Church.[1] The Church carried out a range of charitable activities including the establishment, funding and running of what were called hospitals, which in fact catered for a wider range of needs than medical care. These hospitals provided shelter for the poor, the aged, the sick and disabled. It is interesting to note at the outset that the relief of the sick by charity was traditionally linked with assisting the poor.

The Church's charitable activities were mainly funded by wealthy individuals. Some of this funding was through pure donation but some of the funding was involuntary. Where a man of means died intestate,[2] one third of his estate was customarily applied *ad pias causas*[3] by the ecclesiastical courts, which had exclusive jurisdiction over wills, probate and intestacies until the early 15th century.

The ecclesiastical courts also developed the doctrine of cy-près[4] to save charitable gifts which could not be carried out or where the object of the gift was uncertain, which, in the case of a private legacy in a will, would mean that it would fail.[5]

---

1 See generally: *Charities, Trusts and Social Welfare* M Chesterman (Weidenfeld & Nicholson, 1979).

2 Without making a will.

3 For pious means.

4 Cy-près which literally means 'as near as' derives from the Norman French which was the language used in the courts in the Middle Ages and signifies that, if the charitable trust is altered, any new purpose must be as close to the original as possible.

5 *History of the Law of Charity 1532–1827* G Jones (Cambridge University Press, 1969) p 5.

As a result of the decline of the Church's influence in temporal matters – the dissolution of the monasteries and the strengthening of the mortmain prohibitions[1] against making gifts of land to ecclesiastical institutions – and the sociological changes in the Tudor period, the provision of charity became more secular. The rise of the merchant classes in the emerging trading towns was coupled with a change in agricultural production from mainly arable to livestock farming. This was less labour-intensive and so resulted in a demographic shift to the towns from the countryside. Many found new trades and occupations but many did not. As a result of this change wealthy merchants were more inclined to give to the unemployed poor than to the ecclesiastical institutions.

The State's response to these prevailing social conditions was to pass a number of statutes designed to deal with poverty and to encourage charitable giving.[2] In the context of these charitable trends, the importance of encouraging charitable giving to hospitals was recognised by two statutes. One validated gifts to hospitals whose name had been misspelt in the deed of transfer whilst the other conferred corporate status on hospitals to enable them to hold property donated in their own name.[3] Recognition of the importance of charitable giving generally was also reflected in the Statute of Charitable Uses 1601 which provided a framework for the supervision of charities.[4] The preamble to that statute forms the basis for the modern law of charitable status.[5] At this stage, health care was no longer the preserve of the Church but was also provided (where provision existed) by secular individualistic philanthropy which was promoted and encouraged by the State.

By the 18th century, there had been a move away from charitable acts of private individuals towards collective provision. This manifested itself in the increasing use of unincorporated associations rather than trusts to govern voluntary societies, which would then raise funds for charitable projects (including health care) by public subscription. An example of this was the increase in the establishment of voluntary hospitals in

1 This medieval legislation restricted the conveyance of land by preventing it from being devised under a will into the dead hand of perpetual corporations.

2 Poor Relief Act 39 Eliz I C3; Charitable Uses Act 39 Eliz I C6; Charitable Uses Act 43 Eliz I C4.

3 Hospitals Misnamed Act 14 Eliz I C4; Incorporation Act 39 Eliz I C5.

4 Charitable Uses Act 43 Eliz I C4.

5 See **10.2**.

London by public subscription adding to the small number of hospitals that had existed there in the 16th century.[1]

Whereas the medieval hospital had been a refuge for the poor and infirm, travellers, pilgrims and the homeless, in the 18th century it was more specifically directed towards the relief of the sick.[2] Nevertheless, the commitment remained to the treatment of the poor sick rather than the sick in general. A more radical change had come about in medical knowledge and the development of the medical profession. It began to evolve from its medieval traditions to a more scientific discipline based on research. Hospitals were very often viewed by the medical profession as places of teaching and research.[3]

A prominent feature of 19th century health care was the development in the relief of the poor sick by charitable means through the dispensary movement. The dispensary movement provided free medical advice and treatment to the poor. Dispensary doctors would also make house calls to patients who were unable to attend the dispensary through sickness.[4] Through treating patients in the community, doctors learned more about poverty and poor hygiene as a cause of disease.[5]

1.2 VICTORIAN CHARITY AND HEALTH CARE

In the 19th century, greater focus was placed upon the morality of the recipient. The Poor Law Amendment Act 1834 was based on the premise that relief under the Poor Law should always be less desirable from the recipient's point of view than obtaining waged employment.[6] State policy was also reflected in private philanthropy in the form of the Charity Organisation Society.[7] This society, headed by leading middle-class citizens, sought to direct charitable relief towards the deserving poor (those who were poor because of misfortune rather than choice). Emphasis was placed on self-help as opposed to reliance. The Charity Organisation Society devoted much time to a perceived abuse of hospital outpatient departments by those who could afford to pay for treatment

1 *Charities, Trusts, and Social Welfare* M Chesterman (Weidenfeld & Nicholson, 1979) p 24. It is estimated that approximately two-thirds of all income for voluntary hospitals came from public subscription: see *English Philanthropy 1660–1960* D Owen (Oxford University Press, 1965) p 48.
2 *Ibid* M Chesterman, p 37.
3 *Ibid* p 40.
4 *Ibid* p 121.
5 *Ibid* p 121.
6 *Ibid* p 42.
7 *Ibid* p 44.

and improving poor hospital administration.[1] Despite this, on the whole, health care was considered morally neutral and 19th century philanthropists contributed greatly to the establishment and maintenance of the voluntary hospitals, homes for the disabled and medical research.

One of the main methods of fund-raising was the subscriber's letter which would admit the holder to the charity wards of the hospital. A subscriber's letter was issued to those who donated sufficient funds to the hospital and, in turn, the subscriber would usually pass on his letters to his servants. Without a subscriber's letter, it was extremely difficult to gain admission to a voluntary hospital although emergency cases were generally admitted at the discretion of the governors. This system could cause great hardship.[2]

The Metropolitan Poor Act 1867 made provision for Poor Law infirmaries which were independent from the workhouses,[3] and sick paupers, fever cases, the mentally ill and patients with venereal disease and other chronic disorders increasingly found themselves accommodated in these Poor Law institutions.[4] F K Prochaska[5] has made the point that the voluntary hospitals accelerated this process because they traditionally turned away this type of patient. Infectious cases and aged paupers made uneconomical use of beds and were of little interest to researchers in medical schools. Acute cases gave a better return in terms of cure and hospital fund-raisers knew that a quick recovery would impress subscribers as a visible sign of their generosity.[6]

1.3 THE BEGINNINGS OF STATE FUNDING

A major development in the funding of health care took place in 1913 with the enactment of the National Insurance Act which made provision for a compulsory contributions health scheme which offered care from a 'panel doctor' for about 12 million workers. The intention of the Act was to relieve poverty caused by illness.

---

1 *English Philanthropy 1660–1960* D Owen (Oxford University Press, 1965) p 230.

2 *An Illustrated History of the Royal Free Hospital* L A Amidon (The Special Trustees of the Royal Free Hospital, 1996).

3 The Poor Law Amendment Act 1868 authorised provincial authorities to establish separate infirmaries.

4 See generally *Philanthropy and the Hospitals of London; The Kings Fund 1897–1990* F K Prochaska (Clarendon Press, 1992).

5 *Ibid* p 5.

6 *Ibid* p 5.

The First World War brought with it increasing State involvement in health care. During the War, the War Office made grants to voluntary hospitals and, in 1915, it offered per capita grants to hospitals for receiving war pensioners. Even with this assistance, the demands created by the war found the voluntary hospitals coming under financial strain. The situation was serious enough for the government to appoint a special committee to look at their future – the Cave Committee.[1] The Committee recommended a temporary injection of funding rather than permanent State intervention. This proved a short-term solution to what was to become a long-term funding problem.

In the 1930s, the State moved towards acceptance of responsibility for health care. The Local Government Act 1929, by implication, imposed responsibility on local authorities for meeting the health needs of their districts either by establishing institutions or by arrangements with voluntary hospitals.[2] The aim of this legislation was to dismantle the administrative structure of the old poor law system and to bring poor law infirmaries and fever hospitals into line with municipal provision under the control of elected local authorities.[3] The effect of this was an expansion of the public sector, so that by the 1940s fewer than one-third of hospital beds in England were under voluntary management.[4] By the start of the Second World War, voluntary hospitals were on the verge of bankruptcy.[5]

1.4 THE ARRIVAL OF THE NHS

The post-war Labour government pursued a policy of passing legislation which would set a social minimum below which citizens would not be allowed to fall. The Beveridge Report paved the way for many pieces of social legislation designed to achieve this aim and included the National Health Service Act 1946. The National Health Service was designed to provide universal health care in contrast to the charitable notion of treating only the poor sick.

At this point, one can see that charity has traditionally played a major role in providing for the health care of the poor sick. Furthermore, it is only in recent times that the State has sought to take over the role of providing a

1 Voluntary Hospitals (Cave) Committee (Cmd 1335) 1921.
2 *English Philanthropy 1660–1960* D Owen (Oxford University Press, 1965) p 529.
3 *Philanthropy and the Hospitals of London* F K Prochaska (Clarendon Press, 1992).
4 *Ibid* D Owen, p 529.
5 *Ibid* p 529.

comprehensive health service for everyone. In recent years, charity in the health sector has been rediscovered and is starting to influence profoundly the provision of health for the nation. In 1948, when the National Health Service came into being, it was true to say that charity was the junior partner to the public sector. Today, this is no longer the case.

Although the role of charity was becoming increasingly important towards the end of the 1980s, it is following the introduction of the internal market of purchasers and providers by the National Health Service and Community Care Act 1990 that charity has come to play a crucial part. At this stage, an examination of the uses to which charity was put following the introduction of the National Health Service is required to show how the role it could play in providing health care for the nation was rediscovered. First, some explanation of the structure of the National Health Service and its development is needed.

Chapter 2

THE STRUCTURE OF THE NATIONAL HEALTH SERVICE

2.1 THE LEGAL FRAMEWORK

The National Health Service was established on 5 April 1948 under the provisions of the National Health Service Act 1946[1] which nationalised most voluntary hospitals and their endowments. Previously, they had been regarded as charitable. The National Health Service was designed to take over the administration and, to a large extent, the funding of the provision of national health care from individual local fund-raising initiatives by voluntary groups. The original idea was to introduce a co-ordinated system of voluntary and municipal hospitals based on local government. In the event, central government is ultimately responsible for the National Health Service. Today, with the purchaser/provider split and the introduction of self-governing NHS Trusts, there has been an attempt to allow the National Health Service to become responsive to local needs and this book argues that charity has a part to play in this development. However, a number of difficulties remain such as the distinction between health care and social care[2] and planning problems which are becoming more of an issue with the evolution of the mixed

---

1 Section 1(1) of the National Health Service Act 1946. The National Health Service was initially administered by Regional Hospital Boards. Individual hospitals or groups of hospitals were managed by hospital governors. Some health functions were carried out by local authorities designated as Local Health Authorities. Later on, the Minister of Health acquired the power to designate a hospital, or group of hospitals, providing facilities for university students, as a university hospital. In such cases, the Hospital Management Committee became a University Hospital Management Committee (s 5 of the Health Services and Public Health Act 1968). On 1 April 1974, Regional Hospital Boards, Hospital Management Committees, University Hospital Management Committees, Boards of Governors and Local Health Authorities were abolished or discontinued (except for twelve preserved Boards of Governors) and replaced by Regional Health Authorities, and Area Health Authorities (Training). Some regional boundary changes were involved and, in general, Regional Health Authorities and Area Health Authorities (Training) were responsible for larger areas than the organisations they replaced (National Health Service Reorganisation Act 1973).

2 See Chapter 8.

health economy in which charity is increasingly playing an important role.[1]

The legal framework for the provision of health services today is contained in the National Health Service Act 1977 as amended,[2] most importantly, by the National Health Service and Community Care Act 1990 which implemented the recommendations of the White Paper 'Working for Patients'.[3]

According to the 1977 Act, the Secretary of State for Health is under a duty to:

> 'continue the promotion in England and Wales of a comprehensive health service designed to secure improvement:
>
> (a) in the physical and mental health of the people of those countries, and;
> (b) in the prevention, diagnosis and treatment of illness, and
>
> for that purpose to provide or secure the effective provision of services'[4]

The National Health Service Act 1977[5] goes on to place a duty on the Secretary of State to provide the following services:

(a) hospital accommodation;
(b) other accommodation for the purpose of any service provided under the National Health Service Act 1977;
(c) medical, dental, nursing and ambulance services;
(d) such other facilities for the care of expectant mothers and young children as he considers are appropriate as part of the Health Service;
(e) such other facilities for the prevention of illness, the care of persons suffering from illness and the after-care of persons who have suffered from illness as the Secretary of State considers are appropriate as part of the health service; and
(f) such other services as are required for the diagnosis and treatment of illness.

1 See Chapter 4.
2 The National Health Service Act 1977 was a consolidating measure repealing and replacing the various health service Acts which followed the National Health Service Act 1946. They were the National Health Service Acts 1952, 1961 and the major part of the National Health Service (Amendment) Act 1949 and the National Health Service Reorganisation Act 1973.
3 Department of Health, 'Working for Patients' (Cm 555) 1989.
4 National Health Service Act 1977, s 1(1).
5 *Ibid* s 3. In addition, the Secretary of State is required to make provision for the medical and dental inspection of school children and to provide a family planning service (s 5(1)).

The services are to be provided free of charge except where the making and recovery of charges is expressly provided for by or under any enactment.[1]

There are two points to note. First, although the legislation talks about the Secretary of State having a duty to promote the establishment of a comprehensive health service, this duty has consistently been interpreted by the courts in relation to the resources at his disposal. This will be discussed at greater length further on in this book.[2] Second, all the services listed by the National Health Service Act 1977 could be classed as the relief of the sick and therefore charitable in law so long as they are organised on a non-profit making basis. That is not to say that the provision of such services would need to be free of charge in order to be charitable. The duty of the Secretary of State to provide such services can be fulfilled in part by sub-contracting to charities, and, if sufficient resources are not available from the State, the community can be encouraged to establish charities to finance such services through fund-raising.

2.2 LOCAL ADMINISTRATION

In order to carry out these duties the Secretary of State was required by the National Health Service Act 1977 to establish Regional Health Authorities, District Health Authorities, Family Health Service Authorities (District Health Authorities and Family Health Service Authorities have since 1 April 1996 been replaced by new Health Authorities which have taken over all their functions) and Special Health Authorities. The Secretary of State is empowered to direct a Regional Health Authority (in Wales a Health Authority, previously a District Health Authority) or a Special Health Authority to exercise his functions on his behalf and they must comply with such directions.[3] A Regional Health Authority may in turn direct any Health Authority within its region to exercise any of those functions.[4] The Secretary of State may also direct a Regional Health Authority to secure that specified functions are or are not to be carried out by a Health Authority.[5]

Under the National Health Service Act 1977 the principal function of the District Health Authorities (now Health Authorities) was to provide and

1 National Health Service Act 1977, s 1(2).
2 See Chapter 7.
3 National Health Service Act 1977, s 13(1).
4 *Ibid* s 14(1).
5 *Ibid* s 14(2).

manage local hospital services. The policy behind the National Health Service and Community Care Act 1990 was to create an internal market in health care by introducing a 'purchaser/provider split'. Under this arrangement, Health Authorities and general practitioners (GPs) who have fund-holder status became purchasers of hospital services for their patients. Hospitals, the 'provider units', became self-governing Trusts, selling their services to the purchasers, competing with each other and with private sector providers.

Although the most recent White Paper talks about ending competition and replacing it with a duty placed on health service bodies to co-operate with each other in the provision of the National Health Service, in fact it is fairer to say that the internal market will be retained. The idea is that GP fundholders will be replaced by Primary Care Groups which will be run by a variety of health care professionals such as GPs, health visitors, district nurses, school nurses and pharmacists, whose responsibility will be, inter alia, to promote the health of the local community, develop primary care and to commission health services.[1]

The 1990 Act empowers the Secretary of State by statutory instrument to establish NHS Trusts to assume responsibility for the ownership and management of hospitals or other establishments or facilities which were previously managed or provided by Regional, District or Special Health Authorities or to provide and manage other hospitals and facilities.[2] The Secretary of State has established NHS Trusts for the provision of a wide variety of services including hospital, ambulance, mental health and community care services.

An NHS Trust is a self-governing corporate entity, managed by an independent board of directors (known as trustees) accountable directly to the Secretary of State and capable of owning assets and running their own business as a 'provider unit' from which a purchasing authority buys services supplied by such hospitals, community health services, ambulance services and other provider bodies. NHS Trusts are under a duty to break even, taking one year with another, and to achieve such objectives as are set by the Secretary of State.[3] The Secretary of State may dissolve an NHS Trust by order made by statutory instrument, subject to a requirement that the relevant bodies are previously consulted and that staff interests are taken into account.[4]

---

1 *The new NHS. Modern. Dependable* (The Stationery Office, 1997).

2 National Health Service and Community Care Act 1990, s 5(1) and Sch 2, para 1(2).

3 *Ibid* s 10.

4 *Ibid* Sch 2, para 30; National Health Service Trust (Consultation on Dissolution) Regulations 1991, SI 1991/1347, as amended by SI 1992/2905.

The 'internal market' in health care creates the opportunity for different health service bodies to sell goods or services to, and purchase goods and services from, one another, and to purchase them from the private sector and charities. An NHS contract is an arrangement under which one health service body – 'the acquirer' or the 'purchaser' – arranges for another health service body – 'the provider' – to 'sell' it the goods and services[1] which it reasonably requires to fulfill its functions.[2] The term 'health service body' includes Health Authorities, NHS Trusts, general medical practitioners with fund-holding practices recognised by the Regional Health Authority,[3] the Dental Practice Board, the Public Health Laboratory Service Board and the Secretary of State.

There is a remarkable similarity between NHS Trusts and large service-providing national charities[4] in receipt of public funding. NHS Trusts are run by independent boards of trustees responsible for their own finances and accountable to the Secretary of State. Large service providing national charities, such as Scope, are also run by independent boards of trustees responsible for their own budgets and answerable to the Charity Commission. Both NHS Trusts and charities are in receipt of public funds. Large national charities providing services have traditionally raised funds from the general public to make up the additional resources needed to carry out their objects at the level desired but, in recent years, NHS Trusts have increasingly run public charitable appeals sometimes on a national basis. NHS Trusts have carried on this trend and have started to see the funds generated by public charitable appeals as essential to their viability.

2.3 THE PRIVATE FINANCE INITIATIVE

It is likely that the need for charitable funds will become greater with the development of the Private Finance Initiative ('PFI') in the National Health Service. In many ways, the developing role of the PFI has run along parallel lines to the role charity has played in the National Health Service. Initially, private finance was encouraged in non-essential areas just as charity initially provided for non-essential amenities when the National Health Service was created. These non-core areas included 'income generation' activities which involved hospitals using their spare capacity to make some money from projects such as car parks, advertising

---

1 National Health Service and Community Care Act 1990, s 26(3). 'Goods' includes accommodation and 'services' includes services of any description.

2 *Ibid* s 4(1).

3 *Ibid* ss 14 to 17 which make provision in relation to fund-holding practices.

4 *The Gift of Health* M Lattimer (Directory of Social Change, 1996) p 70.

or leasing shop space. However, there is no reason why the PFI should not eventually expand to what most people regard as core services. Indeed, charitable funds now not only provide for non-essential amenities but also cover medical services and vital equipment. Under the most radical PFI proposals a consortium of private firms would finance, build and manage a hospital in return for a long lease committing the National Health Service to buying its services.

The spirit of the age, partnership funding, has encouraged initiatives such as the PFI and charitable fund-raising. The idea behind partnership funding is that the government will match the contribution made by the private sector or the charitable sector (or both) in financing projects for the benefit of the public. Health is but one area that has come under the influence of this trend and its full effect can be gauged by looking across the board from environmental projects to arts funding.

In this climate and with the development of the PFI, charity has a major role to play in the provision of health care for the nation. As the forerunner of partnership funding and the PFI, it is not an overstatement to claim that the development of its role in the National Health Service from providing non-essential amenities to providing core medical services has helped shape the future of health care in England and Wales.

Chapter 3

THE ROLE OF CHARITY IN THE MIXED HEALTH CARE ECONOMY

3.1 ST BARTHOLOMEW'S HOSPITAL

The combined effect of the creation of the 'internal market' in the National Health Service, the climate of partnership public funding, the evolution of the PFI, the growth of charitable funding and the boom in private health care, both within the National Health Service and in the private and charity sectors, has led to mixed-economy health care. The most obvious recent example of this is the story behind the proposal to save St Bartholomew's Hospital in London (which demonstrates in particular the potential importance of charity within that mixed economy).[1] St Bartholomew's Hospital was founded in 1123 as a hospital for the poor sick, an almshouse and a shelter for the homeless and pilgrims. Faced with closure, a proposal was put forward to create a new charity 'The Royal Hospital of St Bartholomew Charitable Foundation'. It was proposed that its trustees would be City businessmen with fund-raising ability. The working capital was to come from charitable donations, mainly from City institutions. It was contemplated that patients would have their bills paid by either the National Health Service, their employers, insurance policies or out of their own pockets. Although this proposal was not implemented, because the future of St Bartholomew's has been secured following a further review,[2] the model proposed for St Bartholomew's offers a possible format for the future of health care nationally. Rather than health service bodies setting up charities to raise funds to cover shortfalls in funding, health service bodies could instead seek to become charities themselves and charge the State the cost of providing health care for those patients who are not covered by insurance or other arrangements. Charities have traditionally been able to charge for their services so long as those services are available to the general public so this in itself would not be a novel concept.

1 (1996) *The Independent*, 27 May.
2 *Health Services in London – A Strategic Review* (The Stationery Office, 1998).

3.2 GREAT ORMOND STREET

In fact the model offered by the St Bartholomew proposals is not new. The Great Ormond Street Hospital Appeal prevented its closure after raising £54 million and securing public funding from the Department of Health for its future viability. Today this hospital is funded by a combination of charitable and public funding. Similarly, Tadworth Court Children's Hospital (now known as the Children's Trust, Tadworth), which provides health care for children with profound disabilities or long term terminal illness, was threatened with closure in 1982. Local people and staff launched a charitable appeal which was backed by a consortium of charities including Mencap, the Cystic Fibrosis Research Trust and the Spastics Society (now known as Scope). The consortium was invited to form a charitable trust to take over the management of the hospital thereby taking it out of the National Health Service. On 1 April 1984, Tadworth Court left the National Health Service. It relies on charitable support and a major government grant-in-aid to cover fees paid under contract for services delivered. Lattimer[1] observes that although the stories of the Children's Trust, Tadworth and Great Ormond Street Hospital provide examples of how successful charity can be in providing for health care needs, the question remains as to whether their success can be repeated nationally. Both the Children's Trust, Tadworth and Great Ormond Street Hospital are situated in affluent parts of London. Would other hospital appeals be so successful in poorer parts of England and Wales?

3.3 HEALTH CARE CHARITIES – THE WAY FORWARD?

This concern is part of a wider issue. It can be argued that the charitable sector as a whole lacks direction and as a result some needs are left unmet whilst others are over-met. Some areas of charity lack popular support or public funding, whereas others have several charities catering for the same need. Should there be one cancer charity providing for all types of cancer or various charities raising funds for particular types of cancer? The charity sector will continue to lack direction and planning so long as the Charity Commissioners in practice continue to decide most issues of

1 *The Gift of Health*, M Lattimer (Directory of Social Change, 1996) p 47.

charitable status.[1] This is because the Charity Commissioners respond to applications made to them concerning individual institutions which may or may not be charitable according to law, rather than looking at what should be charitable in broad terms and then encouraging institutions to apply for charitable status. This means that the charity sector is influenced by the Charity Commissioners, but not led by them. Chris Ham[2] has suggested that the way forward is to establish an agency to support the development of the charity sector and provide access to public funds. He suggested that National Lottery funds should be set aside for investment in health care. This idea was taken up by Tony Blair in the 1997 general election campaign. To develop this idea further by looking at the health sector the agency could take a strategic decision about what is charitable for the relief of the sick on an across-the-board basis (ie from acupuncture to Zen-based relaxation techniques) and therefore which forms of health care should be subsidised by the general public through tax reliefs. In addition, the agency could take a national view of resource allocation and allocate and make available funds when and where they were most needed. In this way the charity health sector could be strategically planned on an equitable basis. By holding the purse-strings, the agency would have the power to lead the charity sector, rather than merely allowing it to develop in an ad hoc fashion. An agency of this nature would also be in a position to plan health care and the prevention of sickness rather than simply funding a sickness service.[3] The agency could, perhaps, implement a funding regime which gave 100 per cent funding to high priority areas and then offer partnership funding to charities on a sliding scale according to the importance placed on various treatments. Before doing so, a decision would need to be made on the definition of ill health and what the National Health Service should provide for. For example, should conditions such as dwarfism be considered as illnesses? Is infertility an illness? These issues are explored further in **7.1**.

---

1 The Charity Commissioners decide most cases of charitable status in England and Wales under their power to register charities under the Charities Act 1993. They exercise this jurisdiction concurrently with the High Court, but the High Court rarely decides cases of charitable status simply because the Charity Commissioners do not charge a fee for registering charities whereas the expense of applying to the High Court for a declaration that an organisation is charitable is in most cases prohibitive.

2 *Public, Private or Community – What Next for the NHS?* C Ham (Demos, 1996) p 46.

3 The Royal Commission on the National Health Service considered the view that the National Health Service was a sickness service rather than a health service and concluded (although it had reservations) that more should be invested in preventative medicine (Royal Commission on the National Health Service (Cmnd 7615) 1979) para 4.23.

Chapter 4

CHARITABLE FUNDS IN THE NHS PRE- AND POST-1948

4.1 INTRODUCTION

Although charitable appeals for the National Health Service have mushroomed in recent years, it is important not to overlook pre-existing charities which have been funding certain areas since their creation. A good place to start looking at the role that charity has played over the years is to see what happened to the property held on charitable trust when the National Health Service was created. This property, insofar as it related to hospitals, was split into two categories: functional property and endowment property.[1]

4.2 FUNCTIONAL PROPERTY

Functional property was defined by s 6 of the National Health Service Act 1946 as: 'premises of a voluntary hospital and ... equipment, furniture, or other moveable property used in or in connection with such premises ... solely for the purposes of that hospital'. This meant that, on 5 April 1948, when the 1946 Act came into force, the site, premises, equipment, furniture and other moveable assets held in connection with voluntary hospitals were transferred to, and vested in, the Minister of Health and freed from existing trusts.[2] Power was given to the Minister to use this property for any of his functions but he was required, so far as practicable, to see that the original charitable objects for which the

---

1 For trust property not held in connection with hospitals, see the National Health Service (Amendment of Trust Instruments) Order 1974, SI 1974/63 (amended by SI 1982/75). This provided for the hospital authorities and offices connected with them and referred to in various trust instruments to be abolished and replaced by Health Authorities but did not alter any trusts.

2 National Health Service Act 1946, s 6 stated that those properties should be transferred to and vested in the health authorities specified by the Secretary of State.

National Health Service Act 1946

Distribution of Charitable Property

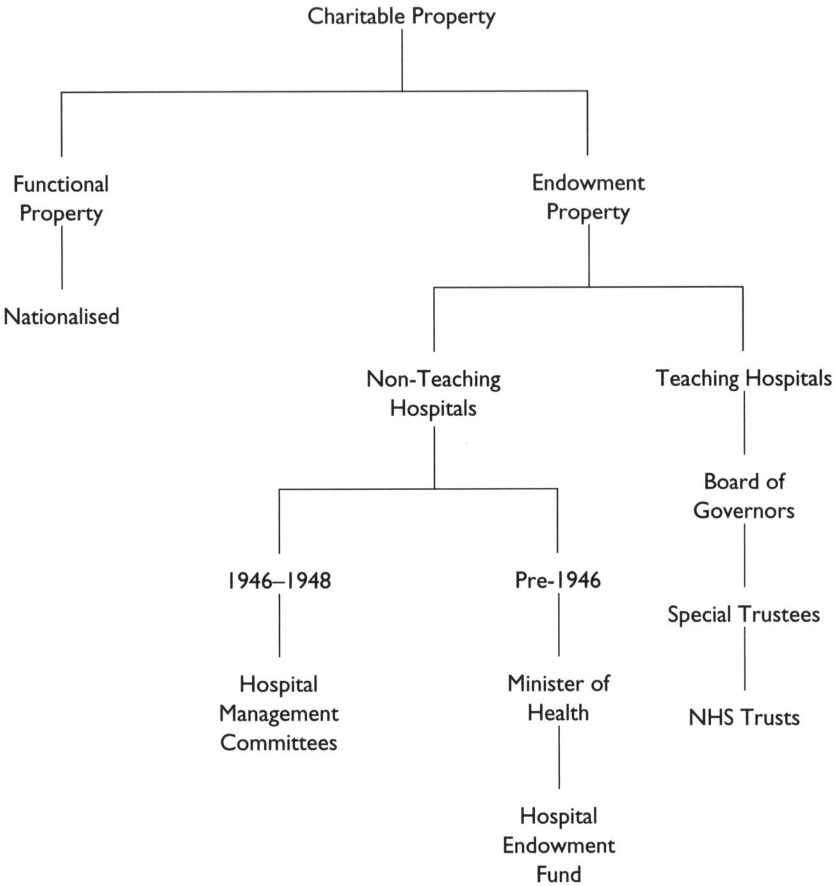

property was used were not prejudiced.[1] In effect, property which had been held on charitable trusts prior to 1946, if it fell within the definition of functional property, was nationalised and became the property of the State.

1 Where any voluntary hospital was transferred by virtue of the 1946 Act and the character and associations of that hospital were such as to link it with a particular religious denomination then regard was to be had in the general administration of the hospital to the preservation of that character and those associations: see s 3(2) of the National Health Service Act 1977.

4.3 ENDOWMENT PROPERTY

Endowment property is defined by s 7(10) of the National Health Service Act 1946 as 'property held solely for the purposes of [a particular hospital] such as land, other than hospital premises, shares, stocks and bonds, and money'. Effectively, charitable property coming within this definition was, after 5 April 1948, treated in the following ways.[1]

4.3.1 Teaching hospital endowments

The endowments of those voluntary hospitals which had been designated by the Minister of Health as teaching hospitals were transferred free of charitable trusts on 5 April 1948 (the date the National Health Service Act 1946 was brought into force and the starting date for the National Health Service) to Boards of Governors to be held by them on trust for hospital services or research. In 1973,[2] provision was made for the Secretary of State to appoint Special Trustees for the purpose of holding the property of the abolished Boards of Governors where this was the wish of those Boards. The National Health Service and Community Care Act 1990 makes provision for the Secretary of State, after consultation, to transfer by order property held by Special Trustees to the trustees of NHS Trusts, which now govern the teaching hospitals.[3]

4.3.2 Non-teaching hospital endowments

Endowments given to non-teaching hospitals after the passing of the National Health Service Act 1946 and before 5 July 1948 were transferred on the latter date to the Hospital Management Committees managing those hospitals. All other endowments (ie those endowments pre-dating 1946) of non-teaching hospitals were transferred on 5 July 1948 to the Minister of Health and, after discharging liabilities, were placed in a central Hospital Endowment Fund.[4] Although not free from doubt, it is generally assumed that the Hospital Endowment Fund was itself charitable. The income from this Fund was distributed at regular intervals to the Regional Hospital Boards and the Hospital Management Committees in accordance with regulations.

---

1 National Health Service Act 1946, s 7(7) imposed an obligation on the Minister in relation to the Hospital Endowments Fund to secure so far as reasonably practicable that the objects and other conditions were not prejudiced.

2 National Health Service Reorganisation Act 1973, s 29(1).

3 National Health Service and Community Care Act 1990, s 11(6)(a) and (b).

4 National Health Service Act 1946, s 7(4).

4.4 THE FUTURE OF ENDOWMENT PROPERTY HELD ON TRUST

All endowments transferred to Boards of Governors (teaching hospitals), Hospital Management Committees or the Minister of Health (non-teaching hospitals)[1] were transferred subject to a condition imposed on the Boards of Governors and the Hospital Management Committees to secure, so far as reasonably practicable, that the previous objects of the endowments were not prejudiced by the transfer (including any particular conditions intended to preserve the memory of any person or class of persons).[2] The relevant provision is now contained in the National Health Service Act 1977[3] which is widened to enable all endowments, except those held by Special Trustees (teaching hospitals) to be held on trust for such purposes relating to hospital services (including research) or to any other part of the health service associated with any hospital, as the person holding the property thinks fit. Special Trustees continued to be restricted to applying funds in their hospitals alone. The National Health Service Reorganisation Act 1973 required the Secretary of State to wind up the Hospital Endowment Fund and distribute its assets to health service bodies by order.[4] To summarise what is a complex state of affairs, because the teaching hospitals have been so successful at lobbying they have managed to retain their endowment funds whereas the non-teaching hospitals had their funds pooled in the Hospital Endowment Fund. This Fund was eventually nationalised.[5]

4.4.1 Charitable Trusts acquired after the National Health Service Act 1946

The National Health Service Act 1946 did not come into force until an appointed day in 1948.

4.4.2 Charitable Trusts acquired before the appointed day

Trustees holding charitable property, whether endowment or functional, under the trusts of which they were authorised or required to apply the capital for the purposes of a specified hospital within the National Health

1 National Health Service Act 1977, s 93.

2 This particular provision explains why many hospitals have wards named after benefactors or display plaques in memory of donors.

3 National Health Service Act 1977, s 93(4).

4 National Health Service Act 1946, s 60.

5 National Health Service Reorganisation Act 1973, s 23 and the National Health Service (Hospital Endowment Fund – Distribution of Assets) Order 1974, SI 1974/1915.

Service, were authorised or required to make payments to the appropriate hospital authority.[1] Any sums received by a hospital authority were, so far as practicable, to be applied for the purposes specified in the original charitable trust instrument. Insofar as it could not, then the authority would need to apply to the Charity Commissioners for a scheme so that the charitable purposes could be widened.[2]

4.4.3 Charitable Trusts acquired after the appointed day

All hospital authorities were appointed by the National Health Service Act 1946 to accept, hold and administer property held upon trusts for purposes relating to hospital services or to the functions of the Boards of Governors or Hospital Management Committees with respect to research.[3] Within these broad purposes, the property was to be held subject to any particular directions of the donors, who often specified that their gift should be used for a particular hospital, or a particular purpose. These gifts have been subject to interpretation by the court and the Charity Commissioners. For example, the endowment of a hospital bed is a well-established form of charitable giving. Whether the gift is held as a capital endowment for the purchase of a bed or whether the income is to be applied for its maintenance or, even, whether it should be applied for the maintenance of the hospital as a whole, is a matter of construction.[4] Of course, it might be possible to argue that a gift apparently for a particular hospital was in fact intended for much broader application. For example, a gift to research a cure for cancer made payable to a particular hospital might be interpreted as a gift for that particular purpose, irrespective of where it is fulfilled. The issue will depend on the exact terms of the gift. Before the Charities Acts 1992 and 1993, most health

---

1 National Health Service Reorganisation Act, s 23 and the National Health Service (Hospital Endowment Fund – Distribution of Assets) Order 1974, SI 1974/1915.

2 The National Health Service Act 1946 was repealed by s 57 and Sch 5 to the National Health Service Reorganisation Act 1973, which replaced it with s 22, making the same sort of provision without any reference to dates and thus applying to post-1946 trusts. This was re-enacted in National Health Service Act 1977, s 91. Normally the trustees of the charity from whence the funds came would be the persons who would make the application for a scheme, but it is not inconceivable that circumstances might arise in which the funds, having been properly transferred to the authority, could not possibly be applied for the stated purposes of the trusts and would therefore need to be schemed. Certainly, the Charity Commissioners have been known to make schemes in respect of the funds originally received under National Health Service Act 1946, s 60 to widen investment powers.

3 National Health Service Act 1946, s 59; now see National Health Service Act 1977, s 90.

4 See *Re Ginger* [1951] 1 Ch 458; *AG v Belgrave Hospital* [1910] 1 Ch 73 and *Re Adams* [1968] Ch 80.

service bodies did not keep detailed records of the terms of all gifts and legacies, many of which were of little value and on informally expressed trusts.[1]

Whereas the National Health Service Act 1946 empowered all hospital authorities to accept, hold and administer property relating to only hospital services and research,[2] the National Health Reorganisation Act 1973 enabled Health Authorities to accept and administer future endowments for any purpose relating to the health service.[3] A similar power was given to the special trustees of teaching hospitals but only relating to the hospitals for which they were appointed. The 1973 Act enabled trustees who had been given a power or a duty under a trust instrument to apply property for the purposes of a hospital vested in the Secretary of State to, instead, make payments to the appropriate Health Authority or, in the case of a teaching hospital, to the Special Trustees.[4]

4.4.4 Trusteeship of the Charitable Funds

As the National Health Service was reorganised, so provision was made for charitable funds held on trust to be transferred to successor health service bodies.[5]

---

1 Some health service bodies kept a record of: (a) general purpose funds with permanent endowment; (b) general purpose funds which were expendable; or (c) special purpose funds with a note of the purpose and whether income or capital was expendable in each case.

2 National Health Service Act 1946, s 59.

3 National Health Service Reorganisation Act 1973, s 21. See now National Health Service Act 1977, s 90.

4 National Health Service Reorganisation Act 1973, s 22. See now National Health Service Act 1977, s 91.

5 Under National Health Service Reorganisation Act 1973, s 24 all the charitable trust property held by the former hospital authorities immediately before 1 April 1974 was transferred to the newly created health authorities as follows:

(a) trust property held by Regional Health Boards was transferred to Area Health Authorities;

(b) trust property held by the Hospital Management Committees was transferred to Area Health Authorities;

(c) trust property held by Boards of Governors not preserved by order under s 15 of the National Health Reorganisation Act 1973, and that of University Hospital Management Committees was transferred to special trustees appointed by the Secretary of State except in those few cases where the hospital authorities opted under the 1973 Act to leave their trust property transferred instead to the Area Health Authority responsible for administering the hospitals concerned. The Boards of Governors of the 12 London post-graduate teaching hospitals were preserved (see National Health Service (Preservation of Boards of Governors) Order 1974, SI 1974/28) and continued to hold and administer their trust property;

4.5 CONCLUSION

It has been shown that, following the introduction of the National Health Service, charity continued to play a part in funding the health service. Significantly, the endowments of the teaching hospitals were preserved following the introduction of the National Health Service. These endowments are now so substantial that, in any proposed reform involving the teaching hospitals, their presence creates difficult moral and legal questions for the legislators and therefore continues to influence health policy.

(d) trust property held by the Local Health Authorities was transferred to Area Health Authorities. See National Health Service (Transfer of Local Health Authority Trust Property) Order 1974, SI 1974/246.

Where reorganisation causes property to come under the administration of more than one health body, the legislation provides that in such cases the property should be apportioned between the transferee authorities in such proportions as they might agree (see National Health Service Act 1977, s 92(4) and, in default of an agreement, the Secretary of State was empowered to determine the apportionment to make consequential amendments to the trust instrument relating to the property. See National Health Service Act 1977, s 92(5).

Chapter 5

THE REGROWTH IN CHARITABLE FUND-RAISING IN THE NATIONAL HEALTH SERVICE

5.1 FROM AMENITIES TO CORE SERVICES

It was not long after the inception of the National Health Service that the courts recognised that it was charitable to donate funds to National Health Service hospitals despite the responsibility placed on the Minister for Health to provide a comprehensive health service, on the basis that the government was unable to provide sufficient funds to meet all needs.[1]

Following the introduction of the National Health Service, charitable giving continued but it was directed towards amenities rather than core services.[2] Examples of such giving included funds for painting hospital wards, providing toys for child patients and recreational facilities. However, the State found it increasingly difficult to fund all areas of the National Health Service and the emphasis changed from fund-raising for amenities to fund-raising for core activities: specific items of medical equipment such as body scanners, and medical research, particularly in the field of cancer. This change in focus from amenities to core equipment marked the start of fund-raising for everything from core services to buildings.[3]

Appeals such as the Wishing Well Appeal for the Great Ormond Street Hospital have raised funds for rebuilding hospitals and providing other equipment and services which are essential to the National Health

---

1 *Re Perreyman* [1953] 1 All ER 223.

2 This development is described in 'Charity and the NHS – use or abuse?', A Paines, *Private Client Business* (Sweet & Maxwell, 1994) Vol 5, pp 338–345.

3 The change was officially recognised in 1980 when Health Authorities were given the power to engage in activities intended to stimulate the giving (whether on trust or otherwise) of money or other property to assist them in connection with research. The costs of the establishment of a charity for the purpose and cost of fund-raising could be met from public funds and, in addition, Health Authority premises could be used. This power has now been extended to NHS Trusts. See National Health Service Act 1977, s 96A as amended by National Health Service and Community Care Act 1990, s 5 and Sch 2, Pt III, para 23.

Service. Such successful appeals have generated a significant percentage of the National Health Service budget. However, with the acceptance of charitable funds, health service bodies have duties and responsibilities as charity trustees. The uneven fit between charity and the National Health Service now falls to be discussed in relation to the Tomlinson Report.[1] On the one hand, health service bodies want to encourage donors to give funds to assist in the provision of services but, on the other hand, they want freedom to use the funds to suit the changing needs of the health service body. It will be shown in the next chapter that these two interests are sometimes irreconcilable.

1 See Chapter 6.

Chapter 6

LEGAL ISSUES ARISING OUT OF THE ACCEPTANCE OF CHARITABLE FUNDS BY THE NATIONAL HEALTH SERVICE

6.1 GENERAL CHARITABLE FUNDS

The acceptance of charitable funds by the National Health Service carries with it duties and responsibilities which can cause problems if overlooked. The issues involved are well illustrated by the proposals contained in Sir Bernard Tomlinson's 1992 report, 'London's Health Service'. In the event, the Tomlinson proposals have not been implemented because of the controversy caused by them. However, the implications of the proposals throw up some interesting issues in relation to the acceptance of charitable funds by health service bodies which merit further discussion. The report recommended a series of hospital mergers and closures.[1] Many of the hospitals affected are hospitals which, before the creation of the National Health Service, were teaching hospitals. Whereas in the case of voluntary hospitals endowments held were pooled

---

1 For an analysis of how the Tomlinson Report affects endowment funds see 'Hospital Endowments – Casualties of Tomlinson?', B Sage (1993) *NGO Finance Magazine*, 12 February.

Hospital Affected	*Endowments (£ millions)**	*Report's Recommendations*
St Bartholomew's	59.2	Close and transfer to Royal London
Royal London	17.5	—
Middlesex	15.0	Close and transfer to UCH
Royal National Throat Nose & Ear	1.4	Close and transfer to UCH
UCH	7.8	—
St Thomas's	65.4	Management to merge with Guy's
Guy's	53.5	Management to merge with St Thomas's
Westminster and Roehampton	8.3	Westminster only to close and transfer to Charing Cross
Royal Brompton	7.6	Close and transfer to Charing Cross
Royal Marsden (at Fulham and Sutton)	16.7	Fulham branch to close and transfer to Charing Cross
Charing Cross	6.6	If the transfers are not agreed to close

* Book values at 31 March 1991. Current real values are likely to be considerably higher.

in the Hospital Endowments Fund (and later expended for the general purposes of the National Health Service), in the case of endowments for teaching hospitals provision was made in the National Health Service Act 1946 (and subsequent legislation) for the first transfer of these funds to be free of pre-existing trusts, and instead, to be held by the Special Trustees for all or any purposes relating to hospital services, including research. The relevant provision can currently be found in s 95(2) of the National Health Service Act 1977 which provides that:

> 'Special Trustees have power to accept, hold and administer any property on trust for all or any purposes relating to hospital services (including research), or to any other part of the health service associated with hospitals ...'

An interesting question arises as to how existing charitable funds held by Special Trustees would be dealt with if the Tomlinson proposals had been put into effect. These funds are individually registered as charities which hold funds for the purposes set out in s 95(2) of the National Health Service Act 1977. Unless legislation was passed to deal with these funds, they would have needed to be schemed by the Charity Commissioners for merged hospitals, or the hospitals where the patients were moved to. In the event of the closure of the teaching hospitals the question would arise as to what would happen to the charitable endowment funds.

6.2 THE OPTIONS

6.2.1 Amalgamation of charitable funds according to hospital amalgamations

If the two hospitals were amalgamated, the charitable trust funds could be amalgamated. Problems might arise if the amalgamated hospital was around the same size as the individual hospitals involved in the merger. The creation of an endowment fund by the trustees of the various charitable trust funds which faced difficulty in applying its income would almost certainly lead to an inquiry by the Charity Commissioners concerning the widening of the endowment fund's objects by way of a cy-près scheme.[1] This is because charity trustees are under a duty to apply for a scheme in these circumstances.[2] If, on the other hand, the Charity Commissioners amalgamated the charitable trust funds by scheme then an enquiry would be made by the Charity Commissioners as to the desirability of extending the charitable objects. In either case, the trustees

1 Cy-près meaning 'as near as'. For the occasions when a cy-près scheme may be obtained from the Charity Commissioners see Charities Act 1993, s 13.

2 Charities Act 1993, s 13.

could find that the funds become available for wider charitable purposes than they wished.

6.2.2 The charitable funds follow the patients

This is what usually happens with the closure of any National Health Service unit. When a unit is closed and the patients are sent elsewhere, the funds are usually directed to the new unit. As the London teaching hospitals treat patients from a wide catchment area this would mean dissipating the funds all around the UK, and in doing so reducing their spending power. In addition, with the creation of the internal market, one can no longer say where the patients will be treated with any certainty.

6.2.3 Continue

Under this option the charitable trust funds would continue to support as many ongoing activities maintained by the funds as can be identified. The danger here is that the Department of Health or other health service bodies employing the funds may use them to meet running costs. This would beg the question whether it is right for charitable funds to be used to relieve statutory bodies of their responsibilities.[1]

6.2.4 Amalgamate the funds into a pan-London charity

The funds could be amalgamated into a London-wide charitable trust with its own trustees and new purposes as defined by a cy-près scheme.[2] This would be an enormous and problematic task as within the hospitals concerned there are also many funds where the money was given for a specific purpose, such as for a particular piece of medical equipment or for a nurses home, and in some cases the special fund may have its own trust deed[3] or a scheme of the Charity Commissioners.[4]

6.2.5 Nationalise the funds

This would be a politically unpopular move but the Government could point to the National Health Service Act 1946 which did exactly the same thing in respect of the endowments of voluntary hospitals which were not teaching hospitals.[5]

1 See Chapter 9.
2 Charities Act 1993, s 13.
3 For example, a specific charitable bequest in a will. In such circumstances the will itself forms the trust deed.
4 The Charity Commissioners have the power to make schemes for the administration of charities under Charities Act 1993, s 16.
5 *Decisions of the Charity Commissioners*, Vol 3, pp 35–38.

6.3 SPECIFIC CHARITABLE FUNDS

6.3.1 Phillip Harris House

The case of Phillip Harris House at Guy's Hospital provides a topical starting-point for a discussion about funds raised for specific charitable purposes. Phillip Harris House was built with an estimated £40 million raised from charities. Of the £40 million donated, the Special Trustees of Guy's Hospital committed themselves to donating £24 million, and the Imperial Cancer Research Fund used £1.7 million to set up a breast cancer unit in the building. They demanded that, because the activities at Guy's were to be transferred to St Thomas's following the merger of the two hospitals, the Department of Health should provide similar accommodation of a similar quality on the St Thomas's site at no further cost to them. Alternatively, the money should be returned to the donors. Other sizable donations came from the British Kidney Patient Association, Guy's Kidney Patient Association, and from the Phillip Harris Charitable Trust. The legal position concerning ownership of these funds will depend on the wording of the appeal and the terms upon which the funds were donated.

Perhaps with the Tomlinson Report in mind, the Charity Commissioners have given consideration to, and summarised their advice[1] as to, the legal position where health service bodies have received donations for expenditure in connection with the provision, development and maintenance of the premises and equipment of or for NHS hospitals, but cannot apply those donations for the purposes contemplated in the gift, or, after applying the funds, take an administrative decision (which may be forced on them) which has the effect that the facility paid for by those funds ceases to be used as the donor intended.

Where the recipient body is a charity, the Charity Commissioners consider the issue to be clear. The property into which the gift is converted is still held on charitable trusts, and if the trusts fail then it will either be transferred to another charity under an express dissolution clause or alternatively be schemed by the Commissioners for other charitable purposes.[2] The Charity Commissioners point out, by way of contrast, that health service bodies are not themselves regarded as charities and their general corporate property is not subject to any charitable trusts.

1 *Decisions of the Charity Commissioners*, Vol 3, pp 35–38.

2 Charities Act 1993, s 16. If the charity is small, it may be dealt with under Charities Act 1993, ss 74–75.

Where the intending donors have merely promised to make a payment to a health service body but the purpose of the gift is frustrated before the payment is made, no difficulty should arise. There is generally no legal obligation to complete the gift if the recipient can no longer fulfill its side of the bargain. A donor is entitled to change his mind at any time before he actually pays the money unless the proposed recipient has, as a result of the promise, acted to its detriment by incurring expense.

The Charity Commissioners also advise that where funds have been given to a health service body and been spent by it on a single outright purpose for which the gift was intended, the donor has no further interest in the matter legally. By definition, a gift for a simple outright purpose does not accommodate any further objects for the funds once that purpose has been achieved.[1] It follows that unless the donor gives the money on terms which are inconsistent with this outcome, he has no claim against the health service body for a return of the funds in any circumstances. For example, if the terms of the appeal were to build a children's wing at a particular hospital then once it has been built if would not be open to donors to argue that they have any legal claim over the children's wing or the donated funds. In other words the charitable trusts end at this point and the hospital children's wing would be held as part of the health service body's corporate property.[2]

However, where the gift is for the building and maintenance of a hospital building, then there will still be funds of the charity that may, depending on the circumstances, be schemed for similar charitable purposes by the Charity Commissioners. On the face of it, a hospital building which is partly erected in circumstances where there are some funds available towards its completion, then there is a partial failure and the funds donated are returnable to known and non-disclaiming donors or schemed by the Charity Commissioners for similar charitable purposes.[3]

---

1 *Decisions of the Charity Commissioners*, Vol 3, pp 35–38.

2 Legal authorities in support of this principle include *Re Spence* [1938] 1 Ch 96. Where the Court had to consider a testimentary gift of funds for: '... the purchase of a suitable site of land at Stockton-on-Tees and ... the erection on such site of a public hall ... which shall be presented ... to the Corporation of Stockton-on-Tees'. Luxmore J said: '... it seems fairly plain that the site and the public hall are to become part of the property of the Corporation of Stockton-on-Tees and accordingly are to be held like its other property, for the benefit of the borough'. Also, in *Richmond-upon-Thames LBC v AG* (1982) 81 LGR 156, at 168, Warner J's analysis of Luxmore J's judgment was that the latter 'thought ... that once the presentation [of the site and public hall] had taken place ... the charitable trust was at an end'.

3 Charities Act 1993, s 14.

Where the funds provided by the donor remain wholly unspent by the health service body at the moment when it exercises its administrative discretion (or is instructed to act) in such a way as to make the fulfilment of the purpose impracticable, then the purpose has failed from the beginning and the funds will normally be returnable even if the gift is made without any terms as to repayment. Where the money originates from a public appeal for a specific purpose, it will be returnable to the donors, unless they cannot be identified or found or they have executed a written disclaimer.[1]

The health service body may become aware that something is about to happen which would make it impossible for the gift or appeal fund to be applied for its proper purpose. The Charity Commissioners take the view that the health service body should not try to spend the money quickly to prevent any application of the funds being curtailed as the recipient body could be asked to refund the money spent from other resources under its control.[2] They point out that, if the purpose for which funds have been donated has already been fulfilled, the health service body should stop paying funds for that purpose unless there is some very strong reason for continuing. For example, it may be unwise to leave a building half built if it is in a dangerous condition.

6.3.2 The Royal Marsden appeal

Where the purposes of the gift have been put into effect initially by the health service body but subsequently fail, any unspent funds will not normally be returnable unless the terms of the gift provide for it. The Charity Commissioners give as an example the case of a hospital department, supported by a particular charitable gift for its maintenance, which closes or merges with another department leaving charitable funds unspent.[3] This is what happened to the Royal Marsden 'Save the Humans' appeal, which raised £25 million for facilities to be provided at its Fulham branch, whereupon the Tomlinson Report recommended closing the Fulham site and merging with the Charing Cross site nearby at Hammersmith. It could be argued that in such circumstances the point of charitable giving occurs when the funds are donated for a purpose which, at that time, is viable. On that basis, it is irrelevant whether the unit is closed at a later stage because the property will either be held for the general purposes of the charity or on special trusts which will need to be schemed by the Charity Commissioners for the general purposes of the

1 Charities Act 1993, s 14 and the Charities (Cy-près Advertisements, Enquiries and Disclaimer) Regulations 1993.

2 They do not say on what legal basis.

3 *Decisions of the Charity Commissioners*, Vol 3, pp 35–38.

charity. However, the legal position is not completely clear and it could be argued that, in fact, there is a subsequent failure of the charitable trust and that the funds must be applied for similar charitable purposes via a cy-près scheme.

If the terms of the gift include an alternative purpose for the application of the unspent funds then that is how they should be applied.

The precise moment when the purposes of the gift actually take effect has not been fully explored in the legal authorities. For example, charitable funds paid to a building contractor employed to build a new building may be payable in instalments as the building work progresses. The event which frustrates the purposes contemplated in the gift may occur midway through the project, before the building has been used for the purposes contemplated. Even the Charity Commissioners concede that the legal position is unclear as to whether this would constitute a failure *ab initio* or subsequent failure in respect of the unspent balance. The distinction is crucial, in that if the purposes are impossible to fulfill from the start the donor should be reimbursed, but if the failure is subsequent the funds can be applied by way of a scheme for similar charitable purposes.

The Charity Commissioners have traditionally advised charities donating funds to non-charitable bodies similar to health service bodies (such as county schools) that the donating charity should make arrangements to protect its gift. Protective measures may include a lease of the site of any building to the recipient health service body, with the freehold title being owned by the donor charity, or registering a charge against the title. With such protection in place, a health service body which received funds from a charity to build a hospital would have to buy the donor charity out if it wanted to free itself from the restrictions placed on it by the terms of the gift as to the use to which the building could be put.

In many cases, the health service body will not be a trustee of the donor charity as the charity will be run by an independent board of trustees (for example the League of Hospital Friends). The trustees of such charities will either have to dissolve under express powers in their constitutions and pass the funds over to other charities with similar purposes or apply to the Charity Commissioners for a scheme to enable the funds to be applied elsewhere.

There may be situations were charitable funds have already been spent on the construction of hospital buildings. Legal opinion is divided on the issue of ownership of the applied charitable funds. Again the terms of the gift are all-important. It could be argued that the construction of a building is not itself a charitable purpose as it is the charitable use of the building after its construction which enables the charitable purpose to be realised. If the building is never used for charitable purposes then it could be argued that there has been an *ab initio* failure and that the donors have an interest in the property. Arguably, donors could either challenge the closure or ask for their money back. In *Re Ulverston and District New Hospital Buildings Trusts*,[1] a public fund had been created for the construction of a building but the project was abandoned on the passing of the National Health Service Act 1946. The court ruled that money donated by known donors should be repaid since it was for a particular purpose which could not be carried out. That part of the fund coming from anonymous donors or fund-raising events had to be applied cy-près (and this principle is now enshrined in s 14 of the Charities Act 1993).

The acceptance of charitable funds by health service bodies may seem an attractive proposition but those responsible for administering the charitable funds and applying them should be aware of the legal issues involved and plan to avoid potential pitfalls.

1 *Re Ulverston and District New Hospital Buildings Trusts* [1956] Ch 622.

Chapter 7

HEALTH CARE RESOURCES AND THEIR ALLOCATION

7.1 PRIORITIES IN HEALTH CARE

From the inception of the National Health Service it became clear that it would be short of funds to carry out its functions. Aneurin Bevan, the first Secretary of State for the National Health Service, resigned in protest at the introduction of prescription charges in 1951[1] and the question of funding has been in the political arena ever since.

There seems to be a general consensus that health services need to be prioritised but there is no agreement on where the priorities should lie. Should charity provide amenities and the National Health Service provide core services or vice versa? One of the reasons why pressure is being put on funding is that demand for health care has expanded. Ironically, at the time the National Health Service was conceived there was an expectation that the need for health services would decrease. Penicillin had been discovered and advances in medical knowledge enabled the medical profession to treat illnesses which had, in the past, proved fatal. A good example of this is the recent controversy surrounding the availability of the drug inferon for multiple sclerosis. The Multiple Sclerosis Society has pointed out that some health service bodies are providing it whilst others are not on grounds of cost.[2]

In response to this burgeoning demand the National Health Service has started to reassess its priorities. Tattoo removal, for example, is not now universally offered by the National Health Service and many Health Authorities have restricted the availability of in vitro fertilisation, gender reassignment, reversal of sterilisation, cosmetic surgery and complementary medicine.[3] All these areas could be supported by charity and it is

---

1 *Aneurin Bevan* M Foot (Davis-Poynter, 1973) Vol 2, ch 8.

2 (1998) *The Independent*, 11 May.

3 See responses of Health Authorities to the questionnaire issued by the House of Commons Health Committee in 'Priority Setting in the NHS: Purchasing' (HC 227, Session 1993–1994) referred to in *Who Should We Treat? Law, Patients and the NHS* C Newdick (Clarendon Press, 1995) p 5.

interesting to speculate, as the National Health Service redefines its financial priorities, how charity will step in and provide. The point has previously been made in this book[1] that the services listed by the National Health Service Act 1977 relating to the physical and mental health of the population of England and Wales and in the prevention, diagnosis and treatment of illness could all be classed as being for the relief of the sick (both physical and mental health) and therefore charitable in law so long as they are organised on a non-profit making basis. If the State ceases to fund these areas, charity could step in and provide.

It is not a coincidence that charity has been increasingly rediscovered as resources in the National Health Service have become more and more scarce. Inflationary pressures, an expanding demand for health care and an ageing population have all contributed to a scarcity of resources.[2] As the pressure on resources has increased, so greater attention has been given to the efficiency of the National Health Service in order to maximise the use of public funds. Before the National Health Service and Community Care Act 1990, public funds were allocated to hospitals and other health service providers at the start of each financial year and, consequently, there was little incentive to improve performance. In fact, efficiency was penalised because if more patients were treated expenditure increased but income remained static. This was called the 'efficiency trap'.

After a review of the National Health Service by the Thatcher Government a number of proposals were made and published in a White Paper called 'Working for Patients'.[3] Following its publication the National Health Service and Community Care Act 1990 was enacted. The Act introduced the 'internal market' into the National Health Service. The 'internal market' works as follows: the Department of Health allocates money to health authorities and GP fund-holders to enable them to purchase (or commission) health care from hospitals on behalf of patients. The providers of health care in the National Health Service are mainly hospitals which are run by health service bodies. Health service bodies also provide other health care services including ambulance, mental health and community care services. Private hospitals run for profit as well as non-profit making charitable hospitals can also compete for the purchase of medical care by health authorities and GP fund-holders.

---

1 See **2.1**.

2 See *Who Should We Treat? Law, Patients and the NHS* C Newdick (Clarendon Press, 1995) ch 1.

3 *Working for Patients* (HMSO, 1989).

With the growing emphasis on the cost of health care and the limitation of resources to provide for universal health care, increasingly priorities are set and treatment without charge can no longer be taken for granted. It is worth reiterating that the Secretary of State has a duty to 'promote the establishment... of a comprehensive health service'.[1] However, attempts to establish a legal duty to provide health care regardless of the resources at the Secretary of State's disposal have yet to succeed. If an action were to succeed, it would be by establishing negligence on the part of a health service body. Unlikely though this might be, Kennedy and Grubb[2] have suggested that there may be three situations where negligence might be argued – the so called 'benchmark situation', non-provision and curtailed provision.

7.2 (1) THE 'BENCHMARK SITUATION'

The court could question whether a complaint arose out of inadequacies in the delivery of a system of care. If this is the case then it could examine whether the inadequacy amounted to negligence, rather than looking at the wider issue of a failure to provide sufficient resources. In determining the issue of negligence, the court could look at expert evidence as to what could be reasonably expected of a service of the type provided by the health service body. This would then set a benchmark against which any health service body could be judged. A failure to reach the benchmark would amount to a breach of duty. At this stage, a health service body could argue that its failure was due to a lack of resources and that the legal duty of care should be modified to reflect this. Acceptance of this argument by the court would amount to an endorsement of the health service body's policy decision. Rejection by the court would make the health service body liable for its failings and put more pressure on its resources. However, the legal authorities suggest that a court would be unlikely to resist a defence by a health service body that it lacked the resources to fulfill its duty.[3]

1 National Health Service Act 1946, s 1(1).
2 *Medical Law Texts with Materials* I Kennedy and A Grubb (Butterworths, 1994).
3 See *Wilsher v Essex Area Health Authority* [1986] 3 All ER 801, 834 and *Bull v Devon Area Health Authority* [1993] BMLR 117 (CA). For the contrary view see *Knight v Home Office* [1989] 3 All ER 237 (QBD).

7.3 (2) NON-PROVISION

The court could be faced with a complaint, not about an existing system, but about an absence of any provision in circumstances where it should be provided. A claim in negligence would be based on argument that a health service body had breached its duty of care in failing to provide the service. This would involve looking at what a reasonable health service body would do in the circumstances where it lacked the resources to provide the service. It is difficult for a court to establish a duty of care in such circumstances because it is so obviously a question of policy. The courts show a reluctance to intervene in matters of policy which they consider non-justiciable.[1]

7.4 (3) CURTAILED PROVISION

A complaint could result from a reduction in the level of resources devoted to a particular service. The claim would be that a patient was harmed not by reason of the inadequate care delivered but because of the complete absence of care. The court could avoid being drawn into the policy debate by looking at what the health service body undertook to provide and whether, in fact, it did so. If the health service body undertook only to provide a curtailed service then a claim would almost certainly fail.

In *R v Central Birmingham HA ex parte Walker*,[2] Sir John Donaldson MR commented that:

> 'It is not for this Court, or indeed any court, to substitute its own judgement for the judgement of those who are responsible for the allocation of resources. This Court could only intervene where it is satisfied that there was a *prima facie* case, not only of failing to allocate resources in the way in which others would think that resources should be allocated, but of a failure to allocate resources to an extent which was *Wednesbury*[3] unreasonable ... which involves a breach of a public law duty ...'

Increasing financial pressures on health service bodies have resulted in harrowing decisions being reported in the media and litigation to establish rights to health care. In *R v Cambridge Health Care Authority ex parte B*,[4] because of the unavailability of beds in the only National

1 See *R v Secretary of State ex parte Hinks* (1992) 1 BMLR 93.
2 *R v Central Birmingham Health Authority ex parte Walker* (1987) 3 BMLR 32.
3 *Associated Provincial Picture Houses v Wednesbury Corporation* [1947] 2 All ER 680; [1948] 1 KB 223.
4 *R v Cambridge Health Authority ex parte B* [1995] 2 All ER 129.

Health Service hospital prepared to carry out life-saving treatment on a ten-year-old girl suffering from non-Hogkins lymphoma with common acute lymphoblastic leukaemia, the proposed treatment could only be offered privately. The treatment involved a two-stage process, the first being a further course of chemotherapy costing £15,000, with an estimated 10-20 per cent chance of success, and a second stage, if remission was achieved, a second bone marrow transplant costing £60,000 which had a similar chance of success. B's father sought a judicial review of the Health Authority's decision not to treat his child. In rejecting B's claim, Sir Thomas Bingham MR commented that:

> 'Difficult and agonising judgements have to be made as to how a limited budget is best allocated to the maximum number of patients. That is not a judgement that the Court can make.'

He went on to say that a Health Authority could not be accused of a breach of statutory duty if it had funds in its account which had not been spent. Unless the Health Authority had funds to spend on all its patients' needs, that situation would never be reached.

The reluctance of the courts to interfere with public bodies' decisions concerning the allocation of resources reached a high point in the landmark House of Lords decision *R v Gloucestershire County Council and Another ex parte Barry*.[1] Although the case was concerned with community care rather than health care, it has important consequences for the allocation of resources in both areas. Mr Barry had been assessed by the local authority's social services department as requiring home care help twice a week for shopping, collecting his pension, laundry and cleaning, as well as meals on wheels four days a week. Under s 2(1) of the Chronically Sick and Disabled Persons Act 1970, if a local authority is satisfied that it is necessary to make arrangements in order to meet the needs of a chronically sick or disabled person, it is 'the duty of that authority to make those arrangements'. Because of a cut in funding from central Government the local authority informed Mr Barry that it would no longer be able to provide services to meet his full needs as assessed and that the cleaning and laundry services would have to be withdrawn. Despite the fact that the 1970 Act imposes a duty (as opposed to a power) on the local authority to provide services, the House of Lords decided that a chronically sick or disabled person's needs could legitimately be assessed having regard to the availability of resources. Had this decision been applied generally by the courts, then cash-starved local authorities have no option but to pass on the shortfall in funding to those in need, or charities serving those in need.

---

1 *R v Gloucestershire County Council and Another ex parte Barry* [1997] 2 WLR 459.

However, following the decision in *Barry* the courts appear to have retreated from the line that a local authority or health service body is entitled to take into account the availability of resources when assessing needs. In *R v Sefton Borough Council ex parte Help the Aged and others*,[1] the Court of Appeal decided that a local authority was not entitled to take into account lack of resources when deciding whether to provide residential accommodation for elderly persons in need of care and attention not otherwise available to them under s 21(1)(a) of the National Assistance Act 1948. As a matter of statutory construction the Court of Appeal distinguished s 2(1) of the Chronically Sick and Disabled Act 1970 (which was the section under review in *Barry*) from s 2(1)(a) of the National Assistance Act 1948 on the basis that the 1970 Act used the word 'necessary' whereas the similar wording in the 1948 Act did not. This decision restricts the *Barry* case to interpreting s 2(1) of the 1970 Act and so cannot be used to support the general proposition that local authorities and health service bodies can take into account their limited resources when deciding whether they can fulfill their statutory duties or not. In a recent case in North Derbyshire,[2] a Health Authority was restrained by the High Court from refusing to fund an expensive drug for a multiple sclerosis sufferer, contrary to a National Health Service circular issued by the Secretary of State. The case demonstrates a further retreat from the line taken in *Barry*.

What all these cases demonstrate is that if the funds are not available then a health service body is left with the choice of cutting services or making up the shortfall from other sources. In the case of health care, clearly there is an option for health service bodies to establish charities and seek support from the public and the business community. Increasingly, this is the case. Significantly, the treatment for the ten-year-old girl, 'child B',[3] was funded by a private philanthropist.

---

1 *R v Sefton Metropolitan Borough Council ex parte Help the Aged and others* (1997) *The Times*, 23 August.

2 *R v North Derbyshire Health Authority ex parte Fisher* (1997) *The Times*, 2 September.

3 *R v Cambridge Health Authority ex parte B* [1995] 2 All ER 129.

Chapter 8

HEALTH AND COMMUNITY CARE

8.1 HEALTH CARE OR SOCIAL CARE?

A major debate is taking place in the field of health care as to what is a 'health' issue and what is a 'social' issue. The service provided by the National Health Service is generally free, whereas a service provided by the Social Services Department of a local authority is generally subject to a means-tested charge. From a charity's point of view the issue translates into whether it needs to charge the patient for its services. Charities are caught in the middle of this debate since they operate both in the health and social services sectors.

By way of example, help with bathing is free if provided in a person's home by a district nurse, whereas, if provided by a social services care assistant it may be subject to a charge. The argument is repeated in a hundred different ways with such items as incontinence pads, walking sticks and occupational therapy.[1] Whether a charity is providing social care or health care can have important financial implications and may mean that it has to make up shortfalls in funding through fund-raising appeals to the public, or, alternatively, charge its beneficiaries.

There have been some recent examples of health service bodies and local authorities trying to 'pass the buck'. The issue arose in the Court of Appeal in *White v Adjudication Officer*.[2] The case concerned the long-term care of a group of elderly patients with mental illness. Following an assessment of their condition, a psychiatrist advised that treatment in hospital was no longer necessary because the degree of specialist clinical supervision they required was minimal. They were discharged into a nursing home where a dispute arose between the health authority and the local authority as to the responsibility for paying for the cost of their care. The Court of Appeal held that the nursing home was a 'hospital' within the definition of the National Health Service Act 1977 because it was an 'institution for the reception and treatment of persons suffering from mental illness', namely 'mental disorder within the meaning of the Mental Health Act 1983 . . .'.[3] The court was persuaded by

---

1 *Community Care and the Law* L Clements (LAG, 1996) p 157.

2 *White v Adjudication Officer* (1994) 17 BMLR 68.

3 *Ibid* at 68.

the fact that the nursing home had nursing staff, including mental nurses, and that it prescribed drugs.

The distinction between health care and social care has become blurred in recent years because of the move away from institutional health care to community care. Against the background of financial constraints in the public sector caused by pressure on government funding, community care means care by the community including informal and voluntary care. Public services are seen as sustaining care in the community.[1]

8.2 WHO DELIVERS COMMUNITY CARE?

8.2.1 Local Authorities

Local authorities have responsibilities for the welfare of four client groups:[2] the elderly, disabled, children and their families and the mentally disordered. Traditionally, local authorities have been providers of services, but in April 1993 when community care reforms were implemented they became commissioners and planners of services provided by other agencies, including charities. One can readily think of large national charities who carry out charitable work to benefit people in these four categories and will therefore be in a position to act as agents for local authorities. For example, Age Concern, Scope, the National Society for the Prevention of Cruelty to Children and the Mental After-Care Association all act in this capacity.

8.2.2 The National Health Service

The National Health Service and Community Care Act 1990 gave responsibility for allocating resources and commissioning appropriate services within the National Health Service internal market to health service bodies. Although acute health care services are usually provided in hospitals there has inevitably been a shift towards provision in the community. Since 1982 there has been a 25 per cent decrease in the overall number of acute care hospital beds, and a 20 per cent increase in day admissions.[3] Although the Secretary of State for Health has a responsibility to provide after-care facilities for those recovering from illness as there is a shortage of hospital beds there has been a 30 per cent cut in these services since 1990, and some hospitals now no longer maintain

1 *Community Care for Older People: Rights, Remedies and Finance* M Richards (Jordans, 1996) p 14.
2 See Local Authority Social Services Act 1970.
3 *Community Care for Older People: Rights, Remedies and Finance* M Richards (Jordans, 1996) p 18.

continuing care beds at all. The new health service bodies have the power to discharge their duty to provide continuing in-patient care by purchasing beds from the independent or charity sectors.

Within the National Health Service community health services provide for the health care needs of people at home or in residential care who do not require hospital services. One third of National Health Service expenditure is deployed in the community.[1]

8.3 THE PRIVATE SECTOR, THE VOLUNTARY SECTOR AND THE CONTRACT CULTURE

Local authorities and health service bodies can enter into contracts for the provision of services from charities. Local authorities can either give grants, service agreements or contracts, whereas health service bodies can enter into service agreements within the 'internal market' or alternatively can contract services out to charities or the private sector.[2] There has been a move away from local authorities either providing services themselves or giving grants which were not generally legally binding to entering into service agreements and contracts which are. Contracts within the National Health Service between health service bodies do not confer contractual rights or liabilities.[3] Contracts between a health service body and an independent contractor which may be a charity are legally binding between the parties under the common law. However, if statutory functions are contracted out the health service body will ultimately remain liable to members of the public although in turn may have a legal remedy against the independent contractor.[4]

8.4 COMMUNITY CARE SERVICES

Community care services are defined as services which a local authority[5] may provide or arrange under any of the following Acts of Parliament:

---

1 *Community Care for Older People: Rights, Remedies and Finance* M Richards (Jordans, 1996) p 19.
2 The Deregulation and Contracting Out Act 1994.
3 National Health Service and Community Care Act 1990, s 4(3).
4 Deregulation and Contracting Out Act 1994, ss 72(2) and 72(3).
5 National Health Service and Community Care Act 1990, s 46(3).

8.4.1 Part III of the National Assistance Act 1948[1]

Under s 21 local authorities are required to arrange residential accommodation for people over the age of 18 who 'by reason of age, illness, disability or any other circumstances are in need of care or attention which is not otherwise available to them' and, 'accommodation for expectant and nursing mothers who are in need of care and attention which is not otherwise available to them'. Various directions have been made over the years by the Secretary of State and these are consolidated in appendices to Department of Health Circular LAC (93) 10. The Secretary of State has extended the duty to providing temporary accommodation for other people not referred to in s 21 ordinarily resident in the local authority area who are in urgent need of care in unforeseen circumstances.[2] Local authorities must make arrangements for the care and after-care of people with a mental disorder, whether or not they have a settled residence in a particular local authority area. Finally, the Secretary of State gives approval for arrangements by local authorities to provide accommodation which will meet the needs in respect of the prevention, care and after care of illness including nursing home care.

Under s 29, responsibility is placed on local authorities to care for disabled persons aged 18 or over who are blind, deaf, dumb or who suffer from a mental disorder[3] of any description, and other adults who are substantially and permanently handicapped by illness, injury, congenital deformity or such other disabilities as may be prescribed by the Secretary of State. Circular LAC (93) 10 extends the group to people who are partially sighted or hard of hearing. The Secretary of State may approve or direct certain services and the Circular directs local authorities to make arrangements to provide a social work service and social work advice and support to people in their own homes and elsewhere and to provide rehabilitative day care services, occupational, recreational, social and cultural activities. The Secretary of State has also approved, and therefore empowered, local authorities to provide such facilities as holiday homes, subsidised travel and warden-assisted housing schemes.

1 National Assistance Act 1948, s 21 as amended by National Health Service and Community Care Act 1990, s 42.

2 The Secretary of State, on the other hand, merely approves and empowers the making of residential arrangements for people with no settled residence.

3 'Mental disorder' means mental illness, arrested or incomplete development of mind, psychopathic disorder and any other disorder or disability of mind: see Mental Health Act 1983, s 1.

8.4.2 Health Services and Public Health Act 1968

Section 45 enables local authorities, subject to the direction or approval of the Secretary of State, to make arrangements for promoting the welfare of old people. The section is intended to include elderly persons who are not severely disabled, but who could benefit from services which would help to arrest personal or social deterioration. The Secretary of State has chosen only to approve provision rather than issue directions, which means that the section is weaker than ss 21 and 29 of the National Assistance Act 1948. The services which have been approved are the provision of meals and recreation in the home and elsewhere, the identification of needs for services, home care assistance, warden services and the provision of advice and social work support. This Act also confers power on local authorities to employ voluntary agencies such as charities to deliver the services and links it with grant aid.[1] The National Health Service and Community Care Act 1990 has extended this power to enable delegation to private sector providers.

8.4.3 National Health Service Act 1977

Section 21 and Schedule 8 place responsibility on social services authorities to provide health services at the direction or approval of the Secretary of State. The powers include making arrangements for the care of expectant and nursing mothers,[2] for the prevention of illness and for the care or after-care of people suffering from illness.[3] These services are subject to the Secretary of State's approval or directions. Like s 21 of the National Assistance Act 1948, there appears to be some overlap with the duty of health service bodies to provide after-care services.[4] In Circular LAC (93) 10, the Secretary of State directed the provision of after-care facilities for people suffering from mental disorder and also approved arrangements for night-sitter services, recuperative holidays, facilities for social and recreational activities, and meals on wheels for house-bound people not provided for by other legislation. Schedule 8, para 3 imposes a duty on social services authorities to provide home help services for households where such help is required for adults suffering from illness or congenital deformity. There is also a power to provide laundry facilities for such households. The duty is to provide services 'on such a

---

1 Health Services and Public Health Act 1968, s 65.
2 National Health Service Act 1977, Sch 8, para 1.
3 *Ibid* para 2.
4 National Assistance Act 1977, s 3.

scale as is adequate for the needs of their area',[1] and is therefore difficult to claim as of right.

8.4.4 Mental Health Act 1983

Section 117 applies to certain categories of mentally disordered patients who are or have been detained in hospital. It imposes a joint duty on the new Health Authorities and social services authorities to provide after-care services for such persons in co-operation with voluntary agencies such as charities. Although there is some overlap with s 21 of and Sch 8 to the National Health Service Act 1977, it is easier to show that a duty exists under s 117 of the Mental Health Act 1983.[2]

8.4.5 Chronically Sick and Disabled Persons Act 1970 and Disabled Persons (Services, Consultation and Representation) Act 1986

It is the view of the Department of Health that services provided under the 1970 Act are also community care services because they are provided in exercise of a local authority's functions under s 29 of the National Assistance Act 1948.[3] Section 2 of the 1970 Act creates a duty in respect of the disabled or chronically sick. This category of person is already defined by s 29 of the National Assistance Act 1948. A local authority must arrange such of the services specified in s 2 as it is satisfied are necessary to meet the needs of a disabled person. The specified services are:

- provision of practical assistance within the home;
- provision of disability aids and equipment;
- assistance with adaptations to the home;
- provision of meals at home or elsewhere;
- provision of or assistance in getting a telephone or any special equipment to use a telephone;
- provision of, or assistance in, taking advantage of educational or recreational facilities, both inside and outside the home, including provision of, or assistance with, incidental transport;
- provision of holidays.

Section 2 of the 1970 Act does not require an assessment but does require local authorities to satisfy themselves as to the existence of need. This has been interpreted as meaning that the local authority must make up its

---

1 For guidance on the legal interpretation of this duty see *R v Gloucestershire County Council ex parte Mahfood* (1996) 8 Admin LR 181.

2 *R v Ealing District Health Authority ex parte Fox* [1993] 3 All ER 170.

3 See Chronically Sick and Disabled Persons Act 1970, s 1.

mind in each case rather than applying a blanket policy.[1] However, no duty arises until the local authority has made up its mind. The Disabled Persons (Services, Consultation and Representation) Act 1986 strengthens the duties imposed by the 1970 Act. When requested, the local authority must decide whether the needs of a disabled person call for the provision of any welfare services.[2] The request may be made by an individual disabled person or by his carer or by an 'authorised representative' who may be appointed by or on behalf of the disabled person.[3] Some voluntary organisations including charities provide advocacy services for disabled people.

8.5 PROPOSALS FOR REFORM

A report issued by the Kings Fund in 1997 called 'The Future Organisation of Community Care – Options for the integration of health and social care' explored this area. The reason why integration is desirable is that health cannot be isolated from social issues such as housing and social services. This is particularly true in the context of community care. However, the organisational separation between health and social services militates against this integration. Some attempt has been made to integrate the two through joint commissioning but the procedures are complex and concensus is not always achieved. There is a growing belief that if services are placed within one organisation many of the problems of joint commissioning will disappear.

The advantage of a single agency which would then commission health and social services would be that holistic needs assessments and 'one-shop' service provision would be easier. It could also lead to greater democracy. The current emphasis within the National Health Service is reporting upwards to the Executive and the Secretary of State rather than to the local community.

It is feasible that such an agency could have charitable status. The charity could then enter into contracts with the authorities commissioning its services. Health is free at the point of delivery, whereas social care is mainly means-tested. However, there is no reason why the charity could not adopt a charging policy consistent with the existing charging regime. Charities promote the relief of sickness and the welfare of vulnerable groups such as the elderly and the disabled, and there is no reason why the two cannot be integrated in one organisation with charitable status. Such

---

1 *Blyth v Blyth (No 2)* [1966] 2 WLR 634.

2 Disabled Persons (Services Consultation and Representation) Act 1986, s 4.

3 *Ibid* s 1.

a charity would be supervised by the Charity Commission and would therefore be accountable. It could have local trustees and would, by virtue of being a charity, be independent.

Chapter 9

THE PROVISION OF HEALTH CARE: CHARITY OR STATE?

9.1 INTRODUCTION

The role that charity plays in the provision of health care has important implications both for the voluntary sector and the way in which society defines its responsibility to those in need of health care.

It has been shown[1] that charity antedated the establishment of the National Health Service and the provision of State funding. In the Middle Ages, charity was the main provider of health care and even prior to the establishment of the National Health Service over one-third of all hospitals were charitable voluntary hospitals. With the assumption of State responsibility for a range of areas of social policy previously provided for by charity in the 19th and 20th centuries, including education, welfare and health, a key question arose as to what role charity could play (if at all) in meeting the needs of the public.

9.2 THE LEGAL POSITION

This issue was addressed by the Committee on the Law and Practice relating to Charitable Trusts (The Nathan Committee) which reported its conclusions in 1952.[2] The Committee answered the question by looking at the relationship of charity in general to the State, but its conclusion to this general question has particular relevance to the role of charity in the provision of health care in the National Health Service.

The Nathan Committee pointed out that charity had traditionally provided facilities that had been considered to be the responsibility of the State. For example, the Preamble to the Statute of Charitable Uses 1601 (which is regarded as the starting point for the definition of charitable status) expressly mentions the repair of bridges and highways which have been a matter of public obligation from very early days. The assumption

1 See Chapter 1.
2 Cmd 8710, 1952.

by the State of responsibility for funding an area which is charitable in law does not mean that it thereby ceases to be charitable.

The Charity Commissioners have traditionally advised charity trustees that they should not relieve public funds. One can see some sense in this advice as it is aimed at maximising the benefits charitable funds can produce. However, in law, there is no reason why charitable funds cannot be used to help fund statutory authorities such as health service bodies in carrying out their aims, and the school of thought which holds that charities should not be involved in areas where there is already State provision is really making a political rather than a legal point.[1] Legally there is no difference between charities applying their funds in areas where a public authority has a duty to provide and where it has merely a power to provide. The distinction between State and charity funding has become more blurred in the health service than in any other sector. In 1980, health service bodies were given the statutory power to fund-raise for their own statutory functions or research. This power has been specifically extended to health service bodies.[2] It is possible that when charities tender for service providing grants they might be tempted to reduce their charges on the assumption that they can make up the difference through fund raising. The author has no evidence of this being the case at the moment but it is easy to foresee such a trend. In this way, it is possible that charity could relieve public funds by erosion.

9.3 THE RELATIONSHIP BETWEEN CHARITY AND HEALTH CARE BODIES

There are a number of ways in which charity can co-exist with statutory authorities such as health service bodies.

9.3.1 Sub-contracting

This type of arrangement either involves a grant where public funds are simply donated to charities or a contract to provide services where charities become contractually bound to carry out charitable activities on behalf of the statutory authority. In recent years, public authorities have tended to contract with charities to provide services in fulfilment of their statutory responsibilities. The impetus for this has come largely from compulsory competitive tendering and the implementation of com-

---

1 *Charity Law A to Z: Key Questions Answered* J Claricoat and H Phillips (Jordans, 1995) p 96.

2 National Health Service Act 1977, s 96A as amended by National Health Service and Community Care Act 1990, s 5 and Sch 2, Part III, para 23.

munity care following the National Health Service and Community Care Act 1990, which encompasses services formerly provided by local authorities and health service bodies. The internal market within the National Health Service with its purchasers and providers of services is mirrored in the field of community care and the overlap between health care and community care was discussed in Chapter 8.

9.3.2 Filling the gaps in Public Funding

In 1952 the Nathan Committee talked in terms of charities supplying flowers and books to hospital wards.[1] This type of work is still carried out today by charitable bodies such as the League of Hospital Friends, but, as the gaps in public funding widen, charity is increasingly being asked to provide essential goods and services rather than non-essential amenities.

9.3.3 Pioneering

In this type of situation, a need arises that the State has not contemplated or has not provided for. Charities are in a position to meet crises quickly and enthusiastically. For example, Band Aid brought together a number of popular musicians and singers to raise funds for the Ethiopian famine in the early 1980s.

9.4 ADVANTAGES OF CHARITABLE PROVISION

It can be argued that charity encourages the community to decide where their priorities lie. Unpopular causes will not generate the support of the community. Although the aim of the National Health Service was to provide a comprehensive health service, the increasing role of charity provides the opportunity for health care services to grow in response to local needs and priorities. Charity encourages community participation and can help to engender a community spirit.

The government has recognised the desirability of setting local priorities in the White Paper, *The new NHS. Modern. Dependable*, through the introduction of Primary Care Groups which will allow health priorities to evolve from the bottom up.[2]

It is also generally accepted that charities are more efficient in providing services than the State and that charities can provide services cost-effectively because they can draw on support from unpaid volunteers. It can also be argued that the breadth of what qualifies as charitable under

---

1 Cmd 8710, 1952 para 656.
2 *The new NHS. Modern. Dependable* (The Stationery Office, 1997).

the law of England and Wales opens up the possibility of greater choice by the community about what kind of health care meets its needs. The National Health Service has traditionally fostered conventional medicine, but if the community is prepared to fund-raise for alternative medicine then this can be provided by the community through charitable means.[1]

Through the cy-près doctrine, charity can also adapt to advances in medical science or changing circumstances, for example, if a particular disease dies out then funds could be applied cy-près for the next threatening illness.[2]

9.5 DISADVANTAGES OF CHARITABLE PROVISION

The main strength of the voluntary sector is also its main weakness. As charity assumes responsibility for more and more National Health Service functions the National Health Service will inevitably become a local rather than a national provider. The resulting lack of co-ordination may mean that a comprehensive health service is harder to achieve in the future.

Where charitable funds held on trust cannot be effectively carried out for one reason or another, it would be open to the trustees to apply for a cy-près scheme (assuming they do not have the power to vary the objects) to widen the charitable purposes. Just as the doctrine of cy-près can be seen as a flexible advantage to the use of charity in the relief of sickness, it can also be argued that the very need to apply for a cy-près scheme can be disadvantageous in the sense that the scheme making process is a slow one and is necessarily restrictive as charitable funds can only be applied for other charitable purposes 'as near as' the original charitable purposes. A possible solution to this potential problem would be for the Secretary of State for Health to be given the same kind of powers to alter charitable trusts as the Secretary of State for Education and Employment has powers to alter the trusts governing various educational bodies: such alterations allowed under the education legislation are motivated by educational needs dictated by government policy from time to time. It would seem feasible that the Secretary of State for Health could be given similar powers which could be exercised according to health require-

---

1 The scope of what falls within the charitable definition of relief of sickness is discussed earlier in this book. See Chapter 3.

2 *AG v Hicks* (1810) 3 Bro CC 166n; *Law of Mortmain* Highmore (2nd edn) p 336 (leprosy).

ments. This could help to plan the provision of health care rather than simply to allow it to evolve.[1]

Although it has been shown that the idea of charity providing health care is in no way new and that its role has simply been rediscovered in recent years the way in which modern charities make that provision is quite different. The main difference is that most charities providing for health care and welfare are funded by the State. In a survey of the top two hundred fund-raising charities only 57 per cent of their income came from voluntary sources with the remaining 43 per cent coming from local or national government.[2]

Robert Whelan has argued[3] that prior to the creation of the National Health Service and the Welfare State it was taken for granted that people with reasonable incomes would allocate their time and resources to their chosen charities. Through involvement in the voluntary sector people learned to be altruistic and responsible, some experienced moral growth and rich and poor were brought together at a certain point to form a degree of community. In the 19th century there was an explosion of involvement in the voluntary sector. A survey conducted in the 1890s found that the average middle class family devoted 10 per cent of its income to philanthropic works.[4] Whelan argues that today charities are merely an extension of government and, as a result, they lack innovation and independence because they are mere conduits of the State's welfare programme. An example given by Whelan[5] is the Mildmay Mission Hospital. This hospital was opened in the East End of London in 1892 with the aim of preaching the gospel and healing the sick. After functioning as an independent charity for over half a century it was absorbed into the National Health Service in 1948. In the early part of the 1980s the hospital was threatened with closure as part of a rationalisation scheme which decreed that cottage hospitals with fewer than 200 beds were uneconomic. A campaign was launched to revive the Mildmay as an independent voluntary hospital operating outside the National Health Service. Rather than seek support from the general public the organisers sought support from the Regional Health Authority and the Department

---

1 I am indebted to Hilary Phillips for pointing out this possibility to me. For a commentary on the Secretary of State for Education and Employment's statutory powers to alter trusts, see *Charity Law A to Z: Key Questions Answered* J Claricoat and H Phillips (Jordans, 1995).

2 *Charity Trends*, 11th edn (Charities Aid Foundation, 1988) p 114.

3 *The Corrosion of Charity* R Whelan (Institute of Economic Affairs, 1996).

4 *Statistics of Middle Class Expenditure* (British Library of Political and Economic Science) Pamphlet HD6/D267, Table IX.

5 *The Corrosion of Charity* R Whelan (Institute of Economic Affairs, 1996) pp 67–68.

of Health. The property was returned to the League of Friends on a 99-year lease at a peppercorn rent and it reopened in 1985. The intention was to care for the chronically ill, the disabled and the frail, but everything depended on the type of projects the public authorities were prepared to fund. At this time AIDS funding was becoming available out of all proportion to the numbers affected.[1] From 1987, when the Mildmay converted one of its three wards for the care of AIDS patients, its income seemed assured. The government contributed £200,000 and further donations of £280,000 were received by the beginning of 1988. The accounts for 1994 show that 70 per cent of the Mildmay's income comes from the State, and this inevitably places pressure on the hospital to conform to the current fashions in health care funding set by central government.

1 In the financial year 1988/89 the government spent £50.07 per person dying from heart disease on health education and research into its causes. Spending on AIDS health education and research per person dying of the illness in the same period was £289,755.87. See 'The AIDS Scandal', *Economic Affairs*, Vol 11, No 4 (Institute of Economic Affairs, June 1991).

PART 2

PRACTICE – A GUIDE TO CHARITY LAW FOR HEALTH SERVICE BODIES AND THEIR CHARITIES

Chapter 10

THE CHARITABLE PROVISION OF HEALTH CARE

10.1 INTRODUCTION

Before the Charities Acts 1992 and 1993 the Charity Commissioners' practice was to register all NHS charities (unless they were exempted or excepted from registration) under the control of each health service body under one registration number. After 1993 the Charity Commissioners' duty became to register every charity qualifying for registration (unless exempt or excepted from registration) or two or more charities which can be treated as one for the purposes of registration under the Charities (Amendment) Act 1995.

It is currently estimated that there are around 25,000 charities in the trusteeship of health service bodies.[1] Many of these are subject to informal trusts and over the years many have been neglected by health service body trustees because they have failed to keep records, accounts or to carry out some or all of the duties and responsibilities expected of charity trustees. This section aims to advise such trustees as well as potential trustees of new charities about the general requirements of charity law, especially those of particular pertinence to health-related charities, and the various opportunities to maximise charity funds. The Charity Commission NHS Review Section has produced a model declaration of trust for an NHS umbrella charity which sets out the terms for formalising informal trusts held by health service bodies and to help improve and simplify their administration.

It is clear that charity has a major part to play in the funding of health care for the general public. The question is: how wide are the parameters of the legal concept of charity? Put another way, does the legal concept of charity offer wider opportunities for funding health care? It is only by answering this question that health care bodies can appreciate the extent to which charity can complement or replace existing NHS funded services or facilities.

---

1 [1994] Ch Comm Rep 7.

10.2 THE CHARITABLE USES ACT 1601 AND THE CLASSIFICATION OF CHARITABLE PURPOSES

The starting point for determining charitable status is the preamble to the Charitable Uses Act 1601 often referred to as the Statute of Elizabeth I. The preamble includes the following wording: '*Some for Relief of aged, impotent and poor People; Some for Maintenance of Sick and Maimed Soldiers and Mariners …*' as charitable purposes. Although the relief of sickness is not expressly referred to, it has already been shown that the provision of hospitals and the care of hospital patients was recognised as charitable long before the Statute of Elizabeth. Subsequently, the various instances of charitable purpose set out in the preamble were classified by Lord MacNaughton in *Pemsel's* case[1] as falling into four categories: the relief of poverty, the advancement of education, the advancement of religion, and other purposes beneficial to the community. The relief of the sick is included in the category 'other purposes beneficial to the community' but each of the charitable heads overlaps to a certain extent with the provision of health care. Until the *Joseph Rowntree*[2] case, doubt existed as to whether the words 'aged, impotent and poor' were capable of being construed disjunctively, or whether there must always be an element of poverty for a gift for aged or impotent persons to be charitable. The point has been made earlier in this book that traditionally the relief of sickness was associated with the relief of poverty. In this case, it was decided that even where aged and impotent persons were not poor, a gift for their benefit would be charitable so long as they were in need of 'relief'. Such gifts will fall within Lord McNaughton's fourth category, being for other purposes beneficial to the community. In the *Joseph Rowntree* case[3] Gibson J stated that there must be a need to be relieved by the charitable gift, such need being attributable to the age and impotence of the beneficiary.

10.3 BASIC PRINCIPLES

10.3.1 The 'relief of sickness' or 'the protection and preservation of health'?

The Charity Commissioners and the Inland Revenue expect a charity's objects clause to be expressed to be for either 'the relief of sickness' or 'the

1 *Income Tax Special Purposes Commissioners v Pemsel* [1891] AC 531.

2 *Joseph Rowntree Memorial Trust Housing Association v Attorney-General* [1983] Ch 159.

3 *Income Tax Special Purposes Commissioners v Pemsel* [1891] AC 531.

protection and preservation of health'. This is because, in order to be charitable in the field of health care, there has to be a need that is relieved in some way. It follows that an objects clause expressed to be for 'the promotion of health' is not expressed in an exclusively charitable form of wording. Given the increased understanding of the causes of ill-health, ie a good environment and diet, the insistence of the law on there being a need to be relieved might, at first sight, appear unduly restrictive. However, as it will be shown later in this chapter, good health can be promoted incidentally through other categories of charitable provision such as recreation, sports facilities, good housing and the relief of poverty generally.

10.3.2 Public benefit

The general rule is that in order to be charitable in law the charity must exist for the benefit of the public. Public is defined as meaning the 'community or an appreciably important class of the community'[1] rather than for the benefit of private individuals. It should be noted that in the case of charities with objects for the relief of poverty the class of beneficiaries can be very small. It should also be noted that in the case of educational charities, in order to demonstrate public benefit, there is an additional requirement to demonstrate educational value.

A good example of the public benefit test in operation in the case of a charity for the relief of sickness is sometimes found in the case of proposed alternative medicine charities. On occasion, an alternative medical practitioner establishes a charity and appoints puppet trustees. The intention is that the charity will employ and pay the alternative medical practitioner and obtain tax reliefs. However, the Charity Commissioners response to such a proposal is to provisionally reject the application on the basis that the proposed charity is established primarily for the benefit of an individual and that the private benefit to that individual outweighs the public benefit.

Interestingly, although it is common to raise funds for an individually named sick child, such a collection could never be charitable because it would fail the public benefit test.

Charity law has developed by way of analogy in that the courts or the Charity Commissioners determine the charitable status of organisations by making comparisons with existing cases which were themselves determined to be within the spirit of the preamble to the Statute of Elizabeth. The following are examples of areas of health care which have been held to be charitable.

---

1 Per Lord Wrenbury in *Verge v Somerville* [1924] AC 496.

10.3.3 Relief of the aged

With a rapidly ageing population the relief of the aged is of increasing importance. The most common way of relieving the aged is through the provision of a nursing home.[1] However, housing the aged is not charitable in itself; there must be some relief in respect of needs which arise from old age. The accommodation must be suitably adapted to meet the disabilities of old age, for example, ramps, handrails, stairlifts etc, or the beneficiaries must qualify under another head of charity.[2] The alleviation of physical infirmities associated with old age is only one way of relieving the aged. It is equally charitable to meet the needs of the lonely and isolated, provide chiropody, household aids, visitor services and to organise social gatherings, holidays and outings.[3]

10.3.4 Relief of the disabled

The preamble to the Statute of Elizabeth mentions the relief of the impotent. In this context 'impotent' means the physically weak, or disabled. There are many charities providing for the needs of the disabled. Household names include Scope, Mind and Mencap.

10.3.5 Prevention of alcoholism and drug dependency

The rehabilitation of alcoholics and drug addicts falls within the relief of the impotent. It is also charitable to promote temperance by propaganda and to research the causes and cures of intemperance, so long as the results are made available to the public.

10.3.6 Hospitals

On the face of it, any services provided by a hospital are potentially charitable. A hospital which makes a charge for its services can still be charitable so long as it is not run for private profit. A gift to a hospital for the relief of the sick is charitable, irrespective of whether the hospital gives treatment free of charge or not and whether it is funded by the Department of Health through the internal market. It follows that health service bodies can hold and administer charitable gifts.[4] The Court of Appeal in *Re Adams*[5] considered what was meant by a trust for endowing

1 *Re Bradbury* [1950] All ER 1150.

2 *Charity Law A to Z: Key Questions Answered* J Claricoat and H Phillips (Jordans, 1995).

3 *Charities: Law and Practice* 2nd edn, E Cairns (Sweet & Maxwell, 1997).

4 A gift of a capital sum to be invested and the income to be applied for the general purposes of the hospital is charitable, *Re Ginger* [1951] 1 Ch 458.

5 *Re Adams* [1968] Ch 80.

beds for paying patients and in its decision it embraced the idea that the funds could be invested and income applied in improving the services the hospital in question provided. Lord Justice Dankerwerts accepted that it would be perfectly proper to apply income for any of the following improvements:

(a) the provision of better beds, bedding, furniture, crockery, cutlery, floor coverings, curtains and other furnishings and the better maintenance of such things;
(b) the more frequent redecoration of accommodation;
(c) the sound-proofing of rooms;
(d) the provision of telephones and television sets for the use of patients;
(e) the provision of a wider choice and better food;
(f) the provision of a day or sitting room and dining room for patients who are not required to remain in bed .

10.3.7 Services and facilities for the relief of the sick

Services such as bathing, escort services, exchange of library books, foot care, gardening, hair washing, shaving, help in the home, entertainment, physiotherapy in the home, reading, shopping, sitting in, tape recording for the housebound, travelling companions and the provision of a convalescent home have all been held to be charitable by the Charity Commissioners.[1] Care for the carers of the sick is also charitable either through the arrangement of respite breaks or to help close relations to visit or care for patients by providing transport.

10.3.8 Rest homes

Providing a rest home is charitable so long as the occupants are genuinely in need of rest and they form a sufficient section of the community.[2]

10.3.9 Family planning centres

It is charitable 'to preserve and protect the good health both mental and physical of parents, young people and children and to prevent the poverty, hardship and distress caused by unwanted conception'.[3] A charity has also been registered with additional objects of 'advice, treatment and assistance for women who are suffering from any physical or mental illness or distress as a result of or during pregnancy'.[4]

1 See *The Law and Practice Relating to Charities* 2nd edn, H Picarda (Butterworths, 1995).
2 *Re White's Will Trusts* [1951] 1 All ER 528.
3 The Family Planning Association (1969) Ch Com Rep 11, para 25.
4 The British Pregnancy Advisory Service (1976) Ch Com Rep 17–18, para 54–61.

10.3.10 Occupational health in the workplace

There are a number of charities registered with the object of relieving sickness through occupational health schemes. People now spend longer hours working and employers not only have statutory duties relating to the health and safety of their workforce but are often eager actively to promote the good health of their employees in order to prevent absence through sickness.

10.3.11 Alternative medicine

The Charity Commissioners have given guidance[1] to promoters of charities seeking to register institutions with objects to further the practice of unorthodox methods of healing. They have accepted well known therapeutic activities such as acupuncture, osteopathy, faith healing,[2] homeopathy, yoga, herbalism, clinical nutrition and vegetarianism. Counselling has been accepted by the Charity Commissioners as being a charitable activity if carried out in furtherance of a charitable purpose such as the protection of mental health, so long as it is carried out by properly qualified persons. Meditation has also been accepted as charitable in the context of the relief of the sick,[3] as have charities providing occupational therapy such as art therapy, crafts and music.

10.3.12 The Hospital League of Friends

Most hospitals have a league of friends, the majority of which are registered as charities. Funds are raised at a local level for a wide variety of hospital needs and the national body produces a constitution which allows funds raised to be spent not only on amenities but also essentials, such as the construction of hospital buildings.

---

1 (1975) Ch Com Rep.

2 Faith healing was accepted by the courts as being charitable in *Funnel v Stewart* [1996] 1 WLR 288, ChD.

3 The Gaia House Trust was registered as a charity with dual objects, one of which was 'to preserve and enhance physical, mental, emotional and spiritual health by the provision of a centre for the instruction and practice of meditation'.

10.3.13 Holidays

Holidays for the sick and their carers for the purpose of recuperation are accepted as charitable. So too are holidays for the disabled. Some charities take the sick to religious shrines on pilgrimage.[1]

10.3.14 Hospital staff welfare and amenity funds

These are charitable only because their immediate non-charitable purpose of providing benefits to the employees or a particular employee is perceived as being in furtherance of the charitable purposes of the employer hospital, ie relieving the sick.[2]

10.3.15 The advancement of religion in hospitals

The advancement of religion is a charitable purpose. The law does not favour one religion above another and hospitals commonly have a range of chaplains from various denominations and faiths ministering to patients. The advancement of religion in this context includes building and repairing places of worship in the hospital, supporting chaplains, holding services and evangelism.[3]

10.3.16 The relief of poverty

The relief of poverty is a charitable purpose. Some patients lack the financial means to assist their recovery. Examples of such charitable activity include grants for payment of travelling expenses on entering or leaving hospitals, out-patient consultations and convalescent home fees.[4] The link between poverty and health has long been recognised, as has the

---

1 The Handicapped Children's Pilgrimage Trust provides pilgrimages to Lourdes in France for sick and disabled children and their carers. Dis-Abled Together arranges for pilgrimages to a range of religious shrines. For a pilgrimage to be charitable under the charitable head of the advancement of religion rather than for the relief of the sick the edification must be public and part of a programme of religious events. Pilgrimages which are charitable for the advancement of religion can involve the able bodied or the sick or both.

2 The Charity Commissioners advise that it is not necessary to discriminate against those employed in administration or support, as opposed to those directly involved in patient care. They add, however, that the benefits must not go beyond what a good employer would normally provide for its staff. In assessing what a good employer would normally provide it is submitted that one would have regard to what is generally offered in comparable professions by other employers at that particular time. See *NHS Charitable Funds: A Guide* (Charity Commission, November 1994) p 26.

3 See *NHS Charitable Funds: A Guide* (Charity Commission, November 1994) p 24.

4 *Ibid.*

fact that charities for the relief of poverty have the general effect of promoting good health.

10.3.17 The advancement of education

The advancement of education is a charitable purpose. It includes the provision of funds for medical research and the education of staff, such as the training of doctors and nurses and their professional development when they have qualified. Many professional bodies, including the medical professions, are registered as educational charities on the basis that they are providing education for their members and developing a body of knowledge and enhancing professional standards for the benefit of the public. The Royal College of Surgeons is a case in point.

10.3.18 Hospices

The modern hospice movement began in 1967 with the founding of St. Christopher's Hospice in south London by Dame Cicely Saunders. The few hospices which existed before that date were run by religious charities. The story of the modern hospice movement started with Dr Saunders' friendship with David Tansa during the last few months of his terminal illness. Out of this friendship came the vision to develop a radical approach to terminal illness. It involved an holistic approach to pain involving the treatment of physical, social, psychological and spiritual pain.

Hospices were founded because care for the terminally ill was inadequate. The desire for independent charitable status came from a wish to present a new independent model of care. It was felt that the National Health Service would only change its practices towards the terminally ill if it was presented with a clear alternative. In 1995, 75 per cent of the hospices and bed spaces for the terminally ill were funded by charity.[1] Following the introduction of National Health Service funding, hospices have become more integrated with other health services. It has been argued that this has caused a dilution of the ideals which led to the establishment of the hospice movement.[2] The early hospice amateurism has been replaced by increasing professionalism with the work of those specialising in palliative medicine. Professional specialism often leads to careerism. Cynics have pointed to a similar development in the field of AIDS where further medical specialisation tends to focus more on physical needs rather than the holistic approach. Although it is true to say that with

1 *The Gift of Health*, M Lattimer (Directory of Social Change, 1996) p 115.

2 'From Vision to System: The Maturing of the Hospice Movement', published in *Death Rites – Law and Ethics at the End of Life* edited by R Lee and D Morgan, (Routledge, 1994).

integration into the National Health Service hospices have lost something of their independence, one must not overlook the profound influence they have had on the treatment of the dying within the National Health Service. They have provided a different approach to death from that offered by the euthanasia movement.

Hospices stopped receiving grants in April 1994. From that date they have contracted with the National Health Service as part of the internal market. Ironically, this has led to hospices competing with health service bodies for funds. As the National Health Service has itself increased its fund-raising activities the hospices have started to face competition. One wonders how long the distinction between health service bodies and independent charitable hospices will remain.

10.3.19 The use of charities in multi-party disaster litigation for the relief of sickness

The Bhopal Hospital Trust and the Thalidomide Trust demonstrate how independent charities can be used to distribute compensation paid to the victims of major disasters. Deadlocks between litigants and defendant companies can often only be broken by an independent mediator such as a respected charity. The Bhopal Hospital Trust was established to build a hospital for the benefit of the victims of the huge leak of methyl isocyanate gas from Union Carbide's pesticide plant in Bhopal, India in 1984. Union Carbide decided to disinvest in India and the charity was established as an independent body to ensure that the hospital was built after the company left. The funds put into the charity were from the sale of shares in Union Carbide (India) Ltd. Although Union Carbide had agreed to the sale of its 50.9 per cent stake in Union Carbide (India) Ltd the criminal court immediately placed an attachment order on the shares so as to secure the attendance of the company's chairman at a criminal trial. Without the existence of an independent charitable trust the criminal court would probably not have released the proportion of the funds under the order necessary to build the hospital.[1]

The Thalidomide action, which took place between 1958 and 1962, involved a drug which was discovered by a West German pharmaceutical company and marketed in the UK by Distillers Co (Biochemicals) Ltd as a treatment for morning sickness. Although Distillers marketed the drug as a product which was completely safe for both mother and child, in 1961 a British doctor wrote an article in *The Lancet* pointing to the growing numbers of limb malformations in children whose mothers had been taking thalidomide during pregnancy. Of the 430 British children

1 'Breaking the Deadlock at Bhopal' (1994) *Legal Business* 49 (Nov) pp 72–74.

injured, 62 attempted to sue Distillers. In the event, the action in the UK was not successful and it exposed a number of problems in the legal system which militated against multi-party action by litigants injured by drugs. Ultimately, the case was settled as a result of public pressure and a media campaign on behalf of the victims.[1] Distillers placed £20 million in a trust fund. It is expected that this fund will be exhausted within the next 15 years and the thalidomide victims have recently succeeded in persuading Guiness, the company which took over Distillers, to provide more compensation.[2] The idea of using a charity in this way is gaining momentum. It is possible that the legal actions by injured smokers against various tobacco companies might be settled by a proportion of the profits from the tobacco companies being paid into a charitable fund which is then used to pay for the health care of victims of smoking.[3]

However, the problem with these types of charities is that they can only relieve charitable needs such as medical care rather than provide enhanced lifestyles. Careful planning is therefore required by the trustees of such charities to ensue that this is the case. For example, the funding of a holiday would have to be because there is a need for recuperation rather than simply for pleasure.

10.4 THE ROLE OF CHARITY IN MODERN HEALTH CARE

There are a number of issues arising from the definition of the charitable provision of health care. First, the definition is very broad and covers alternative as well as conventional medicine.[4] This means that the increasing role played by charity in the National Health Service offers scope for a wider range of treatment determined by popular support of the community rather than centralised control by the Department of Health. With the scarcity of funds in the National Health Service there is a real debate as to what constitutes illness (for example, infertility) but also as to the type of treatment that should be funded. The role that charity can play is to empower the community to decide these issues by subscribing to a particular charitable appeal rather than another. In the mixed economy of health care charity will have a powerful say in decisions about health care.

---

1 *Drug Injuries and the Pursuit of Compensation* P R Ferguson (Sweet & Maxwell, 1996) pp 4–5.
2 'Thalidomide Victims Given "£3.75m Bail Out"' (1995) *The Independent*, 4 May.
3 (1997) *The Independent*, 6 March.
4 The National Health Service does offer some forms of alternative medicine already, such as homeopathy, but the range is fairly limited at present.

Secondly, charity offers the possibility of tackling the causes of illness. Examples of this are medical research charities and occupational health charities. One of the criticisms of the National Health Service is that it is a sickness service rather than a health service, where an emphasis is placed on responding to illness rather than looking at the causes of illness. For example, the public sanitation movement in the 19th century provides an example of an approach geared to prevention rather than cure.[1]

As Newdick has pointed out,[2] good health and a good health service may have little in common. Many of the most significant improvements in health have come about from improvements in our environment and diet. The combined death rate from scarlet fever, diphtheria, whooping cough and measles among children up to the age of 15 decreased by 90 per cent between 1865 and 1965 before the introduction of antibiotics and immunization. The most important factor was a higher host resistance due to better nutrition.[3] Evidence of this nature raises the question as to whether the National Health Service should be directing its resources more towards promoting good health rather than dealing with ill health.

The Government intends to focus on promoting health in a future Green Paper entitled 'Our Healthier Nation', which will be followed by legislation to place a statutory duty on Health Authorities to improve the health of the population.[4] This will involve the implementation of a local health improvement programme. In order to ensure the success of this programme the Government intends to legislate to place a new statutory duty on health service bodies to work together to improve the health of the local community.

The World Health Organisation describes 'health' as 'a state of complete physical, mental and social well-being and not merely the absence of disease or infirmity'.[5] Such a definition presupposes the absence of poverty, good education, sanitation, good living accommodation, community support, a holiday each year, good food and a pollution free environment. The legal concept of charity is wide enough to cater for each of these areas and it is an interesting thought that if the direction of the

1 Many public amenities, such as sewers, constructed to deal with sanitation were built with funds raised from public subscription. Arguably the statutory purposes upon which these amenities are held are charitable in nature.

2 *Who Should We Treat? Law, Patients and the NHS* C Newdick (Clarendon, 1995).

3 See *The Modern Rise of Population and the Role of Medicine: Dream, Mirage or Nemesis?* (Nuffield Provincial Hospital Trust, 1976) referred to in *Who Should We Treat? op cit* pp 7–8.

4 *The new NHS. Modern. Dependable* (The Stationery Office, 1997).

5 *Who Should We Treat? Law, Patients and the NHS* C Newdick (Clarendon, 1995).

National Health Service were to change charities would be ideally placed to provide for the promotion of good health.

Finally, conventional medicine is regulated by professional bodies such as the British Medical Association and the Royal College of Nurses.[1] These bodies regulate their professions and issue recognised qualifications and practising certificates. By contrast, alternative medicine is largely unregulated and there exists a myriad of qualifications and institutions awarding them. Not all alternative medicine has centrally recognised professional bodies controlling standards and issuing practising certificates. Alternative medicine is largely carried out by private practitioners and by charities. Therefore, the Charity Commissioners have a crucial role to play in validating alternative medicine. In deciding whether an area of alternative medicine is for the public benefit and therefore charitable the Charity Commissioners require the promoters of a charity to adduce evidence in support of their application for charitable status which usually involves expert conventional medical opinion. To date this has not tended to restrict the range of alternative medical charities registered but it does not solve the problem of regulation of professional standards.

1 Both are charitable bodies as are many of the professional bodies regulating conventional medical practice.

Chapter 11

CHARITY TRUSTEES: DUTIES AND RESPONSIBILITIES

11.1 INTRODUCTION

Health service bodies acting as charity trustees of NHS charities or independent boards of charity trustees of charities providing health care need to be aware of the various responsibilities and duties attached to the office of charity trustee. Those administering charitable funds are often unaware of these important duties and responsibilities and this chapter aims to address this.

11.2 CHARITY TRUSTEES

'Charity trustees' are defined in s 97 of the Charities Act 1993 as 'the persons having the general control and management of the administration of a charity'. It follows that a charity trustee is defined by the duties and responsibilities that he or she carries out rather than the titles he or she possesses. The practical consequence of this is that if an employee takes control of a charity's management he may be deemed to be a charity trustee and, as a result, may fall foul of the general rule prohibiting the payment of charity trustees without express authority in the charity's governing instrument or authorisation from the Charity Commission.

Where health service bodies hold charitable funds in their corporate capacity, the Charity Commissioners take the view that the corporate body, rather than its board members, is the charity trustee. It is also their view that if the corporate trustee commits a breach of trust then it will have done so because of its board members and it will be those members who will be held liable to the corporate trustee for their actions. Even if this analysis is correct (and it has been subject to much recent debate[1]), it would be prudent for the board members of the corporate trustee to

---

1 See 'Trusting to a Corporate Solution', R Meakin and J Ward (1996) *NGO Finance Magazine*, Vol 6, Issue 5, October/November, p 52 and 'Unto the Breach – Doing Battle over Trustee Liability', J Claricoat and H Phillips (1997) *NGO Finance Magazine*, Vol 7, Issue 1, January/February, pp 36–38.

ensure that the corporate trustee complies with all its legal duties and responsibilities.

Where charitable funds are held in the name of individual trustees rather than in the name of a corporate health body those individuals will be the charity trustees, for example, special trustees of endowments held by teaching hospitals.[1]

11.3 DUTIES AND RESPONSIBILITIES OF CHARITY TRUSTEES

The duties and responsibilities of charity trustees apply to all charity trustees regardless of whether the charity is unincorporated or incorporated or of whether the charity trustee is a corporate trustee or an individual.

11.3.1 Duty to register the charity with the Charity Commissioners

This duty is imposed by s 3(7) of the Charities Act 1993, where funds are held for charity and the charity has either permanent endowment[2] or the use or occupation of land or has income from all sources in aggregate of more than £1,000 per annum. Certain charities are exempt or excepted from registration but, as a general rule, charities in the health sector tend not to be exempt or excepted. There is no sanction for failing to register.

11.3.2 Duty to comply with the terms of the charity's governing instrument

Charitable funds must be applied for the charitable objects set out in the charity's governing instrument. In carrying out these objects, charity trustees cannot exceed their powers which are also contained in the governing instrument or conferred by law (most of which are contained in the Trustee Act 1925).

Often funds are donated to health service bodies on oral trusts. For example, a grateful patient might give a £100 to redecorate a ward without ever drawing up a formal trust deed. As trusts can be created orally a donation on such terms would in itself, create a charity. In such circumstances, it is open to the trustees, in the absence of evidence to the

1 National Health Act 1977, s 95.
2 Permanent endowment means property, including land, investments or cash which the trustees must retain as capital assets of the charity.

contrary, to declare the trusts to which the funds were donated for in a formal trust deed. In *A-G v Mathieson*[1] the Court of Appeal ruled that trustees have an implied authority to declare the trusts on behalf of the donors which will then be treated as decisive. The declared trusts must accord with the wishes of the original donors.

11.3.3 Duty to secure the effective use of property

The general rule is that responsibility for administering the charity effectively rests with the charity trustees. They should therefore implement proper systems of financial control and should avoid leaving a charity to be run by any particular employee or employees.[2] The Charity Commissioners have published a useful checklist to assist charity trustees in carrying out this duty.[3] Where a health charity makes a grant to a National Health Service body, the Charity Commissioners have advised that the trustees should take steps to protect the grant.[4] Banking arrangements are a particularly important way of controlling the finances of a charity. The Charity Commissioners have advised that cheques should be required to be signed by at least two trustees.[5] An exception could be made where imprest accounts are used and an officer or employee is allowed to operate a separate account fed by authorised payments from a main account for pre-agreed purposes. Such accounts would have a fixed maximum for the value of cheques that could be drawn and the value would necessarily be low.[6] Under no circumstances should charity trustees sign blank cheques.[7]

11.3.4 Duty to act personally

As a general rule, trustees cannot delegate the performance of their duties. This is subject to an important exception contained in s 23, Trustee Act 1925, which allows trustees to delegate functions rather than responsibilities to solicitors, estate agents, bankers, brokers and the like. Although this enables trustees to delegate administrative acts once they have decided what action needs to be taken, it does not allow them to delegate their discretion in making the decisions themselves. This is particularly important in the context of investment management in the charity's governing instrument. Charity trustees should first establish whether

1 *A-G v Mathieson* [1907] 2 Ch 383.
2 See CC8 *Internal Financial Controls for Charities* (Charity Commission, 1996).
3 *Ibid.*
4 See Chapter 6.
5 The Charity Commissioners' Annual Report 1976, para 127 and CC8 *op cit.*
6 *Ibid.*
7 CC8 *Internal Financial Controls for Charities* (Charity Commission, 1996).

they have the power to delegate their investment management. If they do not, they should consider whether they should obtain the power and, if so, whether it is possible simply to amend the charity's governing instrument by adding the power, or whether they have to obtain an order from the Charity Commission. The Charity Commissioners' current policy is only to make orders of this type if funds of £100,000 or more are involved.

Once the express power is in place, care should be taken in exercising it. Charity trustees will remain liable for the acts of their investment manager when exercising their power to delegate unless they appoint someone in good faith whom they reasonably believe has the necessary experience and expertise in making investments and, in addition, they should retain control by either setting limits on the terms of the delegation or by exercising supervision through reporting back provisions. Careful attention should also be paid to the terms of the contract with the investment manager to ensure that the trustees do not risk liability by allowing that manager too much freedom. Although the example of investment management is given, this is a general statement of the law applicable wherever delegation of discretionary powers is involved. Furthermore, where the power to delegate is without limitation and include responsibilities in addition to functions, the persons to whom the trustees are delegatory will be treated as charity trustees.[1]

Where the trustee is a corporate health service body, there are wide statutory powers permitting delegation. Again, subject to what has been said above, the corporate trustee will remain liable for any delegation using its statutory powers.

If the governing instrument of a charity or the statutory powers of a corporate health body include the power to delegate to sub-committees then, unless the trustees or the Board of the corporate body supervise the delegation properly (through the methods outlined above), they may remain liable for any loss caused to the charity as a result of the actions of sub-committees. Often charity trustees wish to delegate to a committee established for a particular purpose such as fund-raising. The Charity Commissioners usually like to see some representation by the trustees even if it is a minority representation.

11.3.5 Duty to act gratuitously

The general rule is that charity trustees must act without payment and must not receive any private benefit as a result of their trusteeship. The

1 See *Charity Law A to Z: Key Questions Answered* J Claricoat and H Phillips (Jordans, 1995).

rule is linked with the trustee's duty not to put himself in a position where he may have a conflict of interest. There is an exception where the benefits are permitted by an express clause in the governing instrument or authority has been obtained from the Charity Commission. The Charity Commissioners will only allow remuneration where extra services are rendered to the charity by the charity trustee, such services being outside the scope of his role as an actual trustee.

When a charity applies for registration it is quite common for its governing instrument to contain a professional charging clause which allows trustees who are, for example, solicitors or accountants to charge for their services. The Charity Commission usually stipulates that such powers are made conditional so that they can only be exercised where a majority of the trustees cannot benefit, and when the trustee seeking remuneration has withdrawn from the meeting where it is discussed. The Charity Commissioners will not object to the inclusion of a power allowing payment for services rendered to a charity where the power is limited to payment of a reasonable sum. If no such limitation is in place then it will require evidence that the payment is not just a gift, details of the services being paid for, the expertise possessed by the trustee in question, how the level of payment has been calculated and the cost of employing someone else to perform any duties which need not necessarily be performed by the trustee.

In general, the Charity Commissioners are not in favour of charity employees also acting as trustees. This is because it creates a conflict of interest between the trustee's own need to be paid as an employee and his duty to act in the best interests of the charity. The Charity Commissioners will, however, consider an application where it can be argued that a particular employee must also act as a trustee in the best interests of the charity.

In the case of charities already in existence, the charity trustees will need to apply for a scheme[1] or an order[2] on the basis that the remuneration is 'expedient in the interests' of the charity or, alternatively, obtain consent from the Charity Commissioners for amendment to the charity's governing instrument to include a power to remunerate.[3] The charity trustees cannot confer a power on themselves to remunerate one of their number because, as a matter of law, they cannot exercise any of their powers to confer a personal benefit upon themselves.[4] The Charity Commissioners will usually approve the application if it can be shown

1 Charities Act 1993, s 16.

2 Charities Act 1993, s 26.

3 If the charity is a company the consent will be under Charities Act 1993, s 64.

4 *Re French Protestant Hospital* [1951] Ch 567.

that the payment is both necessary and in the best interests of the charity.[1] It is also possible to seek authority from the Charity Commissioners for remuneration for particular work and guidelines have been issued as to the factors which will be relevant to such an application.[2] Reasonable out of pocket expenses incurred by trustees in the course of carrying out their duties as trustees can be paid for out of charitable funds. It is advisable for trustees to keep receipts as evidence. Where a health service body is acting as a corporate trustee there is nothing to prevent its Board from being paid by the National Health Service, but where it is proposed that charitable funds should be used, the principles explained above will apply.

11.3.6 Duty to apply the income of a charity

Unless a charity has power in its governing instrument to accumulate income then the trustees must apply that income in furtherance of the charity's objects within a reasonable time. Charity trustees who do not have an express power to accumulate have relied over the years on their implied power to hold income in reserve for various purposes where they consider it necessary for the good administration of the charity. The issue is of particular importance because income is generally exempt from tax if it is both *applicable* and *actually applied* for charitable purposes only.[3] However, the Inland Revenue's usual practice is to exempt income which has either been spent for charitable purposes or has been invested for the benefit of the charity for a reasonable time.

Where charity trustees are relying on an implied power to accumulate income because there is no express power in the governing instrument they must be able to demonstrate that such accumulation is 'necessary' for the good administration of the charity. If they cannot show this then the accumulation would amount to a breach of trust in the case of trustees refusing to apply the funds for the benefit of beneficiaries in obvious need. Alterantively, an accummulation of funds where there was no need would place the trustees under a duty to apply for a scheme of the Charity Commissioners to widen the objects of the change to allow the funds to be applied more widely.[4] Failure to apply for a scheme in such circumstances would be a breach of trust. In the past this has been a grey area but recently the Charity Commissioners have issued guidance as to what they consider acceptable.[5] The Commissioners will always look at

1 *Decisions of the Charity Commissioners* April (HMSO, 1994) pp 18–20.
2 *Ibid* p 22.
3 Income and Corporation Taxes Act 1988, s 505.
4 Charities Act 1993, s 13(5).
5 See CC19 *Charities' Reserves* (Charity Commission, 1997).

the particular position of the charity. For example, medical research charities usually have to build up a designated fund[1] over a number of years. Knowing that the necessary funding is in place is essential because if the funding for a research project dries up before it is completed the funds already committed would be wasted and the research charity may acquire a bad reputation which would affect its ability to find future funding.[2]

11.4 COMPLIANCE DUTIES

11.4.1 Duty to account

The Charities Act 1993 has tightened the accounting requirements for charities. Charity trustees of all charities regardless of size (but excluding charitable companies) are obliged to keep accounting records which:

(a) disclose at any time the financial position of the charity, and;
(b) enable the charity trustees to prepare annual accounts in the required form.

The accounts must be kept for six years. The accounting records must contain day-to-day entries showing all receipts and payments and the nature of each as well as a record of assets and liabilities. Larger charities, in addition, must provide an annual report and annual return. The position may be summarised as follows:

Neither income nor expenditure over £10,000 per annum

(a) accounts must be prepared, but may be on the receipts and payments basis;
(b) a simple annual report must be prepared;
(c) a simple annual return must be sent to the Charity Commissioners;
(d) the accounts need not be independently examined or audited.

Income not over £100,000 but over £10,000 per annum

(a) accounts must be prepared on the accruals basis;
(b) accounts must be subject to outside scrutiny but trustees may choose independent examination rather than an audit;
(c) an annual report must be prepared;

---

1 For a definition of 'designated' see CC19 *Charities' Reserves* (Charity Commission, 1997).

2 'Medical Research Charities and their Reserves Policies', D Garnham, General Secretary of the Association of Medical Research Charities in *Investment Matters* Issue 2 (Cantrade Investment Management Ltd, July 1997).

(d) accounts, report and annual report must be sent to the Charity Commissioners within 10 months of the charity's accounting year end.

Income over expenditure not over £250,000 but over £100,000

(a) accounts must be prepared on the accruals basis;
(b) accounts must be subject to outside scrutiny but trustees may choose independent examination rather than audit;
(c) annual reports must be prepared;
(d) accounts, reports and annual return must be sent to the Charity Commissioners within 10 months of the accounting year end.

Income or expenditure over £250,000 in the current year or either of the two previous years

(a) accounts must be prepared on the accruals basis;
(b) accounts must be audited by an auditor who is qualified to audit the accounts of companies;
(c) an annual report must be prepared;
(d) accounts, report and annual return must be sent to the Charity Commissioners within 10 months of the accounting year end.

11.4.2 Charitable companies

Charitable companies are subject to company law and must prepare accounts and an annual report and file them at Companies House. Small companies which have a balance sheet total of not more than £1.4 million are exempt from the need to have their accounts audited. A charitable company which has a gross income of £90,000 or less may deliver unaudited accounts to Companies House. Where the company's gross income is between £90,000 and £250,000 unaudited accounts may be submitted, but they must be accompanied by an accountant's report stating that the accounts are in agreement with the company's accounting records, have been prepared in accordance with the companies legislation and that they are exempt from the auditing requirements. Under the exemption a company may submit an abbreviated balance sheet with notes. So far as the Charity Commissioners are concerned, charitable company accounts are acceptable if they are prepared in conformity with their Statement of Recommended Practice ('SORP'). Charitable companies should file their annual report, accounts and annual return with the Charity Commissioners if their income or expenditure is over £10,000 per annum. The annual report must conform with the requirements of the Charities Act 1993.

In addition, all charities are required by the Charities Act 1993 to provide a copy of their latest accounts within two months to any member of the public who requests it (upon payment of a reasonable fee).

11.4.3 Duty to disclose charitable status in stationery

If a registered charity has gross income in its last financial year exceeding £10,000 the fact that it is a registered charity must be stated in English in legible characters:

(a) in all notices, advertisements and other documents issued by or on behalf of the charity in soliciting money or other property for the benefit of that charity;
(b) in all bills of exchange, promissory notes, endorsements, cheques and orders for money or goods purporting to be signed on behalf of the charity; and,
(c) in all bills rendered by it and in all its invoices, receipts and letters of credit.[1]

In addition, charitable companies must make the following disclosures:

(a) the company name must be painted or fixed in an easily legible form in a conspicuous position outside any place where the charity does business.[2]
(b) the company name must be mentioned in legible characters in

- all business letters, all notices and other official publications of the company;
- all bills of exchange, promissory notes, endorsements, cheques and orders for money or goods purporting to be signed by or on behalf of the charitable company; and
- all its bills, invoices, receipts and letters of credit.[3]

(c) the name of the charitable company must be engraved in legible characters on its seal (if it uses one).[4]
(d) the address of the company's registered office must be stated in legible characters in all business letters and order forms.[5]
(e) if the charitable company name does not include the word 'charity' or 'charitable' the fact that it is a charity must be stated in English in legible characters

- in all business letters, notices and other official publications;

1 Charities Act 1993, s 5. There is a penalty for non-compliance.
2 Companies Act 1985, s 348(1).
3 *Ibid* s 349(1).
4 *Ibid* s 350(1).
5 *Ibid* s 351(1).

- in all bills of exchange, promissory notes, endorsements, cheques and orders for money or goods purporting to be signed on behalf of the company;
- in all conveyances purporting to be executed by the company; and
- in all bills rendered by it and in all its invoices, receipts and letters of credit.[1]

(f) a charitable company must not state the name of any of its directors (otherwise than in the text or as a signatory) on any business letter on which the company's name appears unless the names of all directors are shown.[2]

(g) the following must also be stated in the company's business letters and order forms:

- place of registration (ie England);
- registered number; and
- because the company is exempt from the obligation to use the word 'limited' as part of its name, the fact that the company is a limited company.[3]

11.4.4 Personal liability

Crucial to the issue of the personal liability of charity trustees in relation to third parties is the type of governing instrument the charity has. A charity can be constituted in a variety of ways but as most health care charities will be either a trust or a company the discussion in this section is confined to these two types.

The general rule is that a trustee is entitled to be indemnified against all reasonable costs and expenses incurred in the performance of his duties as a trustee provided that those costs and expenses were properly incurred.[4]

11.5 CHARITABLE TRUSTS

11.5.1 Liability as a charity trustee

Failure to carry out the responsibilities and duties of a charity trustee, as previously outlined, will mean that the charity trustee has committed a breach of trust. The standard of care generally required of a charity

1 Charities Act 1993, s 68(1).
2 Companies Act 1985, s 305(1).
3 *Ibid* s 351(1).
4 Trustee Act 1925, s 30.

trustee in administering trust assets is that of an ordinary prudent man of business in relation to his own affairs.[1] A higher duty of care is expected when investing trust funds: that which an ordinary prudent man would observe in making an investment for people he was morally obliged to provide for,[2] although failure to meet this standard will not usually result in liability if the breach of trust amounts to no more than an error of judgement in circumstances where the trustee has acted in good faith, with reasonable care, prudence and circumspection.[3] An even higher standard of care is expected of paid trustees which, in a modern context, usually means professional trustees. A professional trustee will be held accountable for delivering the special skills that he holds himself out as possessing.[4]

11.5.2 Extent of liability

As a general rule, a trustee must make good any loss caused to the trust resulting from his breach of trust. Where a trustee has profited from his office or received unauthorised renumeration (in the absence of express authority in the trust deed) then he must account for the profit he has made or the remuneration received.

11.5.3 Individual liability as a charity trustee

The general rule is that a trustee is liable only for his own acts and defaults and not those of his co-trustees.[5] Having said that, the law does not exempt a passive trustee from responsibility for a breach of trust.

11.5.4 Joint and several liability to third parties

If one of the trustees is sued then he can seek a contribution from his fellow trustees.[6] Trustees can be held jointly and severally liable vis à vis a third party which means that that third party can choose either to sue one individual trustee or all of them. It is then up to the trustees to seek contributions between themselves according to where the culpability lies.[7]

---

1 *Learoyd v Whiteley* (1887) 12 AC 728.
2 *Ibid.*
3 *Re Luckings Will Trust* [1968] 1 WLR 866.
4 *Re Rosenthal* [1972] 1 WLR 1373; see also *Hanbury & Maudsley* in *Modern Equity* 11th edn, R H Maudsley and J E Martin (Stevens) p 520.
5 Trustee Act 1925, s 30.
6 Civil Liability (Contribution) Act 1978.
7 *Ibid.*

11.5.5 Liability to third parties

(1) *Contractual liability*
A trust has no legal existence apart from its trustees. It follows that contracts will be entered into in the names of the trustees and they will be personally liable to fulfill those contracts. However, so long as the trust has sufficient assets to meet the contractual liability and so long as the contracts are entered into within the powers of the charity and are in furtherance of the charity's objects, although a trustee will be personally liable he will usually be entitled to be indemnified from the assets of the charity. In the case of NHS charities, the health service body, as a corporate body, will be the corporate trustee and any contracts will be entered into in its name rather than the names of the individual charity trustees. In this case the health service body will, in the first instance, be personally liable rather than individuals.

(2) *Liability in tort*
A trustee may also be personally liable for negligent acts and omissions involving a breach of duty, for example, as an occupier of land or as an employer for work related injuries. Innocent breaches of duty in good faith will not usually result in personal liability and in some circumstances the trustees will be able to indemnify themselves from trust assets.[1]

(3) *Insufficient trust assets to cover liability*
Even if trustees have not committed a breach of trust, if they face contractual or tortious liability and the trust has insufficient funds to cover that liability the trustees will have to make up any shortfall from their own resources.

11.6 CHARITABLE COMPANIES

Very often the promoters of a charity will know from the outset that they will be involved in entering into contracts for goods and services, employing people or undertaking financial commitments in excess of the assets that the charity expects to receive in the short term. In these circumstances it makes sense to consider setting up the charity as a company rather than a trust to take advantage of limited liability. Health service bodies as corporate bodies can act as corporate trustee, with all the benefits of limited liability. However, sometimes the promoters of a charity will prefer to set up a separate charity independent from the health service body and, if so, they will need to decide whether to constitute the

1 Where they have acted honestly and reasonably and ought fairly to be excused for the breach of trust and for omitting to obtain the directions of the court: Trustee Act 1925, s 61.

charity as a trust or a company. It will be a question of judgement whether a charity should be formed as a trust or a company. On the one hand there is the extra administration involved in dealing with Companies House as well as the Charity Commission. For example, notification of a change of directorship needs to be sent to Companies House and there is a separate regime for annual returns, reports and accounts.[1] On the other hand, the use of a charitable company instead of a trust does confer limited liability on the directors in certain circumstances.

11.6.1 Limited liability?

(1) *Fiduciary duties*
Fiduciary duties are imposed on the directors of charitable companies by both company and charity law and such directors are subject to the same fiduciary duties as trustees of a charitable trust, so that a breach of duty may result in personal liability in the same way. Like the trustees of a charitable trust the directors are under a duty to apply the company's assets for the objects of the company and to act within the powers set out in the memorandum of association. Directors may not ratify any act outside the powers set out in the memorandum by special resolution without the prior written approval of the Charity Commissioners.[2]

Company law forbids transactions where the interests of a director conflict with the interests of the company,[3] but some of these transactions can be approved by a general meeting of the members either before, or be ratified by the members after, the transactions have taken place. However, in certain cases, the prior written consent of the Charity Commissioners will also be required before the members can approve or ratify.[4] Examples include payments for loss of office or retirement or the acquisition of assets from a director.

(2) *Contractual liability*
Contracts will in practice be entered into in the name of the company, which is a separate legal entity from the director trustees. As a result, the directors will not usually be liable where they have entered into a contract in the best interests of the company and where they are acting within the powers set out in the memorandum of association. It follows that even if the company does not have sufficient assets to cover its contractual liability the directors will not necessarily be liable. Nevertheless, the directors may be liable in certain circumstances including:

1 See **11.4.2**.
2 Charities Act 1993, s 65(4).
3 Companies Act 1985, Part X.
4 Charities Act 1993, s 66.

(a) where they have acted as agents of the charitable company in contracts collateral with any main contract made between third parties and the charitable company; or
(b) where they breach warranty of authority in their dealings with a third party by expressly or impliedly misrepresenting their authority to bind the charitable company and the third party suffers a loss by acting in good faith on such misrepresentation.

Although the doctrine of ultra vires has been abolished in respect of commercial companies,[1] it has been preserved to a certain extent in the case of charitable companies.[2] Where a person transacts with a charitable company and gives full consideration and is unaware that the transaction is not within the powers set out in the charitable company's memorandum of association or the powers of the directors, then that transaction will be valid. The burden of proof is on the person alleging that the transaction was not permitted.[3] However, it should be noted that if the charitable company has complied with the requirement to state on its business documents that it is a 'charity' where its name does not include the word 'charity' or the word 'charitable' then the person transacting with the charitable company should be on notice to check the powers.[4]

(3) *Negligence*

The directors of a company may incur personal liability for losses caused to third parties as a result of their negligence. Company directors have been held liable where they have failed to meet the standard of care expected in law of the ordinary reasonable man. In addition, third party liability for negligence may arise from a breach of the directors' duty as employers owed to employees or as occupiers to visitors (even where they are trespassing).

(4) *Wrongful trading*

The directors of a company may be held personally liable for 'wrongful trading' under the Insolvency Act 1986 if they realise that the company is insolvent and that there is no reasonable prospect of avoiding liquidation, and if, at that point, they do not take steps to minimise the potential loss to the company's creditors and ensure that the company ceases trading.

1 Companies Act 1985, ss 35 and 35A.
2 Charities Act 1993, s 65.
3 Charities Act 1993, s 65(3)(a) and (b).
4 Charities Act 1993, s 68.

11.7 CORPORATE TRUSTEE

Usually the health service body will act as trustee. Health service bodies are themselves corporate bodies and they will therefore hold general assets governed by the charities legislation. Where a health service body acts as a trustee of charitable funds it will do so as a corporate trustee. There are some special features about a corporate trustee which need to be noted.

11.7.1 What is a corporate trustee?

A corporate trustee is a corporate body which acts as a trustee of a trust, charitable or otherwise. It can hold assets in its own name, contract in its own name, and sue and be sued in its own name. It follows that any contracts will be entered into in the name of the corporate trustee rather than its directors and where the corporate trustee is a health service body, so long as the contract is within the powers set out in the statute governing the health service body, liability will usually rest with the health service body rather than its directors.[1]

11.7.2 How can a corporate trustee be appointed?

Depending on the powers in the instrument that governs the charity, a corporate trustee can be appointed by deed when the charity is formed or later on. If the powers of appointment are too restrictive, a corporate trustee can be appointed by a Charity Commission Order or Scheme, and, indeed, this may be desirable in many cases as this will automatically confer 'trust corporation' status on the corporate body (which is a separate legal concept from a corporate trustee). Having trust corporation status enables a corporate trustee to act as sole trustee in some circumstances where more than one trustee would normally be needed.[2] The current trustees can be appointed as directors of the corporate body so that when the corporate trustee is appointed they can retire as trustees from the charity. This leaves one trustee of the charity which is operated by its directors. Where the corporate trustee is a health service body, it is not uncommon for the operation of the charity to be delegated to a dedicated committee.

11.7.3 Following the appointment of the corporate trustee who are the charity trustees?

The corporate trustee will be a trustee as it will hold assets belonging to the charity. In addition, s 97 of the Charities Act 1993 defines 'charity

1 See **11.6** for circumstances where the directors can be held liable despite contracts being entered into in the name of the corporate entity.

2 See **11.7.5** below for the distinction between a trust corporation and a corporate trustee.

trustees' as 'the persons having the general control and management of the administration of the charity'. There has been some recent debate as to whether the directors of a corporate trustee are charity trustees within the s 97 definition. In the author's opinion, the better view is that they are charity trustees, but recent advice from the Charity Commissioners has been that only the corporate trustee is a charity trustee. The Charity Commissioners have expressed the view that if the directors of a corporate body cause the corporate trustee to commit a breach of trust the corporate trustee will be liable as charity trustee but, at the same time, the directors will correspondingly be liable to the corporate trustee for any loss caused by that breach. In the author's view, even if the Charity Commissioners' analysis is correct the directors would simply be liable to the corporate trustee rather than the charity.[1]

11.7.4 Holding property

Depending on the powers set out in its memorandum of association or governing statute (as the case may be), a corporate trustee can hold any type of property, whether land or investments. Having a corporate trustee means that the property can be vested in the name of the corporate trustee rather than the individual director trustees. This means that individual trustees may come and go without the need to worry about vesting property in new trustees or discharging retiring trustees by way of deed in each individual case. This makes life easier from an administrative and legal point of view and avoids the expense of drawing up deeds of appointment and retirement.

11.7.5 Trust corporation status?

Where a corporate trustee is appointed by a Charity Commission Order or Scheme, the effect is to confer the status of a trust corporation on the corporate trustee.[2] This means that the corporate trustee can receive the proceeds of sale of land and other capital sums. Without trust corporation status two or more individuals would have to remain trustees.[3] For this reason, it makes sense to ask the Charity Commission to appoint the corporate trustee by Order or Scheme irrespective of the powers of appointment in the charity's governing instrument. Experience has shown that the Charity Commission is generally sympathetic to such

1 See 'Trusting to a Corporate Solution', R Meakin and J Ward (1996) *NGO Finance Magazine*, Vol 6, Issue 5, October/November, p 52 and 'Unto the Breach – Doing Battle over Trustee Liability', J Claricoat and H Phillips (1997) *NGO Finance Magazine*, Vol 7, Issue 1, January/February, pp 36–38.

2 Charities Act 1993, s 35.

3 Law of Property Act 1925, s 27(2) as amended by Trusts of Land and Appointment of Trustees Act 1996, Sch 3, para 4(8)(a).

approaches. Alternatively, an application can be made to the Lord Chancellor for the conferral of trust corporation status. Trustees of charitable, ecclesiastical and public trusts are entitled to make such an application so long as they act without remuneration or for private profit (other than expenses).[1] Whereas, in the case of a company wishing to act as a commercial trust corporation, it would be required, inter alia, to have a share capital of not less than £250,000 of which not less than £100,000 has been paid up in cash, there is no such capital requirement for a corporate body wishing to act for a charity.

11.7.6 Holding investments

The corporate trustee route is particularly useful now that the Official Custodian no longer holds investments in its name on behalf of charities.[2] Many health charities have large investment portfolios which could be held in the name of a corporate trustee in order to facilitate transfers.

11.8 WAYS OF LIMITING LIABILITY – LIMITING LIABILITY AS A CHARITY TRUSTEE

11.8.1 Keeping records of decisions

Irrespective of the type of governing instrument the charity has, charity trustees face the prospect of personal liability for breaches of trust. However, a charity trustee is only liable in his capacity as a charity trustee for his own acts, receipts, neglects and defaults and not those of his co-trustees, unless the same happens through his own wilful default.[3] It is therefore important that the decisions of the charity trustees are minuted at their meetings and that any dissenting opinions are recorded, as this may have a bearing on potential liability at a future date.

11.8.2 Trustee indemnity insurance

The charity trustees may decide to cover their liability through indemnity insurance. Trustee indemnity insurance covers any personal liability caused by an innocent breach of trust or duty (which may possibly

1 Law of Property (Amendment) Act 1926, s 3.

2 Following the Woodfield Report in 1988 (*Efficiency Scrutiny of the Supervision of Charities*) (HMSO, 1988), which recommended that the Charity Commissioners should concentrate more on the supervision of charities, legislation was introduced to enable the Official Custodian to divest himself of all property vested in him other than land or property vested in him by way of Charity Commission Order. See Charities Act 1992, ss 29 and 30.

3 Trustee Act 1925, s 30(1).

amount to negligence giving rise to third party liability) or against a criminal offence successfully defended by the trustees or innocent wrongful trading under the insolvency legislation the extent of cover will be determined by the terms of the policy. The Charity Commissioners take the view that the purchase of indemnity insurance by charity trustees using charity funds as the conferral of a personal benefit and therefore there needs to be an express power in the charity's governing instrument authorising the payment of premiums. If there is no express power, the Charity Commissioners take the view that, because of the rule that a governing instrument cannot be amended to confer personal benefit on charity trustees,[1] authorisation is required from them to exercise a power of amendment to confer such a power.

An important point to bear in mind is that, in the case of charitable trusts, trustee indemnity insurance will not cover contractual liability where the assets are insufficient.

In the case of criminal offence, indemnity insurance will only cover the trustees where they have successfully defended themselves. This seems rather hard on trustees who are guilty of offences of strict liability caused unknowingly, for example, under the food safety legislation. The author has taken this point up with the Charity Commissioners and has been informed that the Charity Commissioners are reviewing their policy and that this issue will be part of that review.

Although companies legislation has recently removed the statutory preclusion on a company purchasing and maintaining insurance for any officer, or any other person employed by the company as an auditor, against any liability in respect of negligence, default, breach of trust or breach of duty of which they might be guilty in relation to the company, the Charity Commissioners take the view that this power does not enable director/charity trustees to purchase indemnity insurance using charity funds. The Charity Commissioners say that, despite this statutory provision, the directors of a charitable company, as charity trustees, would usually be precluded from personal benefit by the company's memorandum of association and, therefore, their authorisation for an amendment to the memorandum of association to include an express power to take out indemnity insurance would be required. This is a good illustration of the conflict between company law, which is geared to commercial companies, and charity law, which is geared to trusts.

If an application is made to the Charity Commissioners for the inclusion of a power to take out indemnity insurance in a charity's governing instrument, the trustees will need to make out a case that there is a risk of

1 *Re French Protestant Hospital* [1951] Ch 567.

liability and that the cost of the insurance is not disproportionate to that risk. In essence, the type of clause that the Charity Commissioners will accept covers liability for breaches of trust or duty as a result of an honest mistake, but will exclude wilful or reckless acts or omissions which result in such a breach. In the case of a charitable company, the Charity Commissioners are, in principle, prepared to include a clause covering director/charity trustees against personal liability for 'wrongful trading' under the insolvency legislation, provided an exclusion clause is inserted so that director/charity trustees who continue to trade knowing that the company is insolvent or have reckless disregard as to whether it is or not are not covered.

11.8.3 Directions from the court

Section 61 of the Trustee Act 1925 confers power on the court to relieve trustees from actual or potential personal liability, either wholly or partly, for breaches of trust where the trustees have acted 'honestly and reasonably and ought fairly to be excused for the breach of trust and for omitting to obtain the directions of the court'. It is always open to trustees to seek guidance from the court in order to gain protection from actual or potential personal liability. Even if a trustee does not seek such guidance he can claim that he has acted honestly and reasonably and ought fairly to be excused.

11.8.4 Opinion of the Charity Commissioners

The Charity Commissioners have the power under s 29 of the Charities Act 1993 to give their opinion or advice, upon written application by any charity trustee, on any matter affecting the performance of his duties. A charity trustee acting upon such advice will be deemed to have acted in accordance with the terms of his duty unless:

(a) he knows or has reasonable cause to suspect that the opinion or advice was given in ignorance of material facts; or,
(b) the decision of the court has been obtained on the matter or proceedings are pending to obtain one.

If charity trustees seek protection under this provision it is important that they ensure that the opinion or advice is expressed to be pursuant to s 29 of the Charities Act 1993.

11.8.5 Order of the Charity Commissioners

Where charity trustees have doubts about their power to act in a particular way, authority may be obtained from the Charity Commissioners by way of an Order made under s 26 of the Charities Act 1993, irrespective of whether the proposed course of action is within their powers. The trustees must show that the proposed course of action is 'expedient in the interests of the charity'.[1] An Order cannot be made authorising a course of action prohibited by the trusts of the charity or to extend or to alter the charity's purposes.

11.9 WAYS OF LIMITING LIABILITY – LIMITING LIABILITY TO THIRD PARTIES

11.9.1 Indemnities from third parties

When entering into arrangements with third parties it may be possible for the trustees to seek an indemnity against any personal liability. For example, if a fund-raiser entered into a contract with a charity to run a fund-raising event the charity trustees might consider it appropriate to include an indemnity in the fund-raising contract against personal liability arising as a result of the event.

11.9.2 Limiting liability in the contract

If, for example, a charity is formed to construct a hospital, it might be considered wise to insert a clause in the development contract to limit liability to the extent of the assets held by the charity or some other form of limitation.

11.9.3 Insurance

Apart from indemnity insurance, there is a whole range of insurance that can be taken out by the charity trustees on behalf of the charity to protect them from risks. Examples of such insurance are contained in the Charity Commissioners' booklet, *Charities and Insurance*.[2]

11.9.4 Limited liability

The merits of limited liability conferred through the use of a charitable company and a corporate trustee have been discussed earlier.[3] Limited liability does not confer any protection against liability incurred as a charity trustee as opposed to liability incurred to third parties.

---

1 Charities Act 1993, s 26.
2 CC49 *Charities and Insurance* (Charity Commission, 1996).
3 See **11.6**.

Chapter 12

AMALGAMATION OF CHARITABLE FUNDS

12.1 INTRODUCTION

This chapter looks at effective ways of merging funds so that they can be dealt with more efficiently. This is an important consideration for health service bodies who often hold numerous small charitable funds for a variety of particular charitable purposes.

12.2 SPECIAL TRUSTS

Depending on the wording of a particular charitable gift, it will either be held for the general purposes of a health service body, a charity supporting a health service body or as a separate charity governed by its own terms: a special trust. The difficulty with the creation of special trusts is that they demand more administration and their ring-fenced funds are not available to meet ongoing health care needs. In order to avoid this problem, health service bodies can request donors and testators to use a form of wording which shows that the donee will try to respect any preference expressed without being legally committed to do so. Additionally, or alternatively, a health service body could establish a charity with very broad charitable objects and encourage donors and testators to give to the charity unconditionally.

12.3 PERMANENT ENDOWMENT

Permanent endowment is any property, including land or cash, which cannot be used as if it were income. Unless the terms of the governing instrument make it clear that the funds are not permanent endowment then there is a statutory presumption that it is.[1] Modern trust deeds tend to exclude the possibility of permanent endowment in order to prevent restrictions on the way in which the funds can be used.

1 Charities Act 1993, s 96(3).

There will only be one case where a charitable company will have permanent endowment and that will be where it is given property to hold for a particular purpose in which case it will hold that property as trustee. This is because property held for the declared charitable purposes of a charitable company is not held on trust but is held as part of the charitable company's corporate property.[1]

12.4 WAYS OF AMALGAMATING CHARITABLE FUNDS

12.4.1 Using a scheme

A scheme is a legal document by which the Charity Commissioners may, amongst other things, alter the charitable objects of a charity, amalgamate funds or appoint or remove trustees. There are two types of scheme – a cy-près scheme or a scheme for the administration of a charity. A cy-près scheme allows charitable property to be applied for a purpose as near as possible to its original purpose, where the original trusts have failed in some way. Either type of scheme could be used to enable a health service body to amalgamate the charitable funds it administers or to enable the purposes of the charities it is responsible for to be altered so that funds could be used for a more useful purpose.

12.4.2 Using the powers in the governing instrument

A scheme might not be necessary if the governing instrument of the charity has a power to amend the charitable objects in order to widen the charity's purposes. Alternatively, if the governing instrument has a power of dissolution it should be possible (depending on the exact wording) to dissolve the charity and pass the funds over to another NHS charity or health care charity.

12.4.3 Charitable application

Even where a charity's governing instrument does not contain a power of amendment or a power of dissolution it may be possible to transfer the charity's assets over to another charity by a process known as 'charitable application'. The requirements are that the transferor charity and transferee charity either have almost identical objects and that, ideally, the transferor charity has an express power to make grants to other charities or that the transferor charity has a wide object and the transferee charity

---

1 *Liverpool and District Hospital v Attorney-General* [1981] All ER 994.

has a narrow object within the transferer's charity and that the transferor has, ideally, an express power to make grants to other charities.[1]

12.4.4 The small charity provisions

(1) *Transfer of property*

The Charities Act 1993 introduced a statutory procedure for transferring charitable property from one charity to another.[2] In order to take advantage of this provision the transferor charity must:

(a) have a gross income which does not exceed £5,000 in its last financial year;
(b) not hold land on trusts which stipulate that the land is to be used for the purposes of, or for any particular purpose of the charity;
(c) not be a charitable company; and,
(d) not be an exempt charity.

It is not possible to transfer only part of the charitable property; it must all be transferred. However, it may be divided between any number of charities. The receiving charity or charities must be registered unless they are not required to do so (ie they are exempt or excepted from registration). The charity trustees do not have the power to pass a resolution using this statutory procedure unless they are satisfied that the existing charity has ceased to be conducive to a suitable and effective application of the charity's resources and that the purposes of the charity or charities specified in the resolution are as similar in character to the purposes of the transferor charity as is reasonably practicable. Before passing the resolution the trustees of the charity transferring its property must have received written confirmation from the trustees of the transferor charity or charities that they are willing to accept the property.

This procedure is particularly relevant to health service bodies holding numerous small charity funds for various specific charitable purposes of a similar nature. Although the procedure can help to reduce the time and expense of administering many small funds the financial limit of £5,000 gross income, the stipulation that all the property must be transferred and the obligation to transfer only to charities of a similar character often limits its usefulness.

(2) *Altering the charity's trusts*

An alternative to transferring the property of the charity is to alter its trusts, in whole or in part, with modified charitable purposes.[3] Before

1 *IRC v Slater (Helen) Charitable Trust* [1982] Ch 49.
2 Charities Act 1993, s 74.
3 *Ibid* s 74(2)(c).

passing a resolution to this effect the charity trustees must be satisfied that:

(a) the existing purposes of the charity (or, as the case may be, such of them as it is proposed to replace) have ceased to be conducive to a suitable and effective application of the charity's resources; and,
(b) that the purposes specified in the resolution are as similar in character to those existing purposes as is practical in the circumstances.

There is also a provision for the alteration of any of the powers exercisable by the charity trustees in the administration of the charity, or regulating the procedure to be followed in any respect in connection with its administration.[1] The charity need not be registered to take advantage of this statutory provision, but it must:

(a) have a gross income which did not exceed £5,000 in its last financial year;
(b) not hold land on trusts which stipulate that that land is to be used for the purposes of, or any particular purpose of, the charity;
(c) not be a charitable company;
(d) not be an exempt charity.

In essence, this procedure is relevant to small charities which do not have sufficient income and assets to meet the needs of the beneficiaries.

(3) ***Power to spend capital***

Where the charity trustees conclude that they cannot achieve any useful purpose by spending the charity's income alone and where the capital of the charity is termed permanent endowment[2] they may resolve to use the powers contained in Charities Act 1993 to release that capital.[3] This statutory provision applies to both registered and unregistered charities but cannot be used by charities which are exempt from registration. Its application is extremely restricted in that it can only be used by charities which:

(a) have a gross income which did not exceed £1,000 in its last financial year;
(b) do not have land which is held as permanent endowment;
(c) are not charitable companies;

---

1 Charities Act 1993, s 74(2)(d).

2 Permanent endowment is the term applied to charitable property which is held subject to a restriction on its expenditure. A charity is deemed to have permanent endowment unless all property held for its purposes may be expended for those purposes without distinction between capital and income. See Charities Act 1993, s 96(3).

3 *Ibid* s 75.

(d) are not exempt from registration.

Before passing the resolution the charity trustees must consider whether a transfer of the property is reasonably possible but should disregard such a possibility if it would cost too much.

Chapter 13

INVESTMENT OF CHARITY FUNDS

13.1 POWERS OF INVESTMENT

13.1.1 Trustee Investments Act 1961

Unless the trust deed has a wide power of investment beyond that of the Trustee Investments Act 1961, the trustees will need to divide the charity's investments into two parts: one for 'narrower range investments' and one for 'wider range investments'. At the time of the division, the value of the wider range investments must be three times that of the narrower range.[1] Narrower range investments are roughly defined under the Act as income-producing investments such as gilts whereas wider range investments are roughly defined as investments producing capital growth such as equities.

There is a duty under the Trustee Investments Act 1961[2] and under the general law, for charity trustees, when exercising their power of investment, to have regard to the need to diversify, in so far as it is appropriate to the circumstances of the charity and with an eye to the suitability of the type of investment proposed.

13.1.2 Express powers

If the charity has an express power of investment beyond the Trustee Investments Act powers then this will govern the scope of the investments made. Again, charity trustees must have regard to the need to diversify and the suitability of investments, referred to in **13.1.1**.

13.2 ETHICAL INVESTMENT

Trustees of charities providing health care may be concerned that when investing the charity's funds they select ethical investments, bearing in mind the objects of the charity concerned. An ethical investment policy may only be adopted if it is consistent with the trustees' overriding duty

---

1 Charities (Trustee Investments Act 1961) Order 1995, SI 1995/1092.
2 Trustee Investments Act 1961, s 6.

to secure the best possible financial return on the funds invested.[1] However, investments which are contrary to the objects of the charity should be excluded regardless of whether they are good investments or not. For example, a cancer research charity should not invest in tobacco shares. It may also be ethically and legally acceptable to avoid certain kinds of investment on the basis that to make such investments might alienate potential donors and cause the charity to suffer financially or alienate potential recipients of aid.

13.3 POOLING SCHEMES

Where a trustee is a trustee of a number of charities, as is often the case for health service bodies, the trustee can apply to the Charity Commissioners asking them to create a 'pooling scheme' for investment purposes.[2] Under such a scheme the assets of the participating charities are pooled so that they are more easily and more cost-effectively managed for investment purposes. A pooling scheme is legally a separate charity.[3] The Charity Commissioners have the power to confer wider powers of investment on the trustees of the pooled fund.

13.4 COMMON INVESTMENT SCHEMES

A variation on a pooling scheme is a common investment scheme which can be established under the same statutory power but using a separately appointed trustee to manage the investments of the participating charities. As a matter of policy, the Charity Commissioners now insist on the appointment of a corporate trustee independent of the fund manager. All charities have the power, in addition to their investment powers, to invest in common investment schemes.[4] A common investment fund is itself a charity which is registered by the Charity Commissioners.[5] Common investment funds are charitable versions of unit trusts. There are a number of them on the market and each offers its own investment policy. Essentially, trustees can choose between them, depending on whether they want investment geared towards equities, fixed interest

---

1 *Harries and Others v Church of England Commissioners for England and Wales and Another* (1991) *The Times*, 30 October.

2 Charities Act 1993, s 24.

3 *Ibid* s 24(8).

4 *Ibid*. Unless their governing instrument prohibits it: in practice this is rarely the case.

5 *Ibid* s 24(8).

funds, overseas equities or a mixture. Again, the Charity Commissioners have the power to confer wider investment powers. The advantages of common investment funds are obvious. Charities can take advantage of wider powers of investment, lower administration charges, nominee facilities for quicker transactions, the opportunity to receive dividends without tax having been deducted,[1] safekeeping of certificates and regular statements of account.

13.5 COMMON DEPOSIT SCHEMES

The Charity Commissioners also have the power to make schemes for common deposit funds. These enable cash to be pooled so that higher interest rates can be achieved.

1 Tax relief on dividend income passing to charities is to be phased out over a five-year period from 1999. This is as a result of the phasing out of Advance Corporation Tax set out in the Finance Act (No 2) 1997.

Chapter 14

CHARITY FUND-RAISING AND TRADING: TAX AND VAT

14.1 FUND-RAISING

Fund-raising may be defined as the raising of money in a way which does not amount to trading. Fund-raising includes activities such as public appeals for funds and soliciting covenants, legacies and donations. Charities also raise funds by giving something in return to their supporters and when this happens the activity may become a trade with resulting tax consequences. Where a donation is a genuine donation without anything expected in return, the donation may be given tax efficiently, by either covenant or gift aid.[1]

14.1.1 Covenants

Covenanted payments involve the giver promising to make payments for a period of time capable of lasting more than three years. Covenanted donations enable charities to recover basic rate tax paid by the donor. The promise, to be tax-efficient, must be made by way of a deed. The covenanted payment must not be in exchange for any benefit, except those set out below.

The direct tax position in respect of covenanted membership subscriptions is that although, in certain circumstances, membership subscriptions might constitute trading if subscriptions are in return for goods and services, a number of permitted benefits are, however, disregarded by the Inland Revenue. The three main exemptions are:

(a) *Small benefits*
Ordinary small membership subscriptions where less than 25 per cent of the membership subscription is returned to the members in the form of benefits may be covenanted without loss of tax relief.[2]

---

1 The Government is currently reviewing charity taxation. See 'Responses to an invitation for comments on the taxation of charities', R Meakin and R Iferenta in *Baring Asset Management – Top 3000 Charities 1998*: *The Guide to UK Charities* (CaritasData Ltd, 1998).

2 Inland Revenue Press Release, 14 March 1989 and [1990] STC 273.

(b) *Rights of admission*
Charities whose sole or main purpose is
(i) the preservation of property for public benefit; or
(ii) the conservation of wildlife for public benefit,
may offer covenants to the general public for consideration, in the form of rights of admission, free of charge or at a reduced rate to the covenantor and his family, to view the property or the wildlife of which the charity is concerned.[1]

(c) *Literature*
The Inland Revenue disregards the provision of publications in return for covenanted membership subscriptions, if the publications are relevant to, and distributed in furtherance of, the charitable objects of the charity.

It is important to note that the VAT position needs to be taken into account in these situations.

14.1.2 Gift aid

Gift aid payments involve single payments of £250 or more. The rule in the case of gift aid is more restrictive than covenants. Any benefit which the giver or person connected with the giver receives may not exceed 2.5 per cent of the gift or £250 in total.

14.2 TRADING

'Trade' is defined in the relevant tax legislation as '... every trade, manufacture, adventure or concern in the nature of trade'.[2] This circular definition is unhelpful and one has to turn to the decisions of the courts to gain an understanding of what is meant by trading. The courts have established certain 'badges' of what constitutes a trade. For example, repetition of the activity,[3] or a profit motive,[4] or the existence of a selling organisation such as a shop, or the acquisition of items for the purpose of being resold; any of these activities can show that trading exists. The profits from a trade are exempt from income tax in two cases:

(a) where the trade is exercised in the course of the actual carrying out of a primary purpose of the charity; or

---

1 Finance Act 1989, s 59.
2 Income and Corporation Taxes Act 1988, s 832(1).
3 See *British Legion Peterhead Branch Remembrance and Welcome Home Fund v IRC* (1953) 3 STC 84.
4 See *Oxfam v City of Birmingham District Council* [1979] AC 126.

(b) where the work in connection with the trade is mainly carried out by the beneficiaries of the charity.[1]

The first exemption is very important for charities providing health care. For example, it enables a charitable hospital to charge its patients fees without incurring a tax liability. By way of concession, the Inland Revenue regards trading which is ancillary to the carrying out of a primary purpose as exempt from tax.[2] For example, a hospital league of friends might sell paintings by patients participating in art therapy as part of their treatment. The second exemption covers remedial or therapeutic work carried out by beneficiaries, such as the sale of goods manufactured by the beneficiaries of a charity for the disabled. Again it is a very useful exemption for charities providing health care.

In some cases the trade may amount, in part, to a primary purpose trade. For example, a charitable hospital may have a dispensary for drugs for its patients and may also sell sweets and newspapers to visitors. The Inland Revenue operates a concession for such income if the part of the trade which is not within a primary purpose (ie the sale of sweets and newspapers) is small in absolute terms and the turnover of that part of the trade is less than 10 per cent of the whole trade turnover.[3] Income from donations is not taxable. By way of concession the income from the sale of donated goods is exempt from tax. There is also an exemption covering one-off fund-raising events.[4] The profits of a trade carried out by a charity which fall outside the statutory and concessional exemptions will be taxable. However, the Inland Revenue is lenient in the way it views the calculation of profits. Profits are calculated in the same way as any other trading activity and, therefore, the direct expenditure of the trade can normally be deducted along with indirect expenditure such as the proportion of lighting, heating and building repairs and maintenance costs if the trade is carried on on the charity's premises. In addition, the Inland Revenue disregards any special rates given to charities because they are charities. For example, if a charity was given a 40 per cent discount on hiring premises for a charity auction event to raise funds because it was a charity, the Inland Revenue would allow the standard hiring fee charged to non-charity customers to be deducted from the charity's profits from the event. The point is that tax is charged on profit, and if this can be reduced by deducting allowable expenditure then this will reduce the tax liability of the charity.[5]

1 See Income and Corporation Taxes Act 1988, s 505(1)(e).
2 CS2 *Trading by Charities* (Inland Revenue, 1995).
3 *Ibid.*
4 *Ibid.*
5 *Ibid.*

14.3 SPONSORSHIP

Income from sponsorship activities may be treated as taxable trading if the charity is providing advertising in exchange for the payments it receives. The basic distinction is that, in the case of sponsorship, the sponsoring business wants something back in return, usually publicity, and as a result there may be tax implications. By way of contrast, in the case of a donation, nothing is expected in return and, as a result, there will be no tax or VAT implications. A useful way of establishing whether a payment is intended as a sponsorship payment or a donation is to check which budget the funding is coming from. Is the sponsoring business giving from its marketing budget or from its charitable-giving budget? At least this will tell you what is intended. If the sponsoring business intends to make its payments as a marketing expense it may deduct it as a business expense leaving the Inland Revenue to pursue the charity for income received as trading income. It is important to note that there is no reason why the sponsoring business cannot make a donation and then advertise the fact itself. If the funds come out of the sponsoring business's charity budget it will be beyond dispute that this is a donation and there will be no direct tax implications.

For VAT purposes, the relevant question is whether the payment received is a pure donation or whether the charity is providing any goods or services in consideration for the receipt of the payment. A pure donation will be outside the scope of VAT. On the other hand a payment will be subject to VAT if:

- it is made on the condition that the sponsor's name or trading style is advertised or promoted; or
- the sponsor receives some benefit, for example, free tickets, preferential booking rights or free advertising space in a charity event programme.

Merely providing an acknowledgment of the sponsor's contribution, such as providing a flag or sticker or inclusion in a list of supporters, will not bring the contribution within the scope of VAT, however.[1] Where a sponsorship is in connection with a one-off fund-raising event, it will be exempt from VAT.[2]

There is no tax liability for patronage which means that nothing is given in return for a donation except mere acknowledgement. In such circumstances a payment can be made by the sponsor either by gift aid or by covenant. If, however, a charity gives something in return to the

1 For further information, see HM Customs & Excise, VAT Notice 701/1/95.
2 Value Added Tax Act 1994, Sch 9, Group 12, Item 1.

sponsor, for example, the charity plays a part in publicising the business sponsor's affinity with it by including references to the sponsor in publications, posters, etc and at events organised by the charity (other than one-off fund-raising events). The Inland Revenue will regard a reference to a sponsor as an advertisement if it incorporates any of the following:

- sponsor's logo;
- sponsor's corporate colours; or,
- a mention of the sponsor's products or services.

There are other services which a charity might provide in return for sponsorship payments which will be factors in determining whether the payments are trading income. Examples are:

- use of a charity's mailing list;
- use of a charity's logo;
- endorsement of the sponsor's products or services; and,
- exclusive rights to sell goods or services on the charity's premises.[1]

It is therefore important to be clear at the outset whether a business intends to make a donation or a sponsorship payment. If possible, a charity should arrange for the payment to be a donation within the rules or, alternatively, ensure that the sponsorship agreement is with the charity's trading company so that, at least, the tax can be covenanted or paid by gift aid to the charity free of tax so that the charity can claim it back.

14.4 TRADING COMPANIES

The use of a trading company is an important method of mitigating a charity's tax liability. The establishment of a trading company and its relationship with a charity is complex and needs careful consideration.

14.4.1 Establishing the trading company

The Charity Commissioners' traditional view has been that the expense of establishing a trading company is not an application of a charity's funds for charitable purposes which has meant that a charity's funds cannot usually be used. Their usual advice is that the charity should ask supporters to donate funds to cover the cost.

1 CS2 *Trading by Charities* (Inland Revenue, 1995).

14.4.2 Funding the trading company

The Charity Commissioners have traditionally been extremely cautious about charities investing in their trading companies. The reason for this is that such investment is usually risky because at the outset the trading company will have no track record. Legally, an investment by a charity in its trading company when it is set up will nearly always be outside the investment powers of the charity because, broadly speaking, charity trustees have a duty to diversify their investments and to consider their suitability. In practice, a trading company will require a substantial investment and will objectively be less secure than other investments. Despite these tensions between charity law and the spirit of commercial adventure the Charity Commissioners have recently relaxed their policy in this area and are far more accommodating than they used to be.[1] There are two main considerations here:

(i) *The investment powers of the charity*

First, the charity must have investment powers wide enough to invest in a trading company. Second, the trustees must exercise that power having regard to the need to diversify, in so far as it is appropriate to the circumstances of the charity and with an eye to the suitability of the type of investment proposed.[2] The trustees, when making an investment, are under a duty to invest as ordinary prudent men minded to make an investment for the benefit of other people for whom they felt morally bound to provide.[3] In fulfilment of this duty, trustees must avoid hazardous or speculative investment.[4] The Charity Commissioners advise that the investment should be by way of a secured loan on commercial terms rather than by a subscription for shares. This is because in the event of a liquidation of the trading company the repayment of share capital has a lower priority than the repayment of a secured creditor. As a point of practice, at a later date, the directors of the trading company can convert the loan into share capital, thereby converting a liability on the trading company's balance sheet into an increase in shareholder's funds. This may assist the trading company to attract investment from other sources. As a final comment, it would also be wise to take independent advice from someone qualified under the Financial Services Act 1986. This may help protect the trustees from potential liability.

1 CC35 *Charities and Trading* (Charity Commission, 1997).
2 Trustee Investment Act 1961, s 6.
3 *Re Whiteley* [1886] 33 ChD 347 at 355 per Lindley LJ.
4 *Learoyd* v *Whiteley* [1887] 12 AC 728.

(ii) *Tax*

In order to qualify for tax relief the investment in the trading company must be 'qualifying expenditure', if it is a loan, it must be for charitable purposes only, for the benefit of the lending charity and not be for the avoidance of tax. This seems strange in that the purpose of a trading company is to avoid tax and the Charity Commissioners have advised in the past that charity trustees have a duty to avoid unnecessary tax liabilities at the risk of incurring personal liability.[1] The Inland Revenue expects the trustees to prepare:

- market research on the proposed business venture;
- a business plan showing how the trade will be developed;
- a cashflow forecast for at least two years;
- a budget showing prospective capital growth and outgoing expenditure;
- an analysis of working capital requirements;
- projections of future profits.

14.4.3 Bailing the trading company out?

Care should be taken by directors of the trading company not to continue trading if there is no real prospect of the company being able to meet its liabilities. This is 'wrongful trading' under the Insolvency Act 1986 and the directors could face personal liability as a result.

14.4.4 Relationship between the charity and its trading company

One of the Charity Commissioners' main areas of concern is the relationship between a charity and its trading company. In law they are separate entities, one being charitable and the other non-charitable. Any dealings between them must be at arm's length. Charity premises used by the trading company must be taken on lease licence at a proper market rent. Any time spent by charity staff at the trading company must be charged at the proper rate. The Charity Commissioners advise against all the trustees acting as directors of the trading company because of potential conflicts of interest. It can, however, be argued that the trustees should be represented on the Board of the trading company so as to safeguard the charity's investment. In order to inject a level of objectivity into proceedings on both sides, the Charity Commissioners suggest that at least one trustee should not be a director of the trading company and at least one director of the trading company should not be a trustee. They have, however, accepted that there is nothing in law to prevent trustees

1 Charity Commissioners Annual Report 1988, para 44.

being directors of the trading company. Finally, it is important to note that a trustee director will usually hold his position on the Board and will (unless expressly authorised by the charity's governing instrument or by the Charity Commissioners) be liable to account for any profit or remuneration received in his capacity as a director of the trading company.[1]

14.5 TAXATION OF CHARITIES – INCOME TAX

The principal exemption from income tax is contained in ss 505 and 506 of the Income and Corporation Taxes Act 1988 ('ICTA 1988'), which provide exemption from income tax for income of a charity *applicable* to charitable purposes only, and to the extent that it is *actually applied* for solely charitable purposes. Section 9 of ICTA 1988 provides that a similar exemption applies to the income of a charitable corporation. The exemption extends only to income from certain sources. These include the rents and profits of land; interest, annuities and dividends[2] on stocks and shares; annual interest or other annual payments including covenanted payments; interest on bank or building society deposit accounts or derived from loans; and income representing a distribution from a company. By concession, interest that is not annual, such as interest on a current account, is also not taxable if such income is applied for charitable purposes.

14.5.1 Trading in land

Unless a charity can demonstrate that the sale of real property is legitimate realisation of a capital asset, which would more likely be exempt from capital gains tax, the sale may be treated either as trading in land or as a transaction within the scope of s 766 of ICTA 1988, an anti-tax avoidance provision, and therefore liable to income tax.

14.6 TAXATION OF CHARITIES – CAPITAL GAINS TAX

Charities are automatically exempt from capital gains tax arising from the sale of real or personal property if the gains are applied for charitable purposes (s 256 of the Taxation of Chargeable Gains Act 1992 ('TCGA

---

1 *Re Macadam* [1946] Ch 73.

2 Under the Finance (No 2) Act 1997, the payment of tax credits on dividends is to be phased out for charities over a five-year period beginning in 1999.

1992')). This exemption extends also to corporation tax on chargeable gains accruing to charitable companies (TCGA 1992, s 8).

14.7 TAXATION OF CHARITIES – INHERITANCE TAX

For inheritance tax purposes the basic exemption is contained in s 23(1) of the Inheritance Tax Act 1984 ('IHTA 1984') which exempts transfers of value (as defined by IHTA 1984, s 2) which are attributable to property given to charities, that is, property which becomes the property of charities or is held on trust for charitable purposes only. The exemption applies to transfers made by the transferor during his life and via his will on death.

14.8 TAXATION OF CHARITIES – VAT

VAT is a tax on the supply of goods or services made by a taxable person in the course or furtherance of a business. VAT will be important, and potentially a heavy burden, for many charities, both by reason of the supplies they receive and the supplies they may make.

Whether a charity is required or entitled to register for VAT will depend on whether, and the extent to which, it makes supplies of goods or services which are taxable supplies. Taxable supplies are supplies other than exempt supplies and therefore include supplies which are taxable at either the zero rate or the standard rate of 17.5 per cent. A charity will be required to register for VAT if the value of its supplies exceeds the registration threshold. However, provided that a charity makes some taxable supplies, it may choose to register voluntarily for VAT purposes. Whilst this may result in it having to account for VAT on certain supplies it makes, it may have the advantage of enabling th charity to recover some or all of the VAT it is charged. This is an important VAT planning issue for charities which they should consider in the light of their particular circumstances.

In addition, a charity's activities may be business activities or non-business activities. Non-business activities, such as the receipt of a donation (see **14.3**) will not attract VAT.

Where a charity is registered for VAT, its business activities may result in supplies which are standard-rated, zero-rated or exempt from VAT. For example, supplies of advertising space for an event may be standard-rated, supplies of booklets and leaflets or supplies of donated goods may be zero-rated and supplies of welfare services, when made otherwise than for a profit, may be exempt.

A charity may also incur VAT on the supplies of goods or services it receives. If the charity is not registered for VAT, unless it is a body to which the Value Added Tax Act 1994, s 33, or a government department for the purposes of s 41, it will not be able to recover the VAT it has been charged. Where the charity is registered, it may generally recover VAT it has been charged, to the extent that the relevant goods or services are used by the charity to make either zero-rated or standard-rated supplies. Recovery of VAT paid on supplies received will be either by way of a refund or set-off against VAT, for which it would otherwise be obliged to account to Customs & Excise VAT on goods and services it uses to make exempt supplies, or it uses for the purposes of its non-business activities, may not be recovered and will therefore represent a real cost to the charity.

Example

> CH, a charitable hospital, predominantly makes exempt supplies of medical and surgical treatment. It also sub-lets part of its premises as shops and charges VAT on the rents. CH incurs VAT on the rent it pays its landlord and on the services of a cleaning company. CH will be able to recover a proportion of the VAT on its rental payments equal to the proportion of the property it sub-lets. The remainder of the VAT it pays on the property and all the VAT it pays for cleaning services for the hospital will be irrecoverable as it is attributable to its exempt supplies.

However, there is a wide range of reliefs for many suppliers of goods or services made to charities in the form of zero rating of those supplies. For example, certain medical equipment and aids for the disabled are zero-rated.[1] When a charity purchases such medical equipment and aids it must provide a certified declaration to the supplier to enable the supplier to charge VAT at a zero rate. In particular, the supply to a charity providing care or medical or surgical treatment to human beings or animals, or engaging in medical or veterinary research of a medicinal product, where the supply is solely for use by the charity in such care, treatment or research, is zero-rated.[2] VAT on services relating to the construction of building hospices (other than the services, provided by an architect, surveyor or a person acting in a supervisory capacity) and institutions for the disabled, mentally ill, persons dependent on drugs and alcohol, and the elderly and other similar establishments are also zero-rated.[3]

1 See Value Added Tax Act 1994, Sch 8, Groups 12 and 15.
2 *Ibid* Sch 8, Group 15, Item 9.
3 *Ibid* Sch 8, Group 5, Item 2.

The case of *League of Friends of Kingston Hospital v C & E*[1] illustrates the technicalities of VAT law and the need for careful planning when a charity is involved with raising funds for a health service body. In this case, the League of Friends, which was a charity formed to raise funds for the hospital, raised funds for a scanner unit to be installed in the grounds of the hospital. The League of Friends purchased the scanner and contracted with the builders for the construction of a building to house it. The building was erected on land owned by the hospital. The League of Friends claimed that the services supplied to it in the course of construction of the building were zero-rated on the ground that the building was intended to be solely for non-business use by a charity. Customs & Excise rejected the claim for zero-rating on the basis that the building was to be used by the hospital and not for the League of Friends as a charity.

On appeal by the League of Friends, the VAT Tribunal held that in this context 'use' had a functional meaning. The building was used as part of the scanner unit operated by the hospital as principal for the purpose of treating its own patients. The hospital was not itself a charity. The League of Friends' intention was to make the building available to the hospital; but when the building functioned as part of the scanner unit it was used by the hospital and not by the League of Friends. The appeal by the League of Friends was therefore dismissed and zero-rating on the building activities was not allowed.

VAT – community care service contracts

Under the community care regime, charities do not generally receive grants. Instead, they enter into contracts to provide services to local authorities and health service bodies. Whereas a grant given freely and without conditions is generally treated as a donation and outside the scope of VAT, a contract for the provision of services is generally treated as a business activity and therefore may give rise to taxable supplies (although they may be exempt).[2] If the payment of the services is taxable, this means that the charity may need to charge VAT on the consideration it receives if it is registered for VAT or subsequently registers for VAT.

The Charity Tax Reform Group recommends that contracts for the provision of community services should include the following clause:

---

1 *League of Friends of Kingston Hospital v C & E* (1994) VAT Decision 12764.

2 For example, the supply, otherwise than for profit, by a charity or public body (such as a health service body or a local authority) of welfare services and of goods supplied in connection therewith which are directly connected to the provision of care, treatment or instruction designed to promote the physical or mental welfare of elderly, sick, distressed or disabled people. See Value Added Tax Act 1994, Sch 9, Group 7.

> 'Any and all sums paid or payable under or pursuant to this agreement shall be exclusive of Value Added Tax'.

Without this clause, the sum specified in the contract will be assumed to include VAT and the charity will have to account for it to Customs & Excise.

VAT – National Lottery

The Lottery Board's policy is that VAT-registered bodies such as charities cannot include the VAT element in their application because they can recover the VAT in the normal course of events. However, in so far as VAT cannot be recovered, this should be referred to in the Lottery application (in detail) and the Lottery Board will include the otherwise recoverable VAT element in the grant.

14.9 TAXATION OF CHARITIES – LOCAL TAX

The Local Government Finance Act 1988[1] provides that where the ratepayer is a charity, and the property is wholly or mainly used for charitable purposes, the charity will be granted 80 per cent mandatory relief from Unified Business Rate tax. In addition, the charity can apply for 100 per cent relief which can be given at the discretion of the local authority. A property will not pass the 'wholly or mainly used for charitable purposes' test if it is wholly or mainly used for the sale of donated goods to the charity and the proceeds (after deduction of expenses) are applied for the purpose of the charity.[2]

14.10 THE TAX POSITION OF HEALTH SERVICE BODIES

For the purpose of direct taxation a health body includes health authorities and NHS Trusts.[3] They are exempt from income and corporation tax.[4]

The normal provision of care, treatment and medical goods to patients by NHS hospitals will general fall outside the scope of VAT as being a non-business activity. However, where a NHS hospital provides goods or services for consideration to, for example, private patients, then those

---

1 Local Government and Finance Act 1988, s 43(6).
2 *Ibid* s 64(10).
3 Income and Corporation Taxes Act 1988, s 519A.
4 *Ibid* s 519A(1)(a) and (b).

supplies will be within the scope of VAT, unless they are exempt. The provision of care or medical or surgical treatment, and the supply of any goods in connection with it, in any hospital or other institution approved, licensed, registered or exempt from registration by a public general Act of Parliament,[1] is exempt from VAT. This definition includes an NHS hospital. NHS hospitals and trusts will incur VAT on certain of the supplies they receive. However, many of the supplies they receive will be exempt from VAT. For example, the services of doctors, dentists, opticians, nurses, the supply of human blood, human organs or tissue for diagnostic or therapeutic purposes or medical research, the supply, otherwise than for profit, by a charity or public body of welfare services and of goods supplied in connection with them, and the supply of transport services for sick or injured persons in vehicles specially designed for that purpose are exempt for the purposes of VAT.[2]

However, there is also provision for the zero rating of certain supplies of medical and similar equipment and certain services when they are either to be donated to hospitals or certain charitable organisations or are bought by them using charitable funds. The eligible bodies include NHS trusts, charities providing care or medical or surgical treatment for handicapped persons and non-profit-making hospitals. The items which may be zero rated include medical, scientific, computer, video, sterilising, laboratory or refrigeration equipment for use in medical research, training, diagnosis or treatment, ambulances and other vehicles for use with handicapped or terminally sick persons.[3] Zero rating also applies to the repair and maintenance of such goods.[4]

Where a NHS trust does incur VAT on supplies it receives, then to the extent that it uses those supplies to make exempt supplies of, for example, care, treatment or medical goods, it will not be able to recover that VAT. However, a NHS trust may generally recover VAT it has incurred on supplies received for the purposes of its non-business activities, if the Treasury so directs.[5] In practice, the Treasury periodically issues a direction in the *London Gazette* containing a list of eligible government departments and eligible services on which VAT may be recovered.[6] During the public expenditure negotiations the Treasury allots funds to health service bodies and account is taken of any VAT costs involved. Therefore, the NHS executive has warned NHS bodies that if they

1 Value Added Tax Act 1994, Sch 9, Group 7, Item 4.
2 *Ibid* Sch 9, Group 7.
3 *Ibid* Sch 8, Group 15, Items 4 and 5.
4 *Ibid* Sch 8, Group 15, Items 6 and 7.
5 *Ibid* s 41(3).
6 See (1996) *London Gazette*, 2 July.

discover the use of VAT avoidance schemes, then funds will be clawed back equal to the VAT element of funding not required due to the tax avoidance arrangements.[1]

Although gifts to a health service body are exempt from inheritance tax.[2] there are various disadvantages in giving to a health body direct rather than to a charity providing health care. Gift aid is not available because it only applies to charities.[3] The same applies to covenanted payments[4] and the payroll deduction scheme.[5]

A health body may therefore decide to establish a charity to secure the tax advantages of gift aid, covenants and pay-roll giving. Also, given that the public perception is that the government should be providing funds for the National Health Service, soliciting for donations to a charity presents a better image as it will be perceived to be separate from the health body itself.

14.11 PARTICULAR COMMERCIAL OPPORTUNITIES

14.11.1 Medical research and associated contracts

The Charity Commissioners have given guidance to charity trustees[6] entering into arrangements with non-charitable sponsors or partners to assist in medical research programmes. Unless arrangements are put in place for the dissemination of the results of the research within a reasonable time the requirement that the research is being carried out for the public benefit – an essential requirement for charitable status – will not be fulfilled and the activity will not therefore be regarded as charitable. If regularly carried on, the research might represent a taxable trading activity and if it becomes a substantial part of the activities of the charity it should be hived off to a non-charitable trading company. The profits could then be covenanted or paid by gift aid free of tax to the charity. Research, if supplied to an eligible body on behalf of an eligible body is exempt from VAT.[7] 'Eligible body' includes a health service body and a body which is precluded from distributing any profits it makes such as a charity, and applies those profits to the continuance or improvement of such supplies.

---

1 'VAT News' (1997) *The Tax Journal*, 22 December.
2 Inheritance Tax Act 1984, Sch 3.
3 Finance Act 1990, s 25 and Income and Corporation Taxes Act 1988, s 339.
4 Income and Corporation Taxes Act 1988, s 660(3).
5 *Ibid* s 202.
6 CC19 *Charities Reserves* (Charity Commission, 1997).
7 Defined in Value Added Tax Act 1994, Sch 9, Group 6.

It should be noted that if a charity has educational objects, then, as the Charity Commissioners advise, arrangements should be put in place for the research to be made available to the public. However, where a charity has objects for the relief of the sick, the public benefit test would be satisfied by using the research to relieve sickness without the need to publish that research.

The Charity Commissioners consider that charity trustees are under a duty to protect any intellectual property rights arising from research carried out by a charity or commissioned by a charity. Where the intellectual property rights can be applied in furtherance of the objects of the charity, the charity need not charge full value; but where they are commercially exploited, the Charity Commissioners advise that a licensing arrangement should be put in place with a commercial company or through the medium of a non-charitable company wholly owned by the charity and that the intellectual property rights should only be made available at a market rate. This is because an intellectual property right is an asset of the charity and the trustees should fulfill their general duty to act prudently when dealing with the assets of the charity.

14.11.2 Charging for services

Charities can charge for services provided in furtherance of their charitable objects.[1] This is crucial to charities providing health and welfare services, particularly charitable hospitals, hospices and nursing homes. Charges for services in furtherance of a primary purpose will be free of direct tax.[2] In certain circumstances, services may be exempt from VAT.[3]

In *Re Resch's Will Trusts*, a testator bequeathed two thirds of net income of his residuary estate to the Sisters of Charity for the general purposes of St Vincent's Private Hospital. The private hospital (which had 82 beds) was close to a public hospital (which had 500 beds) also run by the Sisters of Charity. It was argued by the next of kin that a gift which in effect excluded the poor was not charitable and that a hospital not open to the

---

1 *Re Resch's Will Trusts* [1969] 1 AC 514.

2 See **14.2** of this book.

3 Such as the supply of care or medical or surgical treatment and goods in connection therewith in a hospital (Value Added Tax Act 1994, Sch 9, Group 7, Item 4) or welfare services supplied, otherwise than for profit by a charity or public body (such as a health service body or a local authority), of welfare services and of goods supplied in connection therewith which are directly connected to the provision of care, treatment or instruction designed to promote the physical or mental welfare of elderly, sick, distressed or disabled persons. See Value Added Tax Act 1994, Sch 9, Group 7.

sick as a whole but only to the poor sick could not be charitable because it was not available to the whole community. Nevertheless, the gift was held to be charitable because the essential element of public benefit was present. Lord Wilberforce remarked that in this particular case the charges were not low, but on the evidence it could not be said that the poor were excluded. Some of the poor were excluded: those who had not contributed sufficiently to a medical benefit scheme or needed to stay longer in the hospital than their benefit would cover or could not get a reduction of or exemption from the charges. On the other hand, he considered the general benefit to the community to include the relief to the beds and hospital staff of the public hospital, the benefit of having a type of nursing and treatment which supplemented that provided by the public hospital and the benefit of the standard of care in the public-funded hospital which arose from the juxtaposition of the two institutions.

Local authorities have not been slow to realise that charities can charge fees for their services, can fund-raise from the general public and secure tax reliefs. Inevitably this gives greater scope for the reduction in public funding.

14.12 BUSINESS AND CHARITIES

The age of corporate philanthropy is over.[1] These days, companies and businesses expect to benefit from giving to charity through a variety of arrangements. However, such arrangements have a number of tax, VAT and charity law implications which should be looked at before companies and charities commit themselves. Charities, companies and businesses can benefit from a number of arrangements. These include sponsorship of charity fund-raising events, product endorsement, affinity cards, secondment of employees and charities established by companies and businesses.

Companies and businesses frequently sponsor fund-raising events run by charities. The following example illustrates the sort of legal issues that can occur in a typical sponsored fund-raising event.

---

1 **14.12** to **14.12.5** were published as an article in *Baring Asset Management – Top 3,000 Charities 1997, the Guide to UK Charities* (CaritasData Ltd, 1997) and are reproduced by the kind permission of CaritasData Ltd.

14.12.1 Example: a music concert

The fund-raising department of a charity providing health care has organised a music concert to raise public awareness and raise funds. The charity has been approached by a company which wishes to sponsor the event. In return for underwriting the running costs, the company wants its logo to be displayed on a large advertising board, and on various posters. Payments by companies and businesses which are not in return for goods or services provided by the charity will normally be treated as charitable donations, rather than trading income, and therefore not taxable in the hands of the charity. In this example, however, the charity is providing an advertising service for the company in return for underwriting the event. As a result, the payments will be treated as trading income and so potentially liable to tax which will have to be accounted for by the charity. Commonly, a charity will play a part in publicising the sponsor's affinity with the charity by including references to the sponsor in publications, posters etc. Provided these references amount to no more than acknowledgements of the sponsor's contributions they will not cause the payments to be regarded as trading income.

References in publications, posters and so on of the sponsoring company's logo, corporate colours or products and services give rise to sponsorship income in the hands of the charity. If the company makes a sponsorship payment in the form of advertising it can claim that the payment is tax deductible. This is on the basis that the payment has been incurred 'wholly or exclusively' for the purposes of the company's business. If, on the other hand, the payment is not sponsorship income but simply a donation, it is in both the charity's and the company's interests to make the payment by gift aid.[1] From the company's point of view, such payments will only qualify for tax deduction if gift aided. From the charity's point of view, if the payment is not sponsorship income then the charity should ensure that the payment is gift aided so that it can claim back the tax. If necessary, the event could be run via the charity's trading company, if it has one, so that the taxable trading income received by the trading company can be covenanted or gift aided to the charity free of tax. VAT also needs to be considered if the charity is registered for VAT. Customs & Excise advise that if a sponsor's contribution is made on condition that its logo is advertised or promoted or if it receives some other type of benefit, then it may be considered to be a taxable supply and subject to VAT.

Returning to the example of the music concert, this means that the charity will need to charge the company VAT for supplying the advertising

---

1 See **14.1.1** and **14.1.2**.

services to the company. If, however, the sponsorship payments are directly connected with the fund-raising event which falls within the VAT 'one-off' fund-raising exemption, they would be exempt from VAT. This means that the charity would not need to charge the company VAT. Again if a charity receives a donation from a company and merely provides a simple acknowledgement of the company's support, this will be outside the scope of VAT and VAT will not be charged to the company.

14.12.2 Product or services endorsement

An increasing number of companies and businesses are promoting their products or services by publicising the benefit to charities of each purchase of the product or service. An example would be a pharmaceutical company stating that for each medical product sold 1p will go to a health care charity. However, following the Charities Act 1992, and subsequent regulations, companies and businesses must now comply with various requirements. The Charities Act 1992 introduced the concept of the 'commercial participator'. Commercial participators are companies or businesses which do not fund-raise for charities as part of their usual business, but which run promotions which encourage people to buy goods or services on the understanding that some proceeds will go to charity. A commercial participator which is giving to a charity must clearly state, usually on the product, the name of the charity or charities which will benefit and either the proportion of the money given for the goods or services sold or supplied, or the sum of money to be donated. In addition, the commercial participator will have to enter into a contract with the charity or charities concerned which complies with the regulations made under the Charities Act 1992. The contractual terms must include the proportion of the money given for goods or services sold or supplied or the amount of the donation to be given by the commercial participator. In addition, any remuneration or expenses must be set out in the agreement. Failure to make a proper statement or enter into a proper contract is a criminal offence, and, in addition, the contract will be unenforceable. Again, the tax and VAT position will follow whether the payments to the charity are genuine donations or not.

14.12.3 Affinity cards

A particular type of commercial participation which has become very popular is affinity card agreements. Many charities have entered into arrangements with banks or financial institutions, whereby the bank issues a credit card bearing the name and logo of the charity. Typically, the bank promotes the card to the charity's supporters by stating that for each card taken out a fee will be paid to the charity by the bank, together with a percentage of the total expenditure on the card.

Customs & Excise are prepared to accept by way of concession[1] that only that proportion of the income which is payment for promotional services provided by the charity to the bank need be subject to VAT at standard rate (typically one fifth of the initial payments but not any subsequent income). Customs & Excise are in effect agreeing to a split between a payment for services (for example the use of the charity's mailing list) which will be subject to VAT, and additional contributions for which the charity does nothing in return and which therefore are treated as donations and are outside the scope of VAT. In order to reap the benefit of the VAT concession the agreement needs to be properly structured.

However, following a recent decision in the Court of Appeal,[2] it may be possible for a charity to claim that it should not be charging any VAT because any payment by a bank in return for promotional services are exempt, being either: 'the making of any advance or the granting of any credit (item 2); or 'the making of arrangements for any transaction comprised in item 1, 2, 3, 4 (item 5).[3] Whether it is worthwhile for a charity to rely on this decision will depend on whether claiming exemption affects its recovery of VAT input tax or its non-attributable VAT input tax and consequently the way in which its partial exemption is calculated.

From an income tax point of view, by way of concession the Inland Revenue allows a charity to split a name and logo agreement as follows:

- a formal agreement between the bank and the charity's trading company for promotional services, such as exploiting the charity's mailing list. In this case the trading company can covenant or gift aid any profits to the charity to avoid paying tax; and,
- an agreement between the bank and the charity for the use of the charity's name and logo. In this case the Inland Revenue seems to be prepared to treat income as royalties. Generally speaking, royalties must be paid under a legal obligation, be pure income profit and annually recurring.

The Inland Revenue has not expressed an opinion on the precise allocation of the income between the two parts of the agreement except to say that they should be realistic.

---

1 C & E VAT Leaflet 701/1/95.
2 *CCE v Civil Service Motoring Association Ltd* [1998] STC 111 (CA).
3 Value Added Tax Act 1994, Sch 9, Group 5.

14.12.4 Secondment of employees

Another popular way for a company to benefit charities is to allow one or more of its employees to work on secondment for a charity on a temporary basis. The costs of employment remain deductible for tax purposes, just as if the employee continued to work for the company. One year is the maximum initial period, although it can be extended provided this is not the intention at the outset.

14.12.5 Company-formed charities

Companies frequently consider setting up their own charities. Depending on the kind of business activities carried out by the company in question, a charity can be created in such a way that there is a natural synergy between the work of the charity and the business of the company. For example, a pharmaceutical company may wish to set up a charity concerned with the prevention of illness. Charities can be structured in such a way that companies marketing similar products in a particular field can jointly fund and put forward representatives to run the charity. By way of illustration, a number of companies have established occupational health charities.

Companies often establish charities to try to change a poor public image. Companies accused of causing pollution could, for example, establish, on an industry-wide basis, an environmental charity or health care charity to combat the effects of that pollution.

Most companies are sensitive to the concerns of their community, and establishing and maintaining a good image is essential to their success. There are numerous ways of achieving good publicity for the company through the medium of a charity, and in the context of health care this might translate into funding community projects such as the League of Friends for local hospitals.

A company can endow charities to fund lectureships and professorial chairs which may help advance an area of knowledge with which the company is concerned.

A happy workforce helps make a business successful and companies, particularly in the financial services industry where the emphasis is on individual performance, are looking to establish their own charities and involve their employees for the purposes of motivation and team building. Finally, one should not overlook the traditional way of assisting employees through the use of company benevolent funds which have a long history of helping employees, former employees and their families in time of financial hardship which is often caused by an inability to work because of sickness.

14.13 FUND-RAISING AND COMMERCIAL PARTICIPATION

14.13.1 Fund-raising agreements

The Charities Act 1992 introduced new controls over professional fund-raisers. A 'professional fund-raiser' is defined by s 58(1) of the Charities Act 1992 as:

'(a) any person who carries on a business which is wholly or primarily engaged in soliciting or otherwise procuring money or other property for charitable, benevolent or philanthropic purposes for gain. This does not include:

(i) a charitable institution, or
(ii) a company connected with a charitable institution (and 'connected' means here that the charity or one or more charities together are able directly or indirectly through nominees to control all the voting rights at a general meeting of the company);

(b) any other person who for reward solicits money or other property for the benefit of a charitable institution. This does not include:

(iii) a person who solicits funds in the course of a fund-raising venture organised by a person who carries on a fund-raising business;
(iv) a charitable institution;
(v) companies connected (as defined above) with a charitable institution;
(vi) officers or employees of a charitable institution or connected company acting in that capacity; or any trustee of a charitable institution acting in his capacity as such;
(vii) any person who is a collector for the purposes of the rule on public collections unless he is also the promoter of the collection. 'Promoter' in this context means the person responsible for organising and controlling the conduct of the appeal (s 65(3) Charities Act 1992);
(viii) any person who solicits funds in the course of a fund-raising appeal organised by a charity or connected company in a radio or television programme;
(ix) any commercial participator;
(x) a person who receives no more than £5 per day or £500 a year in remuneration for fund-raising for a charity or more than £500 in connection with a particular fund-raising venture for a charity.'

Under the legislation any charity dealing with a professional fund-raiser must enter into an agreement with him to regulate their relationship. Such an agreement must specify:

(a) the name and address of each of the parties to the agreement;

(b) the date on which the agreement was signed by or on behalf of each of the parties;
(c) the period for which the agreement is to subsist;
(d) any terms relating to the termination of the agreement prior to the date on which that period expires; and
(e) any terms relating to the variation of the agreement during that period.

The precise terms that must be included in the contract are set out in the Charitable Institutions (Fundraising) Regulations 1994.

The agreement must also contain the following:

(a) a statement of its principal objectives and the methods to be used in pursuit of those objectives;
(b) if there is more than one charitable institution party to the agreement, provision as to the manner in which the proportion in which the institutions which are so party are respectively to benefit under the agreement;
(c) provision as to the amount by way of remuneration or expenses which the professional fund-raiser is to be entitled to receive in respect of things done by him in pursuance of the agreement and the manner in which that amount is to be determined.

14.13.2 Commercial participator agreements

The Charities Act 1992 also introduced rules governing the sponsorship of charities by businesses. Section 59(2) makes it unlawful for a 'commercial participator' to represent that 'charitable contributions' are to be given to, or applied for, the benefit of a charitable institution, unless he does so in accordance with an agreement with the institution satisfying the prescribed requirements. 'Commercial participator' is defined as any person who (a) carries on for gain a business other than a fund-raising business but (b) in the course of that business engages in any promotional venture in the course of which it is represented that charitable contributions are to be given to or applied for the benefit of the institution. 'Charitable contributions' are defined in relation to any representation made by any commercial participator as meaning:

(a) the whole or part of

    (i) the consideration given for goods or services sold or supplied by him, or
    (ii) any proceeds (other than such consideration) of a promotional venture undertaken by him, or

(b) sums given by him by way of donation in connection with the sale of supply of any such goods or services (whether the amount of such sums is determined by reference to the value of any such goods or services or otherwise).

'Promotional venture' means any advertising or sales campaign or any other venture undertaken for promotional purposes.

The Charitable Institutions (Fundraising) Regulations 1994 set out the requirements as to the form and content of an agreement made for the purposes of s 59(2) of the Charities Act 1992.

The agreement between the commercial participator and the relevant charitable institution must be in writing and signed by or on behalf of both parties. The agreement must specify:

(a) the name and address of each of the parties to the agreement;
(b) the date on which the agreement was signed by or on behalf of each of the parties;
(c) the period for which the agreement is to subsist;
(d) any terms relating to the termination of the agreement prior to the date on which that period expires; and
(e) any terms relating to the variation of the agreement during that period.

The agreement must also contain:

(a) a statement of its principal objectives and the methods to be used in pursuit of those objectives;
(b) provisions as to the manner in which these are to be determined;

    (i) the proportion of the consideration given for goods or services sold or supplied by the commercial participator, or of any other proceeds of a promotional venture undertaken by him, which is to be given to or applied for the benefit of the charitable institution; or
    (ii) the sums by way of donations by the commercial participator in connection with the sale of supplies of any goods or services sold or supplied by him which are to be so given or applied; and

(c) provision as to any amount by way of remuneration or expenses which the commercial participator is to be entitled to receive in respect of things done by him in pursuance of the agreement and the manner in which any such amount is to be determined.

The statements of methods to be used in pursuit of the objectives must include in relation to each method specified, a description of the type of charitable contributions which are to be given to or applied for the benefit of the charitable institution and of the circumstances in which they are to be given or applied.

The sponsor must also comply with regulations regarding the transmission of money or other property to the charitable institution (if appropriate) except where inviting customers and contacts to make donations direct. All funds held on behalf of the charity concerned must, unless the sponsor has a reasonable excuse, and notwithstanding any inconsistent term in the s 59 agreement:

(a) in the case of any money and any negotiable instrument which is payable to or to the account of the charitable institution, as soon as is reasonably practicable after its receipt and in any event not later than the expiration of 28 days after that receipt, or such other period as may be agreed with the institution

  (i) be paid to the person or persons having the general control and management of the administration of the institution; or
  (ii) be paid into an account held by a bank or building society in the name of or on behalf of the institution which is under the control of the person, or any of the persons, specified in (i) above and

(b) in the case of any other property be dealt with in accordance with any instructions given for that purpose, either generally or in a particular case, by the charitable institution.

The sponsor is required to hold securely any property in its possession as commercial participator pending the obtaining of such instructions from the charitable institution.

The Regulations also require commercial participators on request and at all reasonable times to make available to the charitable institution any books, documents or other records (however kept) which relate to that institution and are kept for the purposes of the agreement.

In addition to the above requirements, s 60(3) of the Charities Act 1992 requires that when any representation is made by a commercial participator to the effect that charitable contributions are to be given to or applied for the benefit of one or more particular charitable institutions, the representations shall be accompanied by a statement clearly indicating:

(a) the name or names of the institution or institutions concerned;
(b) if there is more than one institution concerned, the proportions in which the institutions are respectively to benefit; and
(c) (in general terms) the method by which it is to be determined:

(i) what proportion of the consideration given for goods or services sold or supplied by him, of any other proceeds of any promotional venture undertaken by him, is to be given to or applied for the benefit of the institution or institutions concerned; or

(ii) what sums by way of donations by him in connection with the sale or supply of any such goods or services are to be so given or applied, as the case may require.

Section 60 of the Charities Act 1992 contains other provisions which may be relevant if representations are to be made, variously, in the course of a radio or television programme, in association with an announcement to the effect that payment may be made in response to the representation made by means of a credit or debit card, or orally (other than speaking directly to the particular person or persons to whom it is addressed and in his or their presence).

It is the responsibility of the professional fundraiser and the commercial participator to ensure that an agreement that satisfies the legislation is entered into. The effect of failing to do so renders the contract unenforceable. Furthermore, the professional fundraiser or commercial participator (as the case may be) would be committing a criminal offence. Furthermore, the charity trustees could seek to restrain them by way of an injunction.

Although it is not for charity trustees to ensure that the legislation is complied with, in practice charity trustees wish to avoid bad publicity, caused by compliance failure, and usually seek their own legal advice.

Chapter 15

AN OVERVIEW

15.1 THE CHANGING ROLE OF CHARITY

One of the main themes of this book is that it has always been charitable to provide health care. In the Middle Ages, charity was the main provider. Even prior to the establishment of the National Health Service, over one third of all hospitals were charitable voluntary hospitals. In the 19th century, the State assumed increasing responsibility for the health care of the nation and this culminated in the introduction of the National Health Service with a statutory duty placed on the Secretary of State to provide a comprehensive health service.[1] Since then, State funding has not kept pace with the increasing demands placed on the health service caused by, among other factors, inflation and an ageing population. As State funding has fallen behind, charity's role has increased. It has been pointed out that there is no legal objection to charity doing more than merely supplementing State funding; it can actually provide for core facilities and services. Indeed, the width of the legal concept of charitable status presents scope for charity to play an even greater role in the provision of the nation's health care than it already does.[2]

It is when one considers the potential role of charity in the context of the mixed health care economy that opportunities can be seen.[3] Today the National Health Service is paid for out of a mix of public funds, charitable funds and private funds. The definition of charity is wide enough to cover the investigation of the causes of illness as well as dealing with the effects of illness. Charity can therefore be used to turn the National Health Service truly into a health service as well as a sickness service. Charity, because it can be used to fund both conventional and complementary medicine, offers local communities the chance to decide what kind of health care they require. They can then bid for partnership funding to match their own fund-raising efforts.

---

1 Now contained in the National Health Service Act 1977, s 1.

2 See Chapter 3.

3 See Chapter 13.

15.2 POTENTIAL STRATEGIC ALLOCATION OF RESOURCES

Although the involvement of charity in the National Health Service can provide opportunities for the public to choose to fund the health care they consider essential, setting priorities from the bottom up does have worrying implications for unpopular causes. One should not lose sight of the fact that the most popular charitable causes have traditionally been sick animals rather than sick humans. This is part of a wider concern about the charity sector in general. It could be argued that the sector lacks direction because the public sets the priorities and, as a result, some causes are over-subscribed while others are unprovided for. This will continue to be the case so long as the Charity Commissioners respond to applications for charitable status from institutions seeking registration rather than first looking at what would be charitable in broad terms and then encouraging institutions to apply for charitable status. The solution, which would also provide an answer to health care planning problems, would be to give an agency such as the Charity Commission a funding role allowing it to allocate public funds including lottery funds. It would then be in a position to take a view about where funding was required and then invite applications for charitable status. It could also allocate funds to newly formed charities along with existing charities. This would enable strategic decisions to be taken on the allocation of resources across the board regardless of the popularity of the cause.

15.3 POINTERS TO THE FUTURE ROLE OF CHARITY

The problems caused by the distinction between 'health' care and 'social' care have been explored in this book.[1] Because both areas have different funding regimes – health care is generally provided free and social services are generally means tested – there is a certain amount of 'passing the buck'. It has been recommended that a single agency should be given the power to commission health and social services from the statutory authorities. Such an agency could have charitable status and make charges consistent with the existing regime.

Charity could also play a greater role if NHS Trusts were given charitable status. There is a remarkable similarity between health service bodies and large service-providing national charities. Like charities, NHS Trusts increasingly use fund-raising to make up shortfalls in public funding. There seems no reason why NHS Trusts could not eventually be given

1 See **8.1**.

charitable status and compete on an equal footing for charitable funds. The St Bartholemew's Hospital example provides a possible model that could work.[1] It will be recalled that the proposal was that St Bartholomew's Hospital should be funded by a charitable endowment, public funds and private funds generated through charges made for services.

There is a need for a structured approach to fund-raising for the National Health Service. It has been shown in this book that the terms of a donation either from an individual donor or a charity can create a special trust the terms of which then have to be complied with.[2] The Tomlinson Report highlighted the problem created by accepting donations subject to conditions when trying to reorganise the health service.[3] The duty on the one hand to respect the wishes of the donor and the responsibility on the other hand to manage charity funds so that they meet the most pressing needs can cause both political and legal difficulties. There is a need on the part of the health service bodies for a greater appreciation of these potential difficulties so that, wherever possible, they can be avoided.

A possible solution to this problem would be to confer on the Secretary of State for Health the same kind of powers enjoyed by the Secretary of State for Education and Employment to alter charitable trusts in accordance with health requirements from time to time. This would help to provide a structured approach to the distribution of charitable assets rather than allowing it to evolve in a haphazard way.[4]

The National Health Service today is supported by a mixture of public, private and charitable funds. The internal market and the contract culture of community care have allowed health care and welfare to evolve in line with market forces. Charity is once again emerging as a significant provider of funds and this book has explored the implications of this rediscovery and pointed towards possible future developments.

---

1 See **3.1**.

2 See **6.3**.

3 See **6.1** and **6.2**.

4 See **9.5**.

APPENDICES

Appendix 1

LEGISLATION

CHARITIES ACT 1992

. . .

PART II

CONTROL OF FUND-RAISING FOR CHARITABLE INSTITUTIONS

Preliminary

58 Interpretation of Part II

(1) In this Part—

'charitable contributions', in relation to any representation made by any commercial participator or other person, means—

(a) the whole or part of—

(i) the consideration given for goods or services sold or supplied by him, or
(ii) any proceeds (other than such consideration) of a promotional venture undertaken by him, or

(b) sums given by him by way of donation in connection with the sale or supply of any such goods or services (whether the amount of such sums is determined by reference to the value of any such goods or services or otherwise);

'charitable institution' means a charity or an institution (other than a charity) which is established for charitable, benevolent or philanthropic purposes;
'charity' means a charity within the meaning of the Charities Act 1993;
'commercial participator', in relation to any charitable institution, means any person (apart from a company connected with the institution) who—

(a) carries on for gain a business other than a fund-raising business, but
(b) in the course of that business, engages in any promotional venture in the course of which it is represented that charitable contributions are to be given to or applied for the benefit of the institution;

'company' has the meaning given by section 97 of the Charities Act 1993;
'the court' means the High Court or a county court;
'credit card' means a card which is a credit-token within the meaning of the Consumer Credit Act 1974;
'debit card' means a card the use of which by its holder to make a payment results in a current account of his at a bank, or at any other institution providing banking services, being debited with the payment;
'fund-raising business' means any business carried on for gain and wholly or primarily engaged in soliciting or otherwise procuring money or other property for charitable, benevolent or philanthropic purposes;
'institution' includes any trust or undertaking;
'professional fund-raiser' means—

(a) any person (apart from a charitable instutiton or company connected with such an institution) who carries on a fund-raising business, or
(b) any other person (apart from a person excluded by virtue of subsection (2) or (3)) who for reward solicits money or other property for the benefit of a charitable institution, if he does so otherwise than in the course of any fund-raising venture undertaken by a person falling within paragraph (a) above;

'promotional venture' means any advertising or sales campaign or any other venture undertaken for promotional purposes;

'radio or television programme' includes any item included in a programme service within the meaning of the Broadcasting Act 1990.

(2) In subsection (1), paragraph (b) of the definition of 'professional fund-raiser' does not apply to any of the following, namely—

(a) any charitable institution or any company connected with any such institution;
(b) any officer or employee of any such institution or company, or any trustee of any such institution, acting (in each case) in his capacity as such;
(c) any person acting as a collector in respect of a public charitable collection (apart from a person who is to be treated as a promoter of such a collection by virtue of section 65(3));
(d) any person who in the course of a relevant programme, that is to say a radio or television programme in the course of which a fund-raising venture is undertaken by—

    (i) a charitable institution, or
    (ii) a company connected with such an institution,

makes any solicitation at the instance of that institution or company; or

(e) any commercial participator;

and for this purpose 'collector' and 'public charitable collection' have the same meaning as in Part III of this Act.

(3) In addition, paragraph (b) of the definition of 'professional fund-raiser' does not apply to a person if he does not receive—

(a) more than—

    (i) £5 per day, or
    (ii) £500 per year,

    by way of remuneration in connection with soliciting money or other property for the benefit of the charitable institution referred to in that paragraph; or
(b) more than £500 by way of remuneration in connection with any fund-raising venture in the course of which he solicits money or other property for the benefit of that institution.

(4) In this Part any reference to charitable purposes, where occurring in the context of a reference to charitable, benevolent or philanthropic purposes, is a reference to charitable purposes whether or not the purposes are charitable within the meaning of any rule of law.

(5) For the purposes of this Part a company is connected with a charitable institution if—

(a) the institution, or
(b) the institution and one or more other charitable institutions, taken together,

is or are entitled (whether directly or through one or more nominees) to exercise, or control the exercise of, the whole of the voting power at any general meeting of the company.

(6) In this Part—

(a) 'represent' and 'solicit' mean respectively represent and solicit in any manner whatever, whether expressly or impliedly and whether done—

    (i) by speaking directly to the person or persons to whom the representation or solicitation is addressed (whether when in his or their presence or not), or

(ii) by means of a statement published in any newspaper, film or radio or television programme,

or otherwise, and references to a representation or solicitation shall be construed accordingly; and

(b) any reference to soliciting or otherwise procuring money or other property is a reference to soliciting or otherwise procuring money or other property whether any consideration is, or is to be, given in return for the money or other property or not.

(7) Where—

(a) any solicitation of money or other property for the benefit of a charitable institution is made in accordance with arrangements between any person and that institution, and
(b) under those arrangements that person will be responsible for receiving on behalf of the institution money or other property given in response to the solicitation.

then (if he would not be so regarded apart from this subsection) that person shall be regarded for the purposes of this Part as soliciting money or other property for the benefit of the institution.

(8) Where any fund-raising venture is undertaken by a professional fund-raiser in the course of a radio or television programme, any solicitation which is made by a person in the course of the programme at the instance of the fund-raiser shall be regarded for the purposes of this Part as made by the fund-raiser and not by that person (and shall be so regarded whether or not the solicitation is made by that person for any reward).

(9) In this Part 'services' includes facilities, and in particular—

(a) access to any premises or event;
(b) membership of any organisation;
(c) the provision of advertising space; and
(d) the provision of any financial facilities;

and references to the supply of services shall be construed accordingly.

(10) The Secretary of State may by order amend subsection (3) by substituting a different sum for any sum for the time being specified there.

Note: Section shown as amended by the Deregulation and Contracting Out Act 1994, s 25.

Control of fund-raising

59 Prohibition on professional fund-raiser etc raising funds for charitable institution without an agreement in prescribed form

(1) It shall be unlawful for a professional fund-raiser to solicit money or other property for the benefit of a charitable institution unless he does so in accordance with an agreement with the institution satisfying the prescribed requirements.

(2) It shall be unlawful for a commercial participator to represent that charitable contributions are to be given to or applied for the benefit of a charitable institution unless he does so in accordance with an agreement with the institution satisfying the prescribed requirements.

(3) Where on the application of a charitable institution the court is satisfied—

(a) that any person has contravened or is contravening subsection (1) or (2) in relation to the institution, and

(b) that, unless restrained, any such contravention is likely to continue or be repeated,

the court may grant an injunction restraining the contravention; and compliance with subsection (1) or (2) shall not be enforceable otherwise than in accordance with this subsection.

(4) Where—

(a) a charitable institution makes any agreement with a professional fund-raiser or a commercial participator by virtue of which—

(i) the professional fund-raiser is authorised to solicit money or other property for the benefit of the institution, or

(ii) the commercial participator is authorised to represent that charitable contributions are to be given to or applied for the benefit of the institution,

as the case may be, but

(b) the agreement does not satisfy the prescribed requirements in any respect,

the agreement shall not be enforceable against the institution except to such extent (if any) as may be provided by an order of the court.

(5) A professional fund-raiser or commercial participator who is a party to such an agreement as is mentioned in subsection (4)(a) shall not be entitled to receive any amount by way of remuneration or expenses in respect of anything done by him in pursuance of the agreement unless—

(a) he is so entitled under any provision of the agreement, and

(b) either—

(i) the agreement satisfies the prescribed requirements, or

(ii) any such provision has effect by virtue of an order of the court under subsection (4).

(6) In this section 'the prescribed requirements' means such requirements as are prescribed by regulations made by virtue of section 64(2)(a).

60 Professional fund-raisers etc required to indicate institutions benefiting and arrangements for remuneration

(1) Where a professional fund-raiser solicits money or other property for the benefit of one or more particular charitable institutions, the solicitation shall be accompanied by a statement clearly indicating—

(a) the name or names of the institution or institutions concerned;

(b) if there is more than one institution concerned, the proportions in which the institutions are respectively to benefit; and

(c) (in general terms) the method by which the fund-raiser's remuneration in connection with the appeal is to be determined.

(2) Where a professional fund-raiser solicits money or other property for charitable, benevolent or philanthropic purposes of any description (rather than for the benefit of one or more particular charitable institutions), the solicitation shall be accompanied by a statement clearly indicating—

(a) the fact that he is soliciting money or other property for those purposes and not for the benefit of any particular charitable institution or institutions;

(b) the method by which it is to be determined how the proceeds of the appeal are to be distributed between different charitable institutions; and
(c) (in general terms) the method by which his remuneration in connection with the appeal is to be determined.

(3) Where any representation is made by a commercial participator to the effect that charitable contributions are to be given to or applied for the benefit of one or more particular charitable institutions, the representation shall be accompanied by a statement clearly indicating—

(a) the name or names of the institution or institutions concerned;
(b) if there is more than one institution concerned, the proportions in which the institutions are respectively to benefit; and
(c) (in general terms) the method by which it is to be determined—
  (i) what proportion of the consideration given for goods or services sold or supplied by him, or of any other proceeds of a promotional venture undertaken by him, is to be given to or applied for the benefit of the institution or institutions concerned, or
  (ii) what sums by way of donations by him in connection with the sale or supply of any such goods or services are to be so given or applied,

as the case may require.

(4) If any such solicitation or representation as is mentioned in any of subsections (1) to (3) is made —

(a) in the course of a radio or television programme, and
(b) in association with an announcement to the effect that payment may be made, in response to the solicitation or representation, by means of a credit or debit card,

the statement required by virtue of subsection (1), (2) or (3) (as the case may be) shall include full details of the right to have refunded under section 61(1) any payment of £50 or more which is so made.

(5) If any such solicitation or representation as is mentioned in any of subsections (1) to (3) is made orally but is not made—

(a) by speaking directly to the particular person or persons to whom it is addressed and in his or their presence, or
(b) in the course of any radio or television programme,

the professional fund-raiser or commercial participator concerned shall, within seven days of any payment of £50 or more being made to him in response to the solicitation or representation, give to the person making the payment a written statement—

  (i) of the matters specified in paragraphs (a) to (c) of that subsection; and
  (ii) including full details of the right to cancel under section 61(2) an agreement made in response to the solicitation or representation, and the right to have refunded under section 61(2) or (3) any payment of £50 or more made in response thereto.

(6) In subsection (5) above the reference to the making of a payment is a reference to the making of a payment of whatever nature and by whatever means, including a payment made by means of a credit card or a debit card; and for the purposes of that subsection—

(a) where the person making any such payment makes it in person, it shall be regarded as made at the time when it is so made;

(b) where the person making any such payment sends it by post, it shall be regarded as made at the time when it is posted; and

(c) where the person making any such payment makes it by giving, by telephone or by means of any other telecommunication apparatus, authority for an account to be debited with the payment, it shall be regarded as made at the time when any such authority is given.

(7) Where any requirement of subsections (1) to (5) is not complied with in relation to any solicitation or representation, the professional fund-raiser or commercial participator concerned shall be guilty of an offence and liable on summary conviction to a fine not exceeding the fifth level on the standard scale.

(8) It shall be a defence for a person charged with any such offence to prove that he took all reasonable precautions and exercised all due diligence to avoid the commission of the offence.

(9) Where the commission by any person of an offence under subsection (7) is due to the act or default of some other person, that other person shall be guilty of the offence; and a person may be charged with and convicted of the offence by virtue of this subsection whether or not proceedings are taken against the first-mentioned person.

(10) In this section—

'the appeal', in relation to any solicitation by a professional fund-raiser, means the campaign or other fund-raising venture in the course of which the solicitation is made;

'telecommunication apparatus' has the same meaning as in the Telecommunications Act 1984.

61 Cancellation of payments and agreements made in response to appeals

(1) Where—

(a) a person ('the donor'), in response to any such solicitation or representation as is mentioned in any of subsections (1) to (3) of section 60 which is made in the course of a radio or television programme, makes any payment of £50 or more to the relevant fund-raiser by means of a credit card or a debit card, but

(b) before the end of the period of seven days beginning with the date of the solicitation or representation, the donor serves on the relevant fund-raiser a notice in writing which, however expressed, indicates the donor's intention to cancel the payment,

the donor shall (subject to subsection (4) below) be entitled to have the payment refunded to him forthwith by the relevant fund-raiser.

(2) Where—

(a) a person ('the donor'), in response to any solicitation or representation falling within subsection (5) of section 60, enters into an agreement with the relevant fund-raiser under which the donor is, or may be, liable to make any payment or payments to the relevant fund-raiser, and the amount or aggregate amount which the donor is, or may be, liable to pay to him under the agreement is £50 or more, but

(b) before the end of the period of seven days beginning with the date when he is given any such written statement as is referred to in that subsection, the donor serves on the relevant fund-raiser a notice in writing which, however expressed, indicates the donor's intention to cancel the agreement,

the notice shall operate, as from the time when it is so served, to cancel the agreement and any liability of any person other than the donor in connection with the making of any such payment or payments, and the donor shall (subject to subsection (4) below) be entitled to have any payment of £50 or more made by him under the agreement refunded to him forthwith by the relevant fund-raiser.

(3) Where, in response to any solicitation or representation falling within subsection (5) of section 60, a person ('the donor')—

(a) makes any payment of £50 or more to the relevant fund-raiser, but
(b) does not enter into any such agreement as is mentioned in subsection (2) above,

then, if before the end of the period of seven days beginning with the date when the donor is given any such written statement as is referred to in subsection (5) of that section, the donor serves on the relevant fund-raiser a notice in writing which, however expressed, indicates the donor's intention to cancel the payment, the donor shall (subject to subsection (4) below) be entitled to have the payment refunded to him forthwith by the relevant fund-raiser.

(4) The right of any person to have a payment refunded to him under any of subsections (1) to (3) above—

(a) is a right to have refunded to him the amount of the payment less any administrative expenses reasonably incurred by the relevant fund-raiser in connection with—

   (i) the making of the refund, or
   (ii) (in the case of a refund under subsection (2)) dealing with the notice of cancellation served by that person; and

(b) shall, in the case of a payment for goods already received, be conditional upon restitution being made by him of the goods in question.

(5) Nothing in subsections (1) to (3) above has effect in relation to any payment made or to be made in respect of services which have been supplied at the time when the relevant notice is served.

(6) In this section any reference to the making of a payment is a reference to the making of a payment of whatever nature and (in the case of subsection (2) or (3)) a payment made by whatever means, including a payment made by means of a credit card or a debit card; and subsection (6) of section 60 shall have effect for determining when a payment is made for the purposes of this section as it has effect for determining when a payment is made for the purposes of subsection (5) of that section.

(7) In this section 'the relevant fund-raiser', in relation to any solicitation or representation, means the professional fund-raiser or commercial participator by whom it is made.

(8) The Secretary of State may by order—

(a) amend any provision of this section by substituting a different sum for the sum for the time being specified there; and
(b) make such consequential amendments in section 60 as he considers appropriate.

62 Right of charitable institution to prevent unauthorised fund-raising

(1) Where on the application of any charitable institution—

(a) the court is satisfied that any person has done or is doing either of the following, namely—

   (i) soliciting money or other property for the benefit of the institution, or

(ii) representing that charitable contributions are to be given to or applied for the benefit of the institution,

and that, unless restrained, he is likely to do further acts of that nature, and

(b) the court is also satisfied as to one or more of the matters specified in subsection (2),

then (subject to subsection (3)) the court may grant an injunction restraining the doing of any such acts.

(2) The matters referred to in subsection (1)(b) are—

(a) that the person in question is using methods of fund-raising to which the institution objects;
(b) that that person is not a fit and proper person to raise funds for the institution; and
(c) where the conduct complained of is the making of such representations as are mentioned in subsection (1)(a)(ii), that the institution does not wish to be associated with the particular promotional or other fund-raising venture in which that person is engaged.

(3) The power to grant an injunction under subsection (1) shall not be exercisable on the application of a charitable institution unless the institution has, not less than 28 days before making the application, served on the person in question a notice in writing—

(a) requesting him to cease forthwith—

(i) soliciting money or other property for the benefit of the institution, or
(ii) representing that charitable contributions are to be given to or applied for the benefit of the institution,

as the case may be; and

(b) stating that, if he does not comply with the notice, the institution will make an application under this section for an injunction.

(4) Where—

(a) a charitable institution has served on any person a notice under subsection (3) ('the relevant notice') and that person has complied with the notice, but
(b) that person has subsequently begun to carry on activities which are the same, or substantially the same, as those in respect of which the relevant notice was served,

the institution shall not, in connection with an application made by it under this section in respect of the activities carried on by that person, be required by virtue of that subsection to serve a further notice on him, if the application is made not more than 12 months after the date of service of the relevant notice.

(5) This section shall not have the effect of authorising a charitable institution to make an application under this section in respect of anything done by a professional fund-raiser or commercial participator in relation to the institution.

63 False statements relating to institutions which are not registered charities

(1) Where—

(a) a person solicits money or other property for the benefit of an institution in association with a representation that the institution is a registered charity, and
(b) the institution is not such a charity,

he shall be guilty of an offence and liable on summary conviction to a fine not exceeding the fifth level on the standard scale.

(1A) In any proceedings for an offence under subsection (1), it shall be a defence for the accused to prove that he believed on reasonable grounds that the institution was a registered charity.

(2) In this section 'registered charity' means a charity which is for the time being registered in the register of charities kept under section 3 of the Charities Act 1993.

Note: Section shown as amended by the Deregulation and Contracting Out Act 1994, s 26.

Supplementary

64 Regulations about fund-raising

(1) The Secretary of State may make such regulations as appear to him to be necessary or desirable for any purposes connected with any of the preceding provisions of this Part.

(2) Without prejudice to the generality of subsection (1), any such regulation may—

- (a) prescribe the form and content of—
  - (i) agreements made for the purposes of section 59, and
  - (ii) notices served under section 62(3);
- (b) require professional fund-raisers or commercial participators who are parties to such agreements with charitable institutions to make available to the institutions books, documents or other records (however kept) which relate to the institutions;
- (c) specify the manner in which money or other property acquired by professional fund-raisers or commercial participators for the benefit of, or otherwise falling to be given to or applied by such persons for the benefit of, charitable institutions is to be transmitted to such institutions;
- (d) provide for any provisions of section 60 or 61 having effect in relation to solicitations or representations made in the course of radio or television programmes to have effect, subject to any modifications specified in the regulations, in relation to solicitations or representations made in the course of such programmes—
  - (i) by charitable institutions, or
  - (ii) by companies connected with such institutions,

and, in that connection, provide for any other provisions of this Part to have effect for the purposes of the regulations subject to any modifications so specified;

- (e) make other provision regulating the raising of funds for charitable, benevolent or philanthropic purposes (whether by professional fund-raisers or commercial participators or otherwise).

(3) In subsection (2)(c) the reference to such money or other property as is there mentioned includes a reference to money or other property which, in the case of a professional fund-raiser or commercial participator—

- (a) has been acquired by him otherwise than in accordance with an agreement with a charitable institution, but
- (b) by reason of any solicitation or representation in consequence of which it has been acquired, is held by him on trust for such an institution.

(4) Regulations under this section may provide that any failure to comply with a specified provision of the regulations shall be an offence punishable on summary conviction by a fine not exceeding the second level on the standard scale.

CHARITIES ACT 1993

(1993 c 10)

ARRANGEMENT OF SECTIONS

PART I

THE CHARITY COMMISSIONERS AND THE OFFICIAL CUSTODIAN FOR CHARITIES

PART II

REGISTRATION AND NAMES OF CHARITIES

Registration of charities

Charity names

PART III

COMMISSIONERS' INFORMATION POWERS

PART IV

APPLICATION OF PROPERTY CY-PRES AND ASSISTANCE AND SUPERVISION OF CHARITIES BY COURT AND COMMISSIONERS

Extended powers of court and variation of charters

Powers of Commissioners to make schemes and act for protection of charities etc

PART VII

INCORPORATION OF CHARITY TRUSTEES

PART VIII

CHARITABLE COMPANIES

PART IX

MISCELLANEOUS

Powers of investment

Disqualification for acting as charity trustee

An Act to consolidate the Charitable Trustees Incorporation Act 1872 and, except for certain spent or transitional provisions, the Charities Act 1960 and Part I of the Charities Act 1992 [27 May 1993]

PART I

THE CHARITY COMMISSIONERS AND THE OFFICIAL CUSTODIAN FOR CHARITIES

1 The Charity Commissioners

(1) There shall continue to be a body of Charity Commissioners for England and Wales, and they shall have such functions as are conferred on them by this Act in addition to any functions under any other enactment for the time being in force.

(2) The provisions of Schedule 1 to this Act shall have effect with respect to the constitution and proceedings of the Commissioners and other matters relating to the Commissioners and their officers and employees.

(3) The Commissioners shall (without prejudice to their specific powers and duties under other enactments) have the general function of promoting the effective use of charitable resources by encouraging the development of better methods of administration, by giving charity trustees information or advice on any matter affecting the charity and by investigating and checking abuses.

(4) It shall be the general object of the Commissioners so to act in the case of any charity (unless it is a matter of altering its purposes) as best to promote and make effective the work of the charity in meeting the needs designated by its trusts; but the Commissioners shall not themselves have power to act in the administration of a charity.

(5) The Commissioners shall, as soon as possible after the end of every year, make to the Secretary of State a report on their operations during that year, and he shall lay a copy of the report before each House of Parliament.

2 The official custodian for charities

(1) There shall continue to be an officer known as the official custodian for charities (in this Act referred to as 'the official custodian') whose function it shall be to act as trustee for charities in the cases provided for by this Act; and the official custodian shall be by that name a corporation sole having perpetual succession and using an official seal which shall be officially and judicially noticed.

(2) Such officer of the Commissioners as they may from time to time designate shall be the official custodian.

(3) The official custodian shall perform his duties in accordance with such general or special directions as may be given him by the Commissioners, and his expenses (except those re-imbursed to him or recovered by him as trustee for any charity) shall be defrayed by the Commissioners.

(4) Anything which is required to or may be done by, to or before the official custodian may be done by, to or before any officer of the Commissioners generally or specially authorised by them to act for him during a vacancy in his office or otherwise.

(5) The official custodian shall not be liable as trustee for any charity in respect of any loss or of the mis-application of any property unless it is occasioned by or through the wilful neglect or default of the custodian or of any person acting for him; but the Consolidated Fund shall be liable to make good to a charity any sums for which the custodian may be liable by reason of any such neglect or default.

(6) The official custodian shall keep such books of account and such records in relation thereto as may be directed by the Treasury and shall prepare accounts in such form, in such manner and at such times as may be so directed.

(7) The accounts so prepared shall be examined and certified by the Comptroller and Auditor General, and the report to be made by the Commissioners to the Secretary of State for any year shall include a copy of the accounts so prepared for any period ending in or with the year and of the certificate and report of the Comptroller and Auditor General with respect to those accounts.

PART II

REGISTRATION AND NAMES OF CHARITIES

Registration of charities

3 The register of charities

(1) The Commissioners shall continue to keep a register of charities, which shall be kept by them in such manner as they think fit.

(2) There shall be entered in the register every charity not excepted by subsection (5) below; and a charity so excepted (other than one excepted by paragraph (a) of that subsection) may be entered in the register at the request of the charity, but (whether or not it was excepted at the time of registration) may at any time, and shall at the request of the charity, be removed from the register.

(3) The register shall contain—

- (a) the name of every registered charity; and
- (b) such other particulars of, and such other information relating to, every such charity as the Commissioners think fit.

(4) Any institution which no longer appears to the Commissioners to be a charity shall be removed from the register, with effect, where the removal is due to any change in its purpose or trusts, from the date of that change; and there shall also be removed from the register any charity which ceases to exist or does not operate.

(5) The following charities are not required to be registered—

- (a) any charity comprised in Schedule 2 to this Act (in this Act referred to as an 'exempt charity');

(b) any charity which is excepted by order or regulations;
(c) any charity which has neither—

(i) any permanent endowment, nor
(ii) the use or occupation of any land,

and whose income from all sources does not in aggregate amount to more than £1,000 a year;

and no charity is required to be registered in respect of any registered place of worship.

(6) With any application for a charity to be registered there shall be supplied to the Commissioners copies of its trusts (or, if they are not set out in any extant document, particulars of them), and such other documents or information as may be prescribed by regulations made by the Secretary of State or as the Commissioners may require for the purpose of the application.

(7) It shall be the duty—

(a) of the charity trustees of any charity which is not registered nor excepted from registration to apply for it to be registered, and to supply the documents and information required by subsection (6) above; and
(b) of the charity trustees (or last charity trustees) of any institution which is for the time being registered to notify the Commissioners if it ceases to exist, or if there is any change in its trusts or in the particulars of it entered in the register, and to supply to the Commissioners particulars of any such change and copies of any new trusts or alterations of the trusts.

(8) The register (including the entries cancelled when institutions are removed from the register) shall be open to public inspection at all reasonable times; and copies (or particulars) of the trusts of any registered charity as supplied to the Commissioners under this section shall, so long as it remains on the register, be kept by them and be open to public inspection at all reasonable times, except in so far as regulations made by the Secretary of State otherwise provide.

(9) Where any information contained in the register is not in documentary form, subsection (8) above shall be construed as requiring the information to be available for public inspection in legible form at all reasonable times.

(10) If the Commissioners so determine, subsection (8) above shall not apply to any particular information contained in the register and specified in their determination.

(11) Nothing in the foregoing subsections shall require any person to supply the Commissioners with copies of schemes for the administration of a charity made otherwise than by the court, or to notify the Commissioners of any change made with respect to a registered charity by such a scheme, or require a person, if he refers the Commissioners to a document or copy already in the possession of the Commissioners, to supply a further copy of the document; but where by virtue of this subsection a copy of any document need not be supplied to the Commissioners, a copy of it, if it relates to a registered charity, shall be open to inspection under subsection (8) above as if supplied to the Commissioners under this section.

(12) If the Secretary of State thinks it expedient to do so—

(a) in consequence of changes in the value of money, or

(b) with a view to extending the scope of the exception provided for by subsection (5)(c) above,

he may by order amend subsection (5)(c) by substituting a different sum for the sum for the time being specified there.

(13) The reference in subsection (5)(b) above to a charity which is excepted by order or regulations is to a charity which—

(a) is for the time being permanently or temporarily excepted by order of the Commissioners; or
(b) is of a description permanently or temporarily excepted by regulations made by the Secretary of State,

and which complies with any conditions of the exception.

(14) In this section 'registered place of worship' means any land or building falling within section 9 of the Places of Worship Registration Act 1855 (that is to say, the land and buildings which if the Charities Act 1960 had not been passed, would by virtue of that section as amended by subsequent enactments be partially exempted from the operation of the Charitable Trusts Act 1853), and for the purposes of this subsection 'building' includes part of a building.

4 Effect of, and claims and objections to, registration

(1) An institution shall for all purposes other than rectification of the register be conclusively presumed to be or to have been a charity at any time when it is or was on the register of charities.

(2) Any person who is or may be affected by the registration of an institution as a charity may, on the ground that it is not a charity, object to its being entered by the Commissioners in the register, or apply to them for it to be removed from the register; and provision may be made by regulations made by the Secretary of State as to the manner in which any such objection or application is to be made, prosecuted or dealt with.

(3) An appeal against any decision of the Commissioners to enter or not to enter an institution in the register of charities, or to remove or not to remove an institution from the register, may be brought in the High Court by the Attorney General, or by the persons who are or claim to be the charity trustees of the institution, or by any person whose objection or application under subsection (2) above is disallowed by the decision.

(4) If there is an appeal to the High Court against any decision of the Commissioners to enter an institution in the register, or not to remove an institution from the register, then until the Commissioners are satisfied whether the decision of the Commissioners is or is not to stand, the entry in the register shall be maintained, but shall be in suspense and marked to indicate that it is in suspense; and for the purposes of subsection (1) above an institution shall be deemed not to be on the register during any period when the entry relating to it is in suspense under this subsection.

(5) Any question affecting the registration or removal from the register of an institution may, notwithstanding that it has been determined by a decision on appeal under subsection (3) above, be considered afresh by the Commissioners and shall not be concluded by that decision, if it appears to the Commissioners that there has been a

change of circumstances or that the decision is inconsistent with a later judicial decision, whether given on such an appeal or not.

5 Status of registered charity (other than small charity) to appear on official publications etc

(1) This section applies to a registered charity if its gross income in its last financial year exceeded £10,000.

(2) Where this section applies to a registered charity, the fact that it is a registered charity shall be stated in legible characters—

(a) in all notices, advertisements and other documents issued by or on behalf of the charity and soliciting money or other property for the benefit of the charity;
(b) in all bills of exchange, promissory notes, endorsements, cheques and orders for money or goods purporting to be signed on behalf of the charity; and
(c) in all bills rendered by it and in all its invoices, receipts and letters of credit.

(2A) The statement required by subsection (2) above shall be in English, except that, in the case of a document which is otherwise wholly in Welsh, the statement may be in Welsh if it consists of or includes the words 'elusen cofrestredig' (the Welsh equivalent of 'registered charity').

(3) Subsection (2)(a) above has effect whether the solicitation is express or implied, and whether the money or other property is to be given for any consideration or not.

(4) If, in the case of a registered charity to which this section applies, any person issues or authorises the issue of any document falling within paragraph (a) or (c) of subsection (2) above which does not contain the statement required by that subsection, he shall be guilty of an offence and liable on summary conviction to a fine not exceeding level 3 on the standard scale.

(5) If, in the case of any such registered charity, any person signs any document falling within paragraph (b) of subsection (2) above which does not contain the statement required by that subsection, he shall be guilty of an offence and liable on summary conviction to a fine not exceeding level 3 on the standard scale.

(6) The Secretary of State may by order amend subsection (1) above by substituting a different sum for the sum for the time being specified there.

Note: Section shown as amended by the Welsh Language Act 1993, ss 32, 35(1), Sch 2; and the Charities Act 1993 (Substitution of Sums) Order 1995 (SI 1995/2696), art 2(1), (2).

Charity names

6 Power of Commissioners to require charity's name to be changed

(1) Where this subsection applies to a charity, the Commissioners may give a direction requiring the name of the charity to be changed, within such period as is specified in the direction, to such other name as the charity trustees may determine with the approval of the Commissioners.

(2) Subsection (1) above applies to a charity if—

(a) it is a registered charity and its name ('the registered name')—

(i) is the same as, or

(ii) is in the opinion of the Commissioners too like,

the name, at the time when the registered name was entered in the register in respect of the charity, of any other charity (whether registered or not);

(b) the name of the charity is in the opinion of the Commissioners likely to mislead the public as to the true nature—

(i) of the purposes of the charity as set out in its trusts, or

(ii) of the activities which the charity carries on under its trusts in pursuit of those purposes;

(c) the name of the charity includes any word or expression for the time being specified in regulations made by the Secretary of State and the inclusion in its name of that word or expression is in the opinion of the Commissioners likely to mislead the public in any respect as to the status of the charity;

(d) the name of the charity is in the opinion of the Commissioners likely to give the impression that the charity is connected in some way with Her Majesty's Government or any local authority, or with any other body of persons or any individual, when it is not so connected; or

(e) the name of the charity is in the opinion of the Commissioners offensive;

and in this subsection any reference to the name of a charity is, in relation to a registered charity, a reference to the name by which it is registered.

(3) Any direction given by virtue of subsection (2)(a) above must be given within twelve months of the time when the registered name was entered in the register in respect of the charity.

(4) Any direction given under this section with respect to a charity shall be given to the charity trustees; and on receiving any such direction the charity trustees shall give effect to it notwithstanding anything in the trusts of the charity.

(5) Where the name of any charity is changed under this section, then (without prejudice to section 3(7)(b) above) it shall be the duty of the charity trustees forthwith to notify the Commissioners of the charity's new name and of the date on which the change occurred.

(6) A change of name by a charity under this section does not affect any rights or obligations of the charity; and any legal proceedings that might have been continued or commenced by or against it in its former name may be continued or commenced by or against it in its new name.

(7) Section 26(3) of the Companies Act 1985 (minor variations in names to be disregarded) shall apply for the purposes of this section as if the reference to section 26(1)(c) of that Act were a reference to subsection (2)(a) above.

(8) Any reference in this section to the charity trustees of a charity shall, in relation to a charity which is a company, be read as a reference to the directors of the company.

(9) Nothing in this section applies to an exempt charity.

7 Effect of direction under s 6 where charity is a company

(1) Where any direction is given under section 6 above with respect to a charity which is a company, the direction shall be taken to require the name of the charity to be changed by resolution of the directors of the company.

(2) Section 380 of the Companies Act 1985 (registration etc of resolutions and agreements) shall apply to any resolution passed by the directors in compliance with any such direction.

(3) Where the name of such a charity is changed in compliance with any such direction, the registrar of companies—

(a) shall, subject to section 26 of the Companies Act 1985 (prohibition on registration of certain names), enter the new name on the register of companies in place of the former name, and
(b) shall issue a certificate of incorporation altered to meet the circumstances of the case;

and the change of name has effect from the date on which the altered certificate is issued.

PART III

COMMISSIONERS' INFORMATION POWERS

8 General power to institute inquiries

(1) The Commissioners may from time to time institute inquiries with regard to charities or a particular charity or class of charities, either generally or for particular purposes, but no such inquiry shall extend to any exempt charity.

(2) The Commissioners may either conduct such an inquiry themselves or appoint a person to conduct it and make a report to them.

(3) For the purposes of any such inquiry the Commissioners, or a person appointed by them to conduct it, may direct any person (subject to the provisions of this section)—

(a) to furnish accounts and statements in writing with respect to any matter in question at the inquiry, being a matter on which he has or can reasonably obtain information, or to return answers in writing to any questions or inquiries addressed to him on any such matter, and to verify any such accounts, statements or answers by statutory declaration;
(b) to furnish copies of documents in his custody or under his control which relate to any matter in question at the inquiry, and to verify any such copies by statutory declaration;
(c) to attend at a specified time and place and give evidence or produce any such documents.

(4) For the purposes of any such inquiry evidence may be taken on oath, and the person conducting the inquiry may for that purpose administer oaths, or may instead of administering an oath require the person examined to make and subscribe a declaration of the truth of the matters about which he is examined.

(5) The Commissioners may pay to any person the necessary expenses of his attendance to give evidence or produce documents for the purpose of an inquiry under this section, and a person shall not be required in obedience to a direction under paragraph (c) of subsection (3) above to go more than ten miles from his place of residence unless those expenses are paid or tendered to him.

(6) Where an inquiry has been held under this section, the Commissioners may either—

(a) cause the report of the person conducting the inquiry, or such other statement of the results of the inquiry as they think fit, to be printed and published, or

(b) publish any such report or statement in some other way which is calculated in their opinion to bring it to the attention of persons who may wish to make representations to them about the action to be taken.

(7) The council of a county or district, the Common Council of the City of London and the council of a London borough may contribute to the expenses of the Commissioners in connection with inquiries under this section into local charities in the council's area.

9 Power to call for documents and search records

(1) The Commissioners may by order—

(a) require any person to furnish them with any information in his possession which relates to any charity and is relevant to the discharge of their functions or of the functions of the official custodian;

(b) require any person who has in his custody or under his control any document which relates to any charity and is relevant to the discharge of their functions or of the functions of the official custodian—

(i) to furnish them with a copy of or extract from the document, or

(ii) (unless the document forms part of the records or other documents of a court or of a public or local authority) to transmit the document itself to them for their inspection.

(2) Any officer of the Commissioners, if so authorised by them, shall be entitled without payment to inspect and take copies of or extracts from the records or other documents of any court, or of any public registry or office of records, for any purpose connected with the discharge of the functions of the Commissioners or of the official custodian.

(3) The Commissioners shall be entitled without payment to keep any copy or extract furnished to them under subsection (1) above; and where a document transmitted to them under that subsection for their inspection relates only to one or more charities and is not held by any person entitled as trustee or otherwise to the custody of it, the Commissioners may keep it or may deliver it to the charity trustees or to any other person who may be so entitled.

(4) No person properly having the custody of documents relating only to an exempt charity shall be required under subsection (1) above to transmit to the Commissioners any of those documents, or to furnish any copy of or extract from any of them.

(5) The rights conferred by subsection (2) above shall, in relation to information recorded otherwise than in legible form, include the right to require the information to be made available in legible form for inspection or for a copy or extract to be made of or from it.

10 Disclosure of information to and by Commissioners

(1) Subject to subsection (2) below and to any express restriction imposed by or under any other enactment, a body or person to whom this section applies may disclose to the Charity Commissioners any information received by that body or person under or for the purposes of any enactment, where the disclosure is made by the body or person for the purpose of enabling or assisting the Commissioners to discharge any of their functions.

(2) Subsection (1) above shall not have effect in relation to the Commissioners of Customs and Excise or the Commissioners of Inland Revenue; but either of those bodies of Commissioners ('the relevant body') may disclose to the Charity Commissioners the following information—

(a) the name and address of any institution which has for any purpose been treated by the relevant body as established for charitable purposes;
(b) information as to the purposes of an institution and the trusts under which it is established or regulated, where the disclosure is made by the relevant body in order to give or obtain assistance in determining whether the institution ought for any purpose to be treated as established for charitable purposes; and
(c) information with respect to an institution which has for any purpose been treated as so established but which appears to the relevant body—

(i) to be, or to have been, carrying on activities which are not charitable, or
(ii) to be, or to have been, applying any of its funds for purposes which are not charitable.

(3) In subsection (2) above, any reference to an institution shall, in relation to the Commissioners of Inland Revenue, be construed as a reference to an institution in England and Wales.

(4) Subject to subsection (5) below, the Charity Commissioners may disclose to a body or person to whom this section applies any information received by them under or for the purposes of any enactment, where the disclosure is made by the Commissioners—

(a) for any purpose connected with the discharge of their functions, and
(b) for the purpose of enabling or assisting that body or person to discharge any of its or his functions.

(5) Where any information disclosed to the Charity Commissioners under subsection (1) or (2) above is so disclosed subject to any express restriction on the disclosure of the information by the Commissioners, the Commissioners' power of disclosure under subsection (4) above shall, in relation to the information, be exercisable by them subject to any such restriction.

(6) This section applies to the following bodies and persons—

(a) any government department (including a Northern Ireland department);
(b) any local authority;
(c) any constable; and
(d) any other body or person discharging functions of a public nature (including a body or person discharging regulatory functions in relation to any description of activities).

(7) In subsection (6)(d) above the reference to any such body or person as is there mentioned shall, in relation to a disclosure by the Charity Commissioners under subsection (4) above, be construed as including a reference to any such body or person in a country or territory outside the United Kingdom.

(8) Nothing in this section shall be construed as affecting any power of disclosure exercisable apart from this section.

(9) In this section 'enactment' includes an enactment comprised in subordinate legislation (within the meaning of the Interpretation Act 1978).

11 Supply of false or misleading information to Commissioners, etc

(1) Any person who knowingly or recklessly provides the Commissioners with information which is false or misleading in a material particular shall be guilty of an offence if the information—

(a) is provided in purported compliance with a requirement imposed by or under this Act; or
(b) is provided otherwise than as mentioned in paragraph (a) above but in circumstances in which the person providing the information intends, or could reasonably be expected to know, that it would be used by the Commissioners for the purpose of discharging their functions under this Act.

(2) Any person who wilfully alters, suppresses, conceals or destroys any document which he is or is liable to be required, by or under this Act, to produce to the Commissioners shall be guilty of an offence.

(3) Any person guilty of an offence under this section shall be liable—

(a) on summary conviction, to a fine not exceeding the statutory maximum;
(b) on conviction on indictment, to imprisonment for a term not exceeding two years or to a fine, or both.

(4) In this section references to the Commissioners include references to any person conducting an inquiry under section 8 above.

12 Data protection

An order under section 30 of the Data Protection Act 1984 (exemption from subject access provisions of data held for the purpose of discharging designated functions in connection with the regulation of financial services etc) may designate for the purposes of that section, as if they were functions conferred by or under such an enactment as is there mentioned, any functions of the Commissioners appearing to the Secretary of State to be—

(a) connected with the protection of charities against misconduct or mismanagement (whether by trustees or other persons) in their administration; or
(b) connected with the protection of the property of charities from loss or misapplication or with the recovery of such property.

PART IV

APPLICATION OF PROPERTY CY-PRES AND ASSISTANCE AND SUPERVISION OF CHARITIES BY COURT AND COMMISSIONERS

Extended powers of court and variation of charters

13 Occasions for applying property cy-près

(1) Subject to subsection (2) below, the circumstances in which the original purposes of a charitable gift can be altered to allow the property given or part of it to be applied cy-près shall be as follows—

(a) where the original purposes, in whole or in part—

(i) have been as far as may be fulfilled; or
(ii) cannot be carried out, or not according to the directions given and to the spirit of the gift; or

(b) where the original purposes provide a use for part only of the property available by virtue of the gift; or
(c) where the property available by virtue of the gift and other property applicable for similar purposes can be more effectively used in conjunction, and to that end can suitably, regard being had to the spirit of the gift, be made applicable to common purposes; or

(d) where the original purposes were laid down by reference to an area which then was but has since ceased to be a unit for some other purpose, or by reference to a class of persons or to an area which has for any reason since ceased to be suitable, regard being had to the spirit of the gift, or to be practical in administering the gift; or

(e) where the original purposes, in whole or in part, have, since they were laid down,—

 (i) been adequately provided for by other means; or

 (ii) ceased, as being useless or harmful to the community or for other reasons, to be in law charitable; or

 (iii) ceased in any other way to provide a suitable and effective method of using the property available by virtue of the gift, regard being had to the spirit of the gift.

(2) Subsection (1) above shall not affect the conditions which must be satisfied in order that property given for charitable purposes may be applied cy-près except in so far as those conditions require a failure of the original purposes.

(3) References in the foregoing subsections to the original purposes of a gift shall be construed, where the application of the property given has been altered or regulated by a scheme or otherwise, as referring to the purposes for which the property is for the time being applicable.

(4) Without prejudice to the power to make schemes in circumstances falling within subsection (1) above, the court may by scheme made under the court's jurisdiction with respect to charities, in any case where the purposes for which the property is held are laid down by reference to any such area as is mentioned in the first column in Schedule 3 to this Act, provide for enlarging the area to any such area as is mentioned in the second column in the same entry in that Schedule.

(5) It is hereby declared that a trust for charitable purposes places a trustee under a duty, where the case permits and requires the property or some part of it to be applied cy-près, to secure its effective use for charity by taking steps to enable it to be so applied.

14 Application cy-près of gifts of donors unknown or disclaiming

(1) Property given for specific charitable purposes which fail shall be applicable cy-près as if given for charitable purposes generally, where it belongs—

(a) to a donor who after—

 (i) the prescribed advertisements and inquiries have been published and made, and

 (ii) the prescribed period beginning with the publication of those advertisements has expired,

cannot be identified or cannot be found; or

(b) to a donor who has executed a disclaimer in the prescribed form of his right to have the property returned.

(2) Where the prescribed advertisements and inquiries have been published and made by or on behalf of trustees with respect to any such property, the trustees shall not be liable to any person in respect of the property if no claim by him to be interested in it is received by them before the expiry of the period mentioned in subsection (1)(a)(ii) above.

(3) For the purposes of this section property shall be conclusively presumed (without any advertisement or inquiry) to belong to donors who cannot be identified, in so far as it consists—

(a) of the proceeds of cash collections made by means of collecting boxes or by other means not adapted for distinguishing one gift from another; or
(b) of the proceeds of any lottery, competition, entertainment, sale or similar money-raising activity, after allowing for property given to provide prizes or articles for sale or otherwise to enable the activity to be undertaken.

(4) The court may by order direct that property not falling within subsection (3) above shall for the purposes of this section be treated (without any advertisement or inquiry) as belonging to donors who cannot be identified where it appears to the court either—

(a) that it would be unreasonable, having regard to the amounts likely to be returned to the donors, to incur expense with a view to returning the property; or
(b) that it would be unreasonable, having regard to the nature, circumstances and amounts of the gifts, and to the lapse of time since the gifts were made, for the donors to expect the property to be returned.

(5) Where property is applied cy-près by virtue of this section, the donor shall be deemed to have parted with all his interest at the time when the gift was made; but where property is so applied as belonging to donors who cannot be identified or cannot be found, and is not so applied by virtue of subsection (3) or (4) above—

(a) the scheme shall specify the total amount of that property; and
(b) the donor of any part of that amount shall be entitled, if he makes a claim not later than six months after the date on which the scheme is made, to recover from the charity for which the property is applied a sum equal to that part, less any expenses properly incurred by the charity trustees after that date in connection with claims relating to his gift; and
(c) the scheme may include directions as to the provision to be made for meeting any such claim.

(6) Where—

(a) any sum is, in accordance with any such directions, set aside for meeting any such claims, but
(b) the aggregate amount of any such claims actually made exceeds the relevant amount,

then, if the Commissioners so direct, each of the donors in question shall be entitled only to such proportion of the relevant amount as the amount of his claim bears to the aggregate amount referred to in paragraph (b) above; and for this purpose 'the relevant amount' means the amount of the sum so set aside for deduction of any expenses properly incurred by the charity trustees in connection with claims relating to the donors' gifts.

(7) For the purposes of this section, charitable purposes shall be deemed to 'fail' where any difficulty in applying property to those purposes makes that property or the part not applicable cy-près available to be returned to the donors.

(8) In this section 'prescribed' means prescribed by regulations made by the Commissioners; and such regulation may, as respects the advertisements which are to be published for the purposes of subsection (1)(a) above, make provision as to the form and content of such advertisements as well as the manner in which they are to be published.

(9) Any regulations made by the Commissioners under this section shall be published by the Commissioners in such manner as they think fit.

(10) In this section, except in so far as the context otherwise requires, references to a donor include persons claiming through or under the original donor, and references to property

given include the property for the time being representing the property originally given or properly derived from it.

(11) This section shall apply to property given for charitable purposes, notwithstanding that it was so given before the commencement of this Act.

15 Charities governed by charter, or by or under statute

(1) Where a Royal charter establishing or regulating a body corporate is amendable by the grant and acceptance of a further charter, a scheme relating to the body corporate or to the administration of property held by the body (including a scheme for the cy-près application of any such property) may be made by the court under the court's jurisdiction with respect to charities notwithstanding that the scheme cannot take effect without the alteration of the charter, but shall be so framed that the scheme, or such part of it as cannot take effect without the alteration of the charter, does not purport to come into operation unless or until Her Majesty thinks fit to amend the charter in such manner as will permit the scheme or that part of it to have effect.

(2) Where under the court's jurisdiction with respect to charities or the corresponding jurisdiction of a court in Northern Ireland, or under powers conferred by this Act or by any Northern Ireland legislation relating to charities, a scheme is made with respect to a body corporate, and it appears to Her Majesty expedient, having regard to the scheme, to amend any Royal charter relating to that body, Her Majesty may, on the application of that body, amend the charter accordingly by Order in Council in any way in which the charter could be amended by the grant and acceptance of a further charter; and any such Order in Council may be revoked or varied in like manner as the charter it amends.

(3) The jurisdiction of the court with respect to charities shall not be excluded or restricted in the case of a charity of any description mentioned in Schedule 4 to this Act by the operation of the enactments or instruments there mentioned in relation to that description, and a scheme established for any such charity may modify or supersede in relation to it the provision made by any such enactment or instrument as if made by a scheme of the court, and may also make any such provision as is authorised by that Schedule.

Powers of Commissioners to make schemes and act for protection of charities etc

16 Concurrent jurisdiction with High Court for certain purposes

(1) Subject to the provisions of this Act, the Commissioners may by order exercise the same jurisdiction and powers as are exercisable by the High Court in charity proceedings for the following purposes—

- (a) establishing a scheme for the administration of a charity;
- (b) appointing, discharging or removing a charity trustee or trustee for a charity, or removing an officer or employee;
- (c) vesting or transferring property, or requiring or entitling any person to call for or make any transfer of property or any payment.

(2) Where the court directs a scheme for the administration of a charity to be established, the court may by order refer the matter to the Commissioners for them to prepare or settle a scheme in accordance with such directions (if any) as the court sees fit to give, and any such order may provide for the scheme to be put into effect by order of the Commissioners as if prepared under subsection (1) above and without any further order of the court.

(3) The Commissioners shall not have jurisdiction under this section to try or determine the title at law or in equity to any property as between a charity or trustee for a charity and a person holding or claiming the property or an interest in it adversely to the charity, or to try or determine any question as to the existence or extent of any charge or trust.

(4) Subject to the following subsections, the Commissioners shall not exercise their jurisdiction under this section as respects any charity, except—

(a) on the application of the charity; or
(b) on an order of the court under subsection (2) above; or
(c) in the case of a charity other than an exempt charity, on the application of the Attorney General.

(5) In the case of a charity which is not an exempt charity and whose income from all sources does not in aggregate exceed £500 a year, the Commissioners may exercise their jurisdiction under this section on the application—

(a) of any one or more of the charity trustees; or
(b) of any person interested in the charity; or
(c) of any two or more inhabitants of the area of the charity if it is a local charity.

(6) Where in the case of a charity, other than an exempt charity, the Commissioners are satisfied that the charity trustees ought in the interests of the charity to apply for a scheme, but have unreasonably refused or neglected to do so and the Commissioners have given the charity trustees an opportunity to make representations to them, the Commissioners may proceed as if an application for a scheme had been made by the charity but the Commissioners shall not have power in a case where they act by virtue of this subsection to alter the purposes of a charity, unless forty years have elapsed from the date of its foundation.

(7) Where—

(a) a charity cannot apply to the Commissioners for a scheme by reason of any vacancy among the charity trustees or the absence or incapacity of any of them, but
(b) such an application is made by such number of the charity trustees as the Commissioners consider appropriate in the circumstances of the case,

the Commissioners may nevertheless proceed as if the application were an application made by the charity.

(8) The Commissioners may on the application of any charity trustee or trustee for a charity exercise their jurisdiction under this section for the purpose of discharging him from his trusteeship.

(9) Before exercising any jurisdiction under this section otherwise than on an order of the court, the Commissioners shall give notice of their intention to do so to each of the charity trustees, except any that cannot be found or has no known address in the United Kingdom or who is party or privy to an application for the exercise of the jurisdiction; and any such notice may be given by post, and, if given by post, may be addressed to the recipient's last known address in the United Kingdom.

(10) The Commissioners shall not exercise their jurisdiction under this section in any case (not referred to them by order of the court) which, by reason of its contentious character, or of any special question of law or of fact which it may involve, or for other reasons, the Commissioners may consider more fit to be adjudicated on by the court.

(11) An appeal against any order of the Commissioners under this section may be brought in the High Court by the Attorney General.

(12) An appeal against any order of the Commissioners under this section may also, at any time within the three months beginning with the day following that on which the order is published, be brought in the High Court by the charity or any of the charity trustees, or by any person removed from any office or employment by the order (unless he is removed with the concurrence of the charity trustees or with the approval of the special visitor, if any, of the charity).

(13) No appeal shall be brought under subsection (12) above except with a certificate of the Commissioners that it is a proper case for an appeal or with the leave of one of the judges of the High Court attached to the Chancery Division.

(14) Where an order of the Commissioners under this section establishes a scheme for the administration of a charity, any person interested in the charity shall have the like right of appeal under subsection (12) above as a charity trustee, and so also, in the case of a charity which is a local charity in any area, shall any two or more inhabitants of the area and the council of any parish or (in Wales) any community comprising the area or any part of it.

(15) If the Secretary of State thinks it expedient to do so—

(a) in consequence of changes in the value of money, or
(b) with a view to increasing the number of charities in respect of which the Commissioners may exercise their jurisdiction under this section in accordance with subsection (5) above,

he may by order amend that subsection by substituting a different sum for the sum for the time being specified there.

17 Further powers to make schemes or alter application of charitable property

(1) Where it appears to the Commissioners that a scheme should be established for the administration of a charity, but also that it is necessary or desirable for the scheme to alter the provision made by an Act of Parliament establishing or regulating the charity or to make any other provision which goes or might go beyond the powers exercisable by them apart from this section, or that it is for any reason proper for the scheme to be subject to parliamentary review, then (subject to subsection (6) below) the Commissioners may settle a scheme accordingly with a view to its being given effect under this section.

(2) A scheme settled by the Commissioners under this section may be given effect by order of the Secretary of State, and a draft of the order shall be laid before Parliament.

(3) Without prejudice to the operation of section 6 of the Statutory Instruments Act 1946 in other cases, in the case of a scheme which goes beyond the powers exercisable apart from this section in altering a statutory provision contained in or having effect under any public general Act of Parliament, the order shall not be made unless the draft has been approved by resolution of each House of Parliament.

(4) Subject to subsection (5) below, any provision of a scheme brought into effect under this section may be modified or superseded by the court or the Commissioners as if it were a scheme brought into effect by order of the Commissioners under section 16 above.

(5) Where subsection (3) above applies to a scheme, the order giving effect to it may direct that the scheme shall not be modified or superseded by a scheme brought into effect otherwise than under this section, and may also direct that that subsection shall apply to any scheme modifying or superseding the scheme to which the order gives effect.

(6) The Commissioners shall not proceed under this section without the like application and the like notice of the charity trustees, as would be required if they were proceeding

(without an order of the court) under section 16 above; but on any application for a scheme, or in a case where they act by virtue of subsection (6) or (7) of that section, the Commissioners may proceed under this section or that section as appears to them appropriate.

(7) Notwithstanding anything in the trusts of a charity, no expenditure incurred in preparing or promoting a Bill in Parliament shall without the consent of the court or the Commissioners be defrayed out of any moneys applicable for the purposes of a charity but this subsection shall not apply in the case of an exempt charity.

(8) Where the Commissioners are satisfied—

(a) that the whole of the income of a charity cannot in existing circumstances be effectively applied for the purposes of the charity; and
(b) that, if those circumstances continue, a scheme might be made for applying the surplus cy-près; and
(c) that it is for any reason not yet desirable to make such a scheme;

then the Commissioners may by order authorise the charity trustees at their discretion (but subject to any conditions imposed by the order) to apply any accrued or accruing income for any purposes for which it might be made applicable by such a scheme, and any application authorised by the order shall be deemed to be within the purposes of the charity.

(9) An order under subsection (8) above shall not exceed to more than £300 out of income accrued before the date of the order, nor to income accruing more than three years after that date, nor to more than £100 out of the income accruing in any of those three years.

18 Power to act for protection of charities

(1) Where, at any time after they have instituted an inquiry under section 8 above with respect to any charity, the Commissioners are satisfied—

(a) that there is or has been any misconduct or mismanagement in the administration of the charity; or
(b) that it is necessary or desirable to act for the purpose of protecting the property of the charity or securing a proper application for the purposes of the charity of that property or of property coming to the charity,

the Commissioners may of their own motion do one or more of the following things—

(i) by order suspend any trustee, charity trustee, officer, agent or employee of the charity from the exercise of his office or employment pending consideration being given to his removal (whether under this section or otherwise);
(ii) by order appoint such number of additional charity trustees as they consider necessary for the proper administration of the charity;
(iii) by order vest any property held by or in trust for the charity in the official custodian, or require the persons in whom any such property is vested to transfer it to him, or appoint any person to transfer any such property to him;
(iv) order any person who holds any property on behalf of the charity, or of any trustee for it, not to part with the property without the approval of the Commissioners;
(v) order any debtor of the charity not to make any payment in or towards the discharge of his liability to the charity without the approval of the Commissioners;

(vi) by order restrict (notwithstanding anything in the trusts of the charity) the transactions which may be entered into, or the nature or amount of the payments which may be made, in the administration of the charity without the approval of the Commissioners;

(vii) by order appoint (in accordance with section 19 below) a receiver and manager in respect of the property and affairs of the charity.

(2) Where, at any time after they have instituted an inquiry under section 8 above with respect to any charity, the Commissioners are satisfied—

(a) that there is or has been any misconduct or mismanagement in the administration of the charity; and
(b) that it is necessary or desirable to act for the purpose of protecting the property of the charity or securing a proper application for the purposes of the charity of that property or of property coming to the charity,

the Commissioners may of their own motion do either or both of the following things—

(i) by order remove any trustee, charity trustee, officer, agent or employee of the charity who has been responsible for or privy to the misconduct or mismanagement or has by his conduct contributed to it or facilitated it;
(ii) by order establish a scheme for the administration of the charity.

(3) The references in subsection (1) or (2) above to misconduct or mismanagement shall (notwithstanding anything in the trusts of the charity) extend to the employment for the remuneration or reward of persons acting in the affairs of the charity, or for other administrative purposes, of sums which are excessive in relation to the property which is or is likely to be applied or applicable for the purposes of the charity.

(4) The Commissioners may also remove a charity trustee by order made of their own motion—

(a) where, within the last five years, the trustee—

(i) having previously been adjudged bankrupt or had his estate sequestrated, has been discharged, or
(ii) having previously made a composition or arrangement with, or granted a trust deed for, his creditors, has been discharged in respect of it;

(b) where the trustee is a corporation in liquidation;
(c) where the trustee is incapable of acting by reason of mental disorder within the meaning of the Mental Health Act 1983;
(d) where the trustee has not acted, and will not declare his willingness or unwillingness to act;
(e) where the trustee is outside England and Wales or cannot be found or does not act, and his absence or failure to act impedes the proper administration of the charity.

(5) The Commissioners may by order made of their own motion appoint a person to be a charity trustee—

(a) in place of a charity trustee removed by them under this section or otherwise;
(b) where there are no charity trustees, or where by reason of vacancies in their number or the absence or incapacity of any of their number the charity cannot apply for the appointment;
(c) where there is a single charity trustee, not being a corporation aggregate, and the Commissioners are of opinion that it is necessary to increase the number for the proper administration of the charity;

(d) where the Commissioners are of opinion that it is necessary for the proper administration of the charity to have an additional charity trustee because one of the existing charity trustees who ought nevertheless to remain a charity trustee either cannot be found or does not act or is outside England and Wales.

(6) The powers of the Commissioners under this section to remove or appoint charity trustees of their own motion shall include power to make any such order with respect to the vesting in or transfer to the charity trustees of any property as the Commissioners could make on the removal or appointment of a charity trustee by them under section 16 above.

(7) Any order under this section for the removal or appointment of a charity trustee or trustee for a charity, or for the vesting or transfer of any property, shall be of the like effects as an order made under section 16 above.

(8) Subject to subsection (9) below, subsections (11) to (13) of section 16 above shall apply to orders under this section as they apply to orders under that section.

(9) The requirement to obtain any such certificate or leave as is mentioned in section 16(13) above shall not apply to—

(a) an appeal by a charity or any of the charity trustees of a charity against an order under subsection (1)(vii) above appointing a receiver and manager in respect of the charity's property and affairs, or
(b) an appeal by a person against an order under subsection (2)(i) or (4)(a) above removing him from his office or employment.

(10) Subsection (14) of section 16 above shall apply to an order under this section which establishes a scheme for the administration of a charity as it applies to such an order under that section.

(11) The power of the Commissioners to make an order under subsection (1)(i) above shall not be exercisable so as to suspend any person from the exercise of his office or employment for a period of more than twelve months; but (without prejudice to the generality of section 89(1) below), any such order made in the case of any person may make provision as respects the period of his suspension for matters arising out of it, and in particular for enabling any person to execute any instrument in his name or otherwise act for him and, in the case of a charity trustee, for adjusting any rules governing the proceedings of the charity trustees to take account of the reduction in the number capable of acting.

(12) Before exercising any jurisdiction under this section otherwise than by virtue of subsection (1) above, the Commissioners shall give notice of their intention to do so to each of the charity trustees, except any that cannot be found or has no known address in the United Kingdom; and any such notice may be given by post and, if given by post, may be addressed to the recipient's last known address in the United Kingdom.

(13) The Commissioners shall, at such intervals as they think fit, review any order made by them under paragraph (i), or any of paragraphs (iii) to (vii), of subsection (1) above; and, if on any such review it appears to them that it would be appropriate to discharge the order in whole or in part, they shall so discharge it (whether subject to any savings or other transitional provisions or not).

(14) If any person contravenes an order under subsection (1)(iv), (v) or (vi) above, he shall be guilty of an offence and liable on summary conviction to a fine not exceeding level 5 on the standard scale.

(15) Subsection (14) above shall not be taken to preclude the bringing of proceedings for breach of trust against any charity trustee or trustee for a charity in respect of a contravention of an order under subsection (1)(iv) or (vi) above (whether proceedings in respect of the contravention are brought against him under subsection (14) above or not).

(16) This section shall not apply to an exempt charity.

19 Supplementary provisions relating to receiver and manager appointed for a charity

(1) The Commissioners may under section 18(1)(vii) above appoint to be receiver and manager in respect of the property and affairs of a charity such person (other than an officer or employee of theirs) as they think fit.

(2) Without prejudice to the generality of section 89(1) below, any order made by the Commissioners under section 18(1)(vii) above may make provision with respect to the functions to be discharged by the receiver and manager appointed by the order; and those functions shall be discharged by him under the supervision of the Commissioners.

(3) In connection with the discharge of those functions any such order may provide—

- (a) for the receiver and manager appointed by the order to have such powers and duties of the charity trustees of the charity concerned (whether arising under this Act or otherwise) as are specified in the order;
- (b) for any powers or duties exercisable or falling to be performed by the receiver and manager by virtue of paragraph (a) above to be exercisable or performed by him to the exclusion of those trustees.

(4) Where a person has been appointed receiver and manager by any such order—

- (a) section 29 below shall apply to him and to his functions as a person so appointed as it applies to a charity trustee of the charity concerned and to his duties as such; and
- (b) the Commissioners may apply to the High Court for directions in relation to any particular matter arising in connection with the discharge of those functions.

(5) The High Court may on an application under subsection (4)(b) above—

- (a) give such directions, or
- (b) make such orders declaring the rights of any persons (whether before the court or not),

as it thinks just; and the costs of any such application shall be paid by the charity concerned.

(6) Regulations made by the Secretary of State may make provision with respect to—

- (a) the appointment and removal of persons appointed in accordance with this section;
- (b) the remuneration of such persons out of the income of the charities concerned;
- (c) the making of reports to the Commissioners by such persons.

(7) Regulations under subsection (6) above may, in particular, authorise the Commissioners—

- (a) to require security for the due discharge of his functions to be given by a person so appointed;
- (b) to determine the amount of such a person's remuneration;
- (c) to disallow any amount of remuneration in such circumstances as are prescribed by the regulations.

20 Publicity for proceedings under ss 16 to 18

(1) The Commissioners shall not make any order under this Act to establish a scheme for the administration of a charity, or submit such a scheme to the court or the Secretary of State for an order giving it effect, unless not less than one month previously there has been given public notice of their proposals, inviting representations to be made to them within a time specified in the notice, being not less than one month from the date of such notice, and, in the case of a scheme relating to a local charity, other than on ecclesiastical charity, in a parish or (in Wales) a community, a draft of the scheme has been communicated to the parish or community council or, in the case of a parish not having a council, to the chairman of the parish meeting.

(2) The Commissioners shall not make any order under this Act to appoint, discharge or remove a charity trustee or trustee for a charity (other than the official custodian), unless not less than one month previously there has been given the like public notice as is required by subsection (1) above for an order establishing a scheme but this subsection shall not apply in the case of—

(a) an order under section 18(1)(ii) above; or
(b) an order discharging or removing a trustee if the Commissioners are of opinion that it is unnecessary and not in his interest to give publicity to the proposal to discharge to remove him.

(3) Before the Commissioners make an order under this Act to remove without his consent a charity trustee or trustee for a charity, or an officer, agent or employee of a charity, the Commissioners shall, unless he cannot be found or has no known address in the United Kingdom, give him not less than one month's notice of their proposal, inviting representations to be made to them within a time specified in the notice.

(4) Where notice is given of any proposals as required by subsections (1) to (3) above, the Commissioners shall take into consideration any representations made to them about the proposals within the time specified in the notice, and may (without further notice) proceed with the proposals either without modification or with such modifications as appear to them to be desirable.

(5) Where the Commissioners make an order which is subject to appeal under subsection (12) of section 16 above the order shall be published either by giving public notice of it or by giving notice of it to all persons entitled to appeal against it under that subsection, as the Commissioners think fit.

(6) Where the Commissioners make an order under this Act to establish a scheme for the administration of a charity, a copy of the order shall, for not less than one month after the order is published, be available for public inspection at all reasonable times at the Commissioners' office and also at some convenient place in the area of the charity, if it is a local charity.

(7) Any notice to be given under this section of any proposals or order shall give such particulars of the proposals or order, or such directions for obtaining information about them, as the Commissioners think sufficient and appropriate, and any public notice shall be given in such manner as they think sufficient and appropriate.

(8) Any notice to be given under this section, other than a public notice, may be given by post and, if given by post, may be addressed to the recipient's last known address in the United Kingdom.

Property vested in official custodian

21 Entrusting charity property to official custodian, and termination of trust

(1) The court may by order—

(a) vest in the official custodian any land held by or in trust for a charity;
(b) authorise or require the persons in whom any such land is vested to transfer it to him; or
(c) appoint any person to transfer any such land to him;

but this subsection does not apply to any interest in land by way of mortgage or other security.

(2) Where property is vested in the official custodian in trust for a charity, the court may make an order discharging him from the trusteeship as respects all or any of that property.

(3) Where the official custodian is discharged from his trusteeship of any property, or the trusts on which he holds any property come to an end, the court may make such vesting orders and give such directions as may seem to the court to be necessary or expedient in consequence.

(4) No person shall be liable for any loss occasioned by his acting in conformity with an order under this section or by his giving effect to anything done in pursuance of such an order, or be excused from so doing by reason of the order having been in any respect improperly obtained.

22 Supplementary provisions as to property vested in official custodian

(1) Subject to the provisions of this Act, where property is vested in the official custodian in trust for a charity, he shall not exercise any powers of management, but he shall as trustee of any property have all the same powers, duties and liabilities, and be entitled to the same rights and immunities, and be subject to the control and orders of the court, as a corporation appointed custodian trustee under section 4 of the Public Trustee Act 1906 except that he shall have no power to charge fees.

(2) Subject to subsection (3) below, where any land is vested in the official custodian in trust for a charity, the charity trustees shall have power in his name and on his behalf to execute and do all assurances and things which they could properly execute or do in their own name and on their own behalf if the land were vested in them.

(3) If any land is so vested in the official custodian by virtue of an order under section 18 above, the power conferred on the charity trustees by subsection (2) above shall not be exercisable by them in relation to any transaction affecting the land, unless the transaction is authorised by order of the court or of the Commissioners.

(4) Where any land is vested in the official custodian in trust for a charity, the charity trustees shall have the like power to make obligations entered into by them binding on the land as if it were vested in them; and any covenant, agreement or condition which is enforceable by or against the custodian by reason of the land being vested in him shall be enforceable by or against the charity trustees as if the land were vested in them.

(5) In relation to a corporate charity, subsections (2), (3) and (4) above shall apply with the substitution of references to the charity for references to the charity trustees.

(6) Subsections (2), (3) and (4) above shall not authorise any charity trustees or charity to impose any personal liability on the official custodian.

(7) Where the official custodian is entitled as trustee for a charity to the custody of securities or documents of title relating to the trust property, he may permit them to be in the possession or under the control of the charity trustees without thereby incurring any liability.

23 Divestment in the case of land subject to Reverter of Sites Act 1987

(1) Where—

(a) any land is vested in the official custodian in trust for a charity, and
(b) it appears to the Commissioners that section 1 of the Reverter of Sites Act 1987 (right of reverter replaced by trust) will, or is likely to, operate in relation to the land at a particular time or in particular circumstances,

the jurisdiction which, under section 16 above, is exercisable by the Commissioners for the purpose of discharging a trustee for a charity may, at any time before section 1 of that Act ('the 1987 Act') operates in relation to the land, be exercised by them of their own motion for the purpose of—

(i) making an order discharging the official custodian from his trusteeship of the land, and
(ii) making such vesting orders and giving such directions as appear to them to be necessary or expedient in consequence.

(2) Where—

(a) section 1 of the 1987 Act has operated in relation to any land which, immediately before the time when that section so operated, was vested in the official custodian in trust for a charity, and
(b) the land remains vested in him but on the trust arising under that section,

the court or the Commissioners (of their own motion) may—

(i) make an order discharging the official custodian from his trusteeship of the land, and
(ii) (subject to the following provisions of this section) make such vesting orders and give such directions as appear to it or them to be necessary or expedient in consequence.

(3) Where any order discharging the official custodian from his trusteeship of any land—

(a) is made by the court under section 21(2) above, or by the Commissioners under section 16 above, on the grounds that section 1 of the 1987 Act will, or is likely to, operate in relation to the land, or
(b) is made by the court or the Commissioners under subsection (2) above,

the persons in whom the land is to be vested on the discharge of the official custodian shall be the relevant charity trustees (as defined in subsection (4) below), unless the court or (as the case may be) the Commissioners is or are satisfied that it would be appropriate for it to be vested in some other persons.

(4) In subsection (3) above 'the relevant charity trustees' means—

(a) in relation to an order made as mentioned in paragraph (a) of that subsection, the charity trustees of the charity in trust for which the land is vested in the official custodian immediately before the time when the order takes effect, or
(b) in relation to an order made under subsection (2) above, the charity trustees of the charity in trust for which the land was vested in the official custodian immediately before the time when section 1 of the 1987 Act operated in relation to the land.

(5) Where—

(a) section 1 of the 1987 Act has operated in relation to any such land as is mentioned in subsection (2)(a) above, and
(b) the land remains vested in the official custodian as mentioned in subsection (2)(b) above,

then (subject to subsection (6) below), all the powers, duties and liabilities that would, apart from this section, be those of the official custodian as trustee of the land shall instead be those of the charity trustees of the charity concerned; and those trustees shall have power in his name and on his behalf to execute and do all assurances and things which they could properly execute or do in their own name and on their own behalf if the land were vested in them.

(6) Subsection (5) above shall not be taken to require or authorise those trustees to sell the land at a time when it remains vested in the official custodian.

(7) Where—

(a) the official custodian has been discharged from his trusteeship of any land by an order under subsection (2) above, and
(b) the land has, in accordance with subsection (3) above, been vested in the charity trustees concerned or (as the case may be) in any persons other than those trustees,

the land shall be held by those trustees, or (as the case may be) by those persons, as trustees on the terms of the trust arising under section 1 of the 1987 Act.

(8) The official custodian shall not be liable to any person in respect of any loss or misapplication of any land vested in him in accordance with that section unless it is occasioned by or through any wilful neglect or default of his or of any person acting for him; but the Consolidated Fund shall be liable to make good to any person any sums for which the official custodian may be liable by reason of any such neglect or default.

(9) In this section any reference to section 1 of the 1987 Act operating in relation to any land is a reference to a trust arising in relation to the land under that section.

Note: Section shown as amended by the Trusts of Land and Appointment of Trustees Act 1996, s 25(1), Sch 3, para 26.

Establishment of common investment or deposit funds

24 Schemes to establish common investment funds

(1) The court or the Commissioners may by order make and bring into effect schemes (in this section referred to as 'common investment schemes') for the establishment of common investment funds under trusts which provide—

(a) for property transferred to the fund by or on behalf of a charity participating in the scheme to be invested under the control of trustees appointed to manage the fund; and
(b) for the participating charities to be entitled (subject to the provisions of the scheme) to the capital and income of the fund in shares determined by reference to the amount or value of the property transferred to it by or on behalf of each of them and to the value of the fund at the time of the transfers.

(2) The court or the Commissioners may make a common investment scheme on the application of any two or more charities.

(3) A common investment scheme may be made in terms admitting any charity to participate, or the scheme may restrict the right to participate in any manner.

(4) A common investment scheme may make provision for, and for all matters connected with, the establishment, investment, management and winding up of the common investment fund, and may in particular include provision—

(a) for remunerating persons appointed trustees to hold or manage the fund or any part of it, with or without provision authorising a person to receive the remuneration notwithstanding that he is also a charity trustee of or trustee for a participating charity;
(b) for restricting the size of the fund, and for regulating as to time, amount or otherwise the right to transfer property to or withdraw it from the fund, and for enabling sums to be advanced out of the fund by way of loan to a participating charity pending the withdrawal of property from the fund by the charity;
(c) for enabling income to be withheld from distribution with a view to avoiding fluctuations in the amounts distributed, and generally for regulating distributions of income;
(d) for enabling money to be borrowed temporarily for the purpose of meeting payments to be made out of the funds;
(e) for enabling questions arising under the scheme as to the right of a charity to participate, or as to the rights of participating charities, or as to any other matter, to be conclusively determined by the decision of the trustees managing the fund or in any other manner;
(f) for regulating the accounts and information to be supplied to participating charities.

(5) A common investment scheme, in addition to the provision for property to be transferred to the fund on the basis that the charity shall be entitled to a share in the capital and income of the fund, may include provision for enabling sums to be deposited by or on behalf of a charity on the basis that (subject to the provisions of the scheme) the charity shall be entitled to repayment of the sums deposited and to interest thereon at a rate determined by or under the scheme; and where a scheme makes any such provision it shall also provide for excluding from the amount of capital and income to be shared between charities participating otherwise than by way of deposit such amounts (not exceeding the amounts properly attributable to the making of deposits) as are from time to time reasonably required in respect of the liabilities of the fund for the repayment of deposits and for the interest on deposits, including amounts required by way of reserve.

(6) Except in so far as a common investment scheme provides to the contrary, the rights under it of a participating charity shall not be capable of being assigned or charged, nor shall any trustee or other person concerned in the management of the common investment fund be required or entitled to take account of any trust or other equity affecting a participating charity or its property or rights.

(7) The powers of investment of every charity shall include power to participate in common investment schemes unless the power is excluded by a provision specifically referring to common investment schemes in the trusts of the charity.

(8) A common investment fund shall be deemed for all purposes to be a charity; and if the scheme admits only exempt charities, the fund shall be an exempt charity for the purposes of this Act.

(9) Subsection (8) above shall apply not only to common investment funds established under the powers of this section, but also to any similar fund established for the exclusive

benefits of charities by or under any enactment relating to any particular charities or class of charity.

25 Schemes to establish common deposit funds

(1) The court or the Commissioners may by order make and bring into effect schemes (in this section referred to as 'common deposit schemes') for the establishment of common deposit funds under trusts which provide—

(a) for sums to be deposited by or on behalf of a charity participating in the scheme and invested under the control of trustees appointed to manage the fund; and
(b) for any such charity to be entitled (subject to the provisions of the scheme) to repayment of any sums so deposited and to interest thereon at a rate determined under the scheme.

(2) Subject to subsection (3) below, the following provisions of section 24 above, namely—

(a) subsections (2) to (4), and
(b) subsections (6) to (9),

shall have effect in relation to common deposit schemes and common deposit funds as they have effect in relation to common investment schemes and common investment funds.

(3) In its application in accordance with subsection (2) above, subsection (4) of that section shall have effect with the substitution for paragraphs (b) and (c) of the following paragraphs—

'(b) for regulating as to time, amount or otherwise the right to repayment of sums deposited in the fund;
(c) for authorising a part of the income for any year to be credited to a reserve account maintained for the purpose of counteracting any losses accruing to the fund, and generally for regulating the manner in which the rate of interest on deposits is to be determined from time to time;'.

Additional powers of Commissioners

26 Power to authorise dealings with charity property etc

(1) Subject to the provisions of this section, where it appears to the Commissioners that any action proposed or contemplated in the administration of a charity is expedient in the interests of the charity, they may by order sanction that action, whether or not it would otherwise be within the powers exercisable by the charity trustees in the administration of the charity; and anything done under the authority of such an order shall be deemed to be properly done in the exercise of those powers.

(2) An order under this section may be made so as to authorise a particular transaction, compromise or the like, or a particular application of property, or so as to give a more general authority, and (without prejudice to the generality of subsection (1) above) may authorise a charity to use common premises, or employ a common staff, or otherwise combine for any purpose of administration, with any other charity.

(3) An order under this section may give directions as to the manner in which any expenditure is to be borne and as to other matters connected with or arising out of the action thereby authorised; and where anything is done in pursuance of an authority given

by any such order, any directions given in connection therewith shall be binding on the charity trustees for the time being as if contained in the trusts of the charity; but any such directions may on the application of the charity be modified or superseded by a further order.

(4) Without prejudice to the generality of subsection (3) above, the directions which may be given by an order under this section shall in particular include directions for meeting any expenditure out of a specified fund, for charging any expenditure to capital or to income, for requiring expenditure charged to capital to be recouped out of income within a specified period, for restricting the costs to be incurred at the expense of the charity, or for the investment of moneys arising from any transaction.

(5) An order under this section may authorise any act notwithstanding that it is prohibited by any of the disabling Acts mentioned in subsection (6) below or that the trusts of the charity provide for the act to be done by or under the authority of the court; but no such order shall authorise the doing of any act expressly prohibited by Act of Parliament other than the disabling Acts or by the trusts of the charity or shall extend or alter the purposes of the charity.

(6) The Acts referred to in subsection (5) above as the disabling Acts are the Ecclesiastical Leases Act 1571, the Ecclesiastical Leases Act 1572, the Ecclesiastical Leases Act 1575 and the Ecclesiastical Leases Act 1836.

(7) An order under this section shall not confer any authority in relation to a building which has been consecrated and of which the use or disposal is regulated, and can be further regulated, by a scheme having effect under the Union of Benefices Measures 1923 to 1952, the Reorganisation Areas Measures 1944 and 1954, the Pastoral Measure 1968 or the Pastoral Measure 1983, the reference to a building being taken to include part of a building and any land which under such a scheme is to be used or disposed of with a building to which the scheme applies.

27 Power to authorise ex gratia payments etc

(1) Subject to subsection (3) below, the Commissioners may by order exercise the same power as is exercisable by the Attorney General to authorise the charity trustees of a charity—

- (a) to make any application of property of the charity, or
- (b) to waive to any extent, on behalf of the charity, its entitlement to receive any property,

in a case where the charity trustees—

- (i) (apart from this section) have no power to do so, but
- (ii) in all the circumstances regard themselves as being under a moral obligation to do so.

(2) The power conferred on the Commissioners by subsection (1) above shall be exercisable by them under the supervision of, and in accordance with such directions as may be given by, the Attorney General; and any such directions may in particular require the Commissioners, in such circumstances as are specified in the directions—

- (a) to refrain from exercising that power; or
- (b) to consult the Attorney General before exercising it.

(3) Where—

- (a) an application is made to the Commissioners for them to exercise that power in a case where they are not precluded from doing so by any such directions, but

(b) they consider that it would nevertheless be desirable for the application to be entertained by the Attorney General rather than by them,

they shall refer the application to the Attorney General.

(4) It is hereby declared that where, in the case of any application made to them as mentioned in subsection (3)(a) above, the Commissioners determine the application by refusing to authorise charity trustees to take any action falling within subsection (1)(a) or (b) above, that refusal shall not preclude the Attorney General, on an application subsequently made to him by the trustees, from authorising the trustees to take that action.

28 Power to give directions about dormant bank accounts of charities

(1) Where the Commissioners—

(a) are informed by a relevant institution—

(i) that it holds one or more accounts in the name of or on behalf of a particular charity ('the relevant charity'), and
(ii) that the account, or (if it so holds two or more accounts) each of the accounts, is dormant, and

(b) are unable, after making reasonable inquiries, to locate that charity or any of its trustees,

they may give a direction under subsection (2) below.

(2) A direction under this subsection is a direction which—

(a) requires the institution concerned to transfer the amount, or (as the case may be) the aggregate amount, standing to the credit of the relevant charity in the account or accounts in question to such other charity as is specified in the direction in accordance with subsection (3) below; or
(b) requires the institution concerned to transfer to each of two or more other charities so specified in the direction such part of that amount or aggregate amount as is there specified in relation to that charity.

(3) The Commissioners may specify in a direction under subsection (2) above such other charity or charities as they consider appropriate, having regard, in a case where the purposes of the relevant charity are known to them, to those purposes and to the purposes of the other charity or charities; but the Commissioners shall not so specify any charity unless they have received from the charity trustees written confirmation that those trustees are willing to accept the amount proposed to be transferred to the charity.

(4) Any amount received by a charity by virtue of this section shall be received by the charity on terms that—

(a) it shall be held and applied by the charity for the purposes of the charity, but
(b) it shall, as property of the charity, nevertheless be subject to any restrictions on expenditure to which it was subject as property of the relevant charity

(5) Where—

(a) the Commissioners have been informed as mentioned in subsection (1)(a) above by any relevant institution, and

(b) before any transfer is made by the institution in pursuance of a direction under subsection (2) above, the institution has, by reason of any circumstances, cause to believe that the account, or (as the case may be) any of the accounts, held by it in the name of or on behalf of the relevant charity is no longer dormant,

the institution shall forthwith notify those circumstances in writing to the Commissioners; and, if it appears to the Commissioners that the account or accounts in question is or are no longer dormant, they shall revoke any direction under subsection (2) above which has previously been given by them to the institution with respect to the relevant charity.

(6) The receipt of any charity trustees or trustee for a charity in respect of any amount received from a relevant institution by virtue of this section shall be a complete discharge of the institution in respect of that amount.

(7) No obligation as to secrecy or other restriction on disclosure (however imposed) shall preclude a relevant institution from disclosing any information to the Commissioners for the purpose of enabling them to discharge their functions under this section.

(8) For the purposes of this section—

(a) an account is dormant if no transaction, other than—

(i) a transaction consisting in a payment into the account, or
(ii) a transaction which the institution holding the account has itself caused to be effected,

has been effected in relation to the account within the period of five years immediately preceding the date when the Commisioners are informed as mentioned in paragraph (a) of subsection (1) above;

(b) a 'relevant institution' means—

(i) the Bank of England;
(ii) an institution which is authorised by the Bank of England to operate a deposit-taking business under Part I of the Banking Act 1987;
(iii) a European deposit-taker as defined in regulation 8(2) of the Banking Coordination (Second Council Directive) Regulations 1992;
(iv) a building society which is authorised by the Building Societies Commission under section 9 of the Building Societies Act 1986 to raise money from its members; or
(v) such other institution mentioned in Schedule 2 to the Banking Act 1987 as the Secretary of State may prescribe by regulations; and

(c) references to the transfer of any amount to a charity are references to its transfer—

(i) to the charity trustees, or
(ii) to any trustee for the charity,

as the charity trustees may determine (and any reference to any amount received by a charity shall be construed accordingly).

(9) For the purpose of determining the matters in respect of which any of the powers conferred by section 8 or 9 above may be exercised it shall be assumed that the Commissioners have no functions under this section in relation to accounts to which this subsection applies (with the result that, for example, a relevant institution shall not, in connection with the functions of the Commissioners under this section, be required under section 8(3)(a) above to furnish any statements, or answer any questions or inquiries, with respect to any such accounts held by the institution).

This subsection applies to accounts which are dormant accounts by virtue of subsection (8)(a) above but would not be such accounts if sub-paragraph (i) of that provision were omitted.

(10) Subsection (1) above shall not apply to any account held in the name of or on behalf of an exempt charity.

29 Power to advise charity trustees

(1) The Commissioners may on the written application of any charity trustee give him their opinion or advice on any matter affecting the performance of his duties as such.

(2) A charity trustee or trustee for a charity acting in accordance with the opinion or advice of the Commissioners given under this section with respect to the charity shall be deemed, as regards his responsibility for so acting, to have acted in accordance with his trust, unless, when he does so, either—

(a) he knows or has reasonable cause to suspect that the opinion or advice was given in ignorance of material facts; or
(b) the decision of the court has been obtained on the matter or proceedings are pending to obtain one.

30 Powers for preservation of charity documents

(1) The Commissioners may provide books in which any deed, will or other document relating to a charity may be enrolled.

(2) The Commissioners may accept for safe keeping any document of or relating to a charity, and the charity trustees or other persons having the custody of documents of or relating to a charity (including a charity which has ceased to exist) may with the consent of the Commissioners deposit them with the Commissioners for safe keeping, except in the case of documents required by some other enactment to be kept elsewhere.

(3) Where a document is enrolled by the Commissioners or is for the time being deposited with them under this section, evidence of its contents may be given by means of a copy certified by any officer of the Commissioners generally or specially authorised by them to act for this purpose; and a document purporting to be such a copy shall be received in evidence without proof of the official position, authority or handwriting of the person certifying it or of the original document being enrolled or deposited as aforesaid.

(4) Regulations made by the Secretary of State may make provision for such documents deposited with the Commissioners under this section as may be prescribed by the regulations to be destroyed or otherwise disposed of after such period or in such circumstances as may be so prescribed.

(5) Subsections (3) and (4) above shall apply to any document transmitted to the Commissioners under section 9 above and kept by them under subsection (3) of that section, as if the document had been deposited with them for safe keeping under this section.

31 Power to order taxation of solicitor's bill

(1) The Commissioners may order that a solicitor's bill of costs for business done for a charity, or for charity trustees or trustees for a charity, shall be taxed, together with the costs of the taxation, by a taxing officer in such division of the High Court as may be specified in the order, or by the taxing officer of any other court having jurisdiction to order the taxation of the bill.

(2) On any order under this section for the taxation of a solicitor's bill the taxation shall proceed, and the taxing officer shall have the same powers and duties, and the costs of the taxation shall be borne, as if the order had been made, on the application of the person chargeable with the bill, by the court in which the costs are taxed.

(3) No order under this section for the taxation of a solicitor's bill shall be made after payment of the bill unless the Commissioners are of opinion that it contains exorbitant charges; and no such order shall in any case be made where the solicitor's costs are not subject to taxation on an order of the High Court by reason either of an agreement as to his remuneration or the lapse of time since payment of the bill.

Legal proceedings relating to charities

32 Proceedings by Commissioners

(1) Subject to subsection (2) below, the Commissioners may exercise the same powers with respect to—

(a) the taking of legal proceedings with reference to charities or the property or affairs of charities, or
(b) the compromise of claims with a view to avoiding or ending such proceedings,

as are exercisable by the Attorney General acting ex officio.

(2) Subsection (1) above does not apply to the power of the Attorney General under section 63(1) below to present a petition for the winding up of a charity.

(3) The practice and procedure to be followed in relation to any proceedings taken by the Commissioners under subsection (1) above shall be the same in all respects (and in particular as regards costs) as if they were proceedings taken by the Attorney General acting ex officio.

(4) No rule of law or practice shall be taken to require the Attorney General to be a party to any such proceedings.

(5) The powers exercisable by the Commissioners by virtue of this section shall be exercisable by them of their own motion, but shall be exercisable only with the agreement of the Attorney General on each occasion.

33 Proceedings by other persons

(1) Charity proceedings may be taken with reference to a charity either by the charity, or by any of the charity trustees, or by any person interested in the charity, or by any two or more inhabitants of the area of the charity if it is a local charity, but not by any other person.

(2) Subject to the following provisions of this section, no charity proceedings relating to a charity (other than an exempt charity) shall be entertained or proceeded with in any court unless the taking of the proceedings is authorised by order of the Commissioners.

(3) The Commissioners shall not, without special reasons, authorise the taking of charity proceedings where in their opinion the case can be dealt with by them under the powers of this Act other than those conferred by section 32 above.

(4) This section shall not require any order for the taking of proceedings in a pending cause or matter or for the bringing of any appeal.

(5) Where the foregoing provisions of this section require the taking of charity proceedings to be authorised by an order of the Commissioners, the proceedings may

nevertheless be entertained or proceeded with if, after the order had been applied for and refused, leave to take the proceedings was obtained from one of the judges of the High Court attached to the Chancery Division.

(6) Nothing in the foregoing subsections shall apply to the taking of proceedings by the Attorney General, with or without a relator, or to the taking of proceedings by the Commissioners in accordance with section 32 above.

(7) Where it appears to the Commissioners, on an application for an order under this section or otherwise, that it is desirable for legal proceedings to be taken with reference to any charity (other than an exempt charity) or its property or affairs, and for the proceedings to be taken by the Attorney General, the Commissioners shall so inform the Attorney General, and send him such statements and particulars as they think necessary to explain the matter.

(8) In this section 'charity proceedings' means proceedings in any court in England or Wales brought under the court's jurisdiction with respect to charities, or brought under the court's jurisdiction with respect to trusts in relation to the administration of a trust for charitable purposes.

34 Report of s 8 inquiry to be evidence in certain proceedings

(1) A copy of the report of the person conducting an inquiry under section 8 above shall, if certified by the Commissioners to be a true copy, be admissible in any proceedings to which this section applies—

(a) as evidence of any fact stated in the report; and
(b) as evidence of the opinion of that person as to any matter referred to in it.

(2) This section applies to—

(a) any legal proceedings instituted by the Commissioners under this Part of this Act; and
(b) any legal proceedings instituted by the Attorney General in respect of a charity.

(3) A document purporting to be a certificate issued for the purposes of subsection (1) above shall be received in evidence and be deemed to be such a certificate, unless the contrary is proved.

Meaning of 'trust corporation'

35 Application of provisions to trust corporations appointed under s 16 or 18

(1) In the definition of 'trust corporation' contained in the following provisions—

(a) section 117(xxx) of the Settled Land Act 1925,
(b) section 68(18) of the Trustee Act 1925,
(c) section 205 (xxviii) of the Law of Property Act 1925,
(d) section 55 (xxvi) of the Administration of Estates Act 1925, and
(e) section 128 of the Supreme Court Act 1981,

the reference to a corporation appointed by the court in any particular case to be a trustee includes a reference to a corporation appointed by the Commissioners under this Act to be a trustee.

(2) This section shall be deemed always to have had effect; but the reference to section 128 of the Supreme Court Act 1981 shall, in relation to any time before 1 January 1982, be

construed as a reference to section 175(1) of the Supreme Court of Judicature (Consolidation) Act 1925.

PART V

CHARITY LAND

36 Restrictions on dispositions

(1) Subject to the following provisions of this section and section 40 below, no land held by or in trust for a charity shall be sold, leased or otherwise disposed of without an order of the court or of the Commissioners.

(2) Subsection (1) above shall not apply to a disposition of such land if—

- (a) the disposition is made to a person who is not—
  - (i) a connected person (as defined in Schedule 5 to this Act), or
  - (ii) a trustee for, or nominee of, a connected person; and
- (b) the requirements of subsection (3) or (5) below have been complied with in relation to it.

(3) Except where the proposed disposition is the granting of such a lease as is mentioned in subsection (5) below, the charity trustees must, before entering into an agreement for the sale, or (as the case may be) for a lease or other disposition, of the land—

- (a) obtain and consider a written report on the proposed disposition from a qualified surveyor instructed by the trustees and acting exclusively for the charity;
- (b) advertise the proposed disposition for such period and in such manner as the surveyor has advised in his report (unless he has there advised that it would not be in the best interests of the charity to advertise the proposed disposition); and
- (c) decide that they are satisfied, having considered the surveyor's report, that the terms on which the disposition is proposed to be made are the best that can reasonably be obtained for the charity.

(4) For the purposes of subsection (3) above a person is a qualified surveyor if—

- (a) he is a fellow or professional associate of the Royal Institution of Chartered Surveyors or of the Incorporated Society of Valuers and Auctioneers or satisfies such other requirement or requirements as may be prescribed by regulations made by the Secretary of State; and
- (b) he is reasonably believed by the charity trustees to have ability in, and experience of, the valuation of land of the particular kind, and in the particular area, in question;

and any report prepared for the purposes of that subsection shall contain such information, and deal with such matters, as may be prescribed by regulations so made.

(5) Where the proposed disposition is the granting of a lease for a term ending not more than seven years after it is granted (other than one granted wholly or partly in consideration of a fine), the charity trustees must, before entering into an agreement for the lease—

- (a) obtain and consider the advice on the proposed disposition of a person who is reasonably believed by the trustees to have the requisite ability and practical experience to provide them with competent advice on the proposed disposition; and

(b) decide that they are satisfied, having considered that person's advice, that the terms on which the disposition is proposed to be made are the best that can reasonably be obtained for the charity.

(6) Where—

(a) any land is held by or in trust for a charity, and
(b) the trusts on which it is so held stipulate that it is to be used for the purposes, or any particular purposes, of the charity,

then (subject to subsections (7) and (8) below and without prejudice to the operation of the preceding provisions of this section) the land shall not be sold, leased or otherwise disposed of unless the charity trustees have previously—

(i) given public notice of the proposed disposition, inviting representations to be made to them within a time specified in the notice, being not less than one month from the date of the notice; and
(ii) taken into consideration any representations made to them within that time about the proposed disposition.

(7) Subsection (6) above shall not apply to any such disposition of land as is there mentioned if—

(a) the disposition is to be effected with a view to acquiring by way of replacement other property which is to be held on the trusts referred to in paragraph (b) of that subsection; or
(b) the disposition is the granting of a lease for a term ending not more than two years after it is granted (other than one granted wholly or partly in consideration of a fine).

(8) The Commissioners may direct—

(a) that subsection (6) above shall not apply to dispositions of land held by or in trust for a charity or class of charities (whether generally or only in the case of a specified class of dispositions or land, or otherwise as may be provided in the direction), or
(b) that that subsection shall not apply to a particular disposition of land held by or in trust for a charity,

if, on an application made to them in writing by or on behalf of the charity or charities in question, the Commissioners are satisfied that it would be in the interests of the charity or charities for them to give the direction.

(9) The restrictions on disposition imposed by this section apply notwithstanding anything in the trusts of a charity; but nothing in this section applies—

(a) to any disposition for which general or special authority is expressly given (without the authority being made subject to the sanction of an order of the court) by any statutory provision contained in or having effect under an Act of Parliament or by any scheme legally established; or
(b) to any disposition of land held by or in trust for a charity which—

(i) is made to another charity otherwise than for the best price that can reasonably be obtained, and
(ii) is authorised to be so made by the trusts of the first-mentioned charity; or

(c) to the granting, by or on behalf of a charity and in accordance with its trusts, or a lease to any beneficiary under those trusts where the lease—

(i) is granted otherwise than for the best rent that can reasonably be obtained; and

(ii) is intended to enable the demised premises to be occupied for the purposes, or any particular purposes, of the charity.

(10) Nothing in this section applies—

(a) to any disposition of land held by or in trust for an exempt charity;
(b) to any disposition of land by way of mortgage or other security; or
(c) to any disposition of an advowson.

(11) In this section 'land' means land in England or Wales.

37 Supplementary provisions relating to dispositions

(1) Any of the following instruments, namely—

(a) any contract for the sale, or for a lease or other disposition, of land which is held by or in trust for a charity, and
(b) any conveyance, transfer, lease or other instrument effecting a disposition of such land,

and state—

(i) that the land is held by or in trust for a charity,
(ii) whether the charity is an exempt charity and whether the disposition is one falling within paragraph (a), (b) or (c) of subsection (9) of section 36 above, and
(iii) if it is not an exempt charity and the disposition is not one falling within any of those paragraphs, that the land is land to which the restrictions on disposition imposed by that section apply.

(2) Where any land held by or in trust for a charity is sold, leased or otherwise disposed of by a disposition to which subsection (1) or (2) of section 36 above applies, the charity trustees shall certify in the instrument by which the disposition is effected—

(a) (where subsection (1) of that section applies) that the disposition has been sanctioned by an order of the court or of the Commissioners (as the case may be), or
(b) (where subsection (2) of that section applies) that the charity trustees have power under the trusts of the charity to effect the disposition, and that they have complied with the provisions of that section so far as applicable to it.

(3) Where subsection (2) above has been complied with in relation to any disposition of land, then in favour of a person who (whether under the disposition or afterwards) acquires an interest in the land for money or money's worth, it shall be conclusively presumed that the facts were as stated in the certificate.

(4) Where—

(a) any land held by or in trust for a charity is sold, leased or otherwise disposed of by a disposition to which subsection (1) or (2) of section 36 above applies, but
(b) subsection (2) above has not been complied with in relation to the disposition,

then in favour of a person who (whether under the disposition or afterwards) in good faith acquires an interest in the land for money or money's worth, the disposition shall be valid whether or not—

(i) the disposition has been sanctioned by an order of the court or of the Commissioners, or
(ii) the charity trustees have power under the trusts of the charity to effect the disposition and have complied with the provisions of that section so far as applicable to it.

(5) Any of the following instruments, namely—

(a) any contract for the sale, or for a lease or other disposition, of land which will, as a result of the disposition, be held by or in trust for a charity, and
(b) any conveyance, transfer, lease or other instrument effecting a disposition of such land,

shall state—

(i) that the land will, as a result of the disposition, be held by or in trust for a charity,
(ii) whether the charity is an exempt charity, and
(iii) if it is not an exempt charity, that the restrictions on disposition imposed by section 36 above will apply to the land (subject to subsection (9) of that section).

(6) . . .

(7) Where—

(a) the disposition to be effected by any such instrument as is mentioned in subsection (1)(b) or (5)(b) above will be a registered disposition, or
(b) any such instrument will on taking effect on an instrument to which section 123(1) of the Land Registration Act 1925 (compulsory registration of title) applies,

the statement which, by virtue of subsection (1) or (5) above, is to be contained in the instrument shall be in such form as may be prescribed.

(8) Where—

(a) an application is duly made—

(i) for registration of a disposition of registered land, or
(ii) for registration of a person's title under a disposition of unregistered land, and

(b) the instrument by which the disposition is effected contains a statement complying with subsections (5) and (7) above, and
(c) the charity by or in trust for which the land is held as a result of the disposition is not an exempt charity,

the registrar shall enter in the register, in respect of the land, a restriction in such form as may be prescribed.

(9) Where—

(a) any such restriction is entered in the register in respect of any land, and
(b) the charity by or in trust for which the land is held becomes an exempt charity,

the charity trustees shall apply to the registrar for the restriction to be withdrawn; and on receiving any application duly made under this subsection the registrar shall withdraw the restriction.

(10) Where—

(a) any registered land is held by or in trust for an exempt charity and the charity ceases to be an exempt charity, or
(b) any registered land becomes, as a result of a declaration of trust by the registered proprietor, land held in trust for a charity (other than an exempt charity),

the charity trustees shall apply to the registrar for such a restriction as is mentioned in subsection (8) above to be entered in the register in respect of the land; and on receiving any application duly made under this subsection the registrar shall enter such a restriction in the register in respect of the land.

(11) In this section—

(a) references to a disposition of land do not include references to—

(i) a disposition of land by way of mortgage or other security,
(ii) any disposition of an advowson, or
(iii) any release of a rentcharge falling within section 40(1) below; and

(b) 'land' means land in England or Wales;

and subsections (7) to (10) above shall be construed as one with the Land Registration Act 1925.

Note: Section shown as amended by the Trusts of Land and Appointment of Trustees Act 1996, s 25(2), Sch 4.

---

38 Restrictions on mortgaging

(1) Subject to subsection (2) below, no mortgage of land held by or in trust for a charity shall be granted without an order of the court or of the Commissioners.

(2) Subsection (1) above shall not apply to a mortgage of any such land by way of security for the repayment of a loan where the charity trustees have, before executing the mortgage, obtained and considered proper advice, given to them in writing, on the matters mentioned in subsection (3) below.

(3) Those matters are—

(a) whether the proposed loan is necessary in order for the charity trustees to be able to pursue the particular course of action in connection with which the loan is sought by them;
(b) whether the terms of the proposed loan are reasonable having regard to the status of the charity as a prospective borrower; and
(c) the ability of the charity to repay on those terms the sum proposed to be borrowed.

(4) For the purposes of subsection (2) above proper advice is the advice of a person—

(a) who is reasonably believed by the charity trustees to be qualified by his ability in and practical experience of financial matters; and
(b) who has no financial interest in the making of the loan in question;

and such advice may constitute proper advice for those purposes notwithstanding that the person giving it does so in the course of his employment as an officer or employee of the charity or of the charity trustees.

(5) This section applies notwithstanding anything in the trusts of a charity; but nothing in this section applies to any mortgage for which general or special authority is given as mentioned in section 36(9)(a) above.

(6) In this section—

'land' means land in England or Wales;
'mortgage' includes a charge.

(7) Nothing in this section applies to an exempt charity.

39 Supplementary provisions relating to mortgaging

(1) Any mortgage of land held by or in trust for a charity shall state—

(a) that the land is held by or in trust for a charity,

(b) whether the charity is an exempt charity and whether the mortgage is one falling within subsection (5) of section 38 above, and
(c) if it is not an exempt charity and the mortgage is not one falling within that subsection, that the mortgage is one to which the restrictions imposed by that section apply;

and where the mortgage will be a registered disposition any such statement shall be in such form as may be prescribed.

(2) Where subsection (1) or (2) of section 38 above applies to any mortgage of land held by or in trust for a charity, the charity trustees shall certify in the mortgage—

(a) (where subsection (1) of that section applies) that the mortgage has been sanctioned by an order of the court or of the Commissioners (as the case may be), or
(b) (where subsection (2) of that section applies) that the charity trustees have power under the trusts of the charity to grant the mortgage, and that they have obtained and considered such advice as is mentioned in that subsection.

(3) Where subsection (2) above has been complied with in relation to any mortgage, then in favour of a person who (whether under the mortgage or afterwards) acquires an interest in the land in question for money or money's worth, it shall be conclusively presumed that the facts were as stated in the certificate.

(4) Where—

(a) subsection (1) or (2) of section 38 above applies to any mortgage of land held by or in trust for a charity, but
(b) subsection (2) above has not been complied with in relation to the mortgage,

then in favour of a person who (whether under the mortgage or afterwards) in good faith acquires an interest in the land for money or money's worth, the mortgage shall be valid whether or not—

(i) the mortgage has been sanctioned by an order of the court or of the Commissioners, or
(ii) the charity trustees have power under the trusts of the charity to grant the mortgage and have obtained and considered such advice as is mentioned in subsection (2) of that section.

(5) . . .

(6) In this section—
'mortgage' includes a charge, and 'mortgagee' shall be construed accordingly;
'land' means land in England or Wales;
'prescribed' and 'registered disposition' have the same meaning as in the Land Registration Act 1925.

Note: Section shown as amended by the Trusts of Land and Appointment of Trustees Act 1996, s 25(2), Sch 4.

---

40 Release of charity rentcharges

(1) Section 36(1) above shall not apply to the release by a charity of a rentcharge which it is entitled to receive if the release is given in consideration of the payment of an amount which is not less than ten times the annual amount of the rentcharge.

(2) Where a charity which is entitled to receive a rentcharge releases it in consideration of the payment of an amount not exceeding £500, any costs incurred by the charity in

connection with proving its title to the rentcharge shall be recoverable by the charity from the person or persons in whose favour the rentcharge is being released.

(3) Neither section 36(1) nor subsection (2) above applies where a rentcharge which a charity is entitled to receive is redeemed under sections 8 to 10 of the Rentcharges Act 1977.

(4) The Secretary of State may by order amend subsection (2) above by substituting a different sum for the sum for the time being specified there.

PART VI

CHARITY ACCOUNTS, REPORTS AND RETURNS

41 Duty to keep accounting records

(1) The charity trustees of a charity shall ensure that accounting records are kept in respect of the charity which are sufficient to show and explain all the charity's transactions, and which are such as to—

- (a) disclose at any time, with reasonable accuracy, the financial position of the charity at that time, and
- (b) enable the trustees to ensure that, where any statements of accounts are prepared by them under section 42(1) below, those statements of accounts comply with the requirements of regulations under that provision.

(2) The accounting records shall in particular contain—

- (a) entries showing from day to day all sums of money received and expended by the charity, and the matters in respect of which the receipt and expenditure takes place; and
- (b) a record of the assets and liabilities of the charity.

(3) The charity trustees of a charity shall preserve any accounting records made for the purposes of this section in respect of the charity for at least six years from the end of the financial year of the charity in which they are made.

(4) Where a charity ceases to exist within the period of six years mentioned in subsection (3) above as it applies to any accounting records, the obligation to preserve those records in accordance with that subsection shall continue to be discharged by the last charity trustees of the charity, unless the Commissioners consent in writing to the records being destroyed or otherwise disposed of.

(5) Nothing in this section applies to a charity which is a company.

42 Annual statements of accounts

(1) The charity trustees of a charity shall (subject to subsection (3) below) prepare in respect of each financial year of the charity a statement of accounts complying with such requirements as to its form and contents as may be prescribed by regulations made by the Secretary of State.

(2) Without prejudice to the generality of subsection (1) above, regulations under that subsection may make provision—

- (a) for any such statement to be prepared in accordance with such methods and principles as are specified or referred to in the regulations;

(b) as to any information to be provided by way of notes to the accounts;

and regulations under that subsection may also make provision for determining the financial years of a charity for the purposes of this Act and any regulations made under it.

(3) Where a charity's gross income in any financial year does not exceed £100,000, the charity trustees may, in respect of that year, elect to prepare the following, namely—

(a) a receipts and payments account, and
(b) a statement of assets and liabilities,

instead of a statement of accounts under subsection (1) above.

(4) The charity trustees of a charity shall preserve—

(a) any statement of accounts prepared by them under subsection (1) above, or
(b) any account and statement prepared by them under subsection (3) above,

for at least six years from the end of the financial year to which any such statement relates or (as the case may be) to which any such account and statement relate.

(5) Subsection (4) of section 41 above shall apply in relation to the preservation of any such statement or account and statement as it applies in relation to the preservation of any accounting records (the references to subsection (3) of that section being read as references to subsection (4) above).

(6) The Secretary of State may by order amend subsection (3) above by substituting a different sum for the sum for the time being specified there.

(7) Nothing in this section applies to a charity which is a company.

Note: Section shown as amended by the Charities Act 1993 (Substitution of Sums) Order 1995 (SI 1995/2696), art 2(1), (3).

---

43 Annual audit or examination of charity accounts

(1) Subsection (2) below applies to a financial year of a charity ('the relevant year') if the charity's gross income or total expenditure in any of the following, namely—

(a) the relevant year,
(b) the financial year of the charity immediately preceding the relevant year (if any), and
(c) the financial year of the charity immediately preceding the year specified in paragraph (b) above (if any),

exceeds £250,000.

(2) If this subsection applies to a financial year of a charity, the accounts of the charity for that year shall be audited by a person who—

(a) is, in accordance with section 25 of the Companies Act 1989 (eligibility for appointment), eligible for appointment as a company auditor, or
(b) is a member of a body for the time being specified in regulations under section 44 below and is under the rules of that body eligible for appointment as auditor of the charity.

(3) If subsection (2) above does not apply to a financial year of a charity and its gross income or total expenditure in that year exceeds £10,000, then (subject to subsection (4)

below) the accounts of the charity for that year shall, at the election of the charity trustees, either—

(a) be examined by an independent examiner, that is to say an independent person who is reasonably believed by the trustees to have the requisite ability and practical experience to carry out a competent examination of the accounts, or
(b) be audited by such a person as is mentioned in subsection (2) above.

(4) Where it appears to the Commissioners—

(a) that subsection (2), or (as the case may be) subsection (3) above, has not been complied with in relation to a financial year of a charity within ten months from the end of that year, or
(b) that, although subsection (2) above does not apply to a financial year of a charity, it would nevertheless be desirable for the accounts of the charity for that year to be audited by such a person as is mentioned in that subsection,

the Commissioners may by order require the accounts of the charity for that year to be audited by such a person as is mentioned in that subsection.

(5) If the Commissioners make an order under subsection (4) above with respect to a charity, then unless—

(a) the order is made by virtue of paragraph (b) of that subsection, and
(b) the charity trustees themselves appoint an auditor in accordance with the order,

the auditor shall be a person appointed by the Commissioners.

(6) The expenses of any audit carried out by an auditor appointed by the Commissioners under subsection (5) above, including the auditor's remuneration, shall be recoverable by the Commissioners—

(a) from the charity trustees of the charity concerned, who shall be personally liable, jointly and severally, for those expenses; or
(b) to the extent that it appears to the Commissioners not to be practical to seek recovery of those expenses in accordance with paragraph (a) above, from the funds of the charity.

(7) The Commissioners may—

(a) give guidance to charity trustees in connection with the selection of a person for appointment as an independent examiner;
(b) give such directions as they think appropriate with respect to the carrying out of an examination in pursuance of subsection (3)(a) above;

and any such guidance or directions may either be of general application or apply to a particular charity only.

(8) The Secretary of State may by order amend subsection (1) or (3) above by substituting a different sum for the sum for the time being specified there.

(9) Nothing in this section applies to a charity which is a company.

Note: Section shown as amended by the Deregulation and Contracting Out Act 1994, s 28 and the Charities Act 1993 (Substitution of Sums) Order 1995 (SI 1995/2696), art 2(1), (4).

---

44 Supplementary provisions relating to audits etc

(1) The Secretary of State may by regulations make provision—

(a) specifying one or more bodies for the purposes of section 43(2)(b) above;

(b) with respect to the duties of an auditor carrying out an audit under section 43 above, including provision with respect to the making by him of a report on—

(i) the statement of accounts prepared for the financial year in question under section 42(1) above, or
(ii) the account and statement so prepared under section 42(3) above,

as the case may be;

(c) with respect to the making by an independent examiner of a report in respect of an examination carried out by him under section 43 above;
(d) conferring on such an auditor or on an independent examiner a right of access with respect to books, documents and other records (however kept) which relate to the charity concerned;
(e) entitling such an auditor or an independent examiner to require, in the case of a charity, information and explanations from past or present charity trustees or trustees for the charity, or from past or present officers or employees of the charity;
(f) enabling the Commissioners, in circumstances specified in the regulations, to dispense with the requirements of section 43(2) or (3) above in the case of a particular charity or in the case of any particular financial year of a charity.

(2) If any person fails to afford an auditor or an independent examiner any facility to which he is entitled by virtue of subsection (1)(d) or (e) above, the Commissioners may by order give—

(a) to that person, or
(b) to the charity trustees for the time being of the charity concerned,

such directions as the Commissioners think appropriate for securing that the default is made good.

(3) Section 727 of the Companies Act 1985 (power of court to grant relief in certain cases) shall have effect in relation to an auditor or independent examiner appointed by a charity in pursuance of section 43 above as it has effect in relation to a person employed as auditor by a company within the meaning of that Act.

45 Annual reports

(1) The charity trustees of a charity shall prepare in respect of each financial year of the charity an annual report containing—

(a) such a report by the trustees on the activities of the charity during that year, and
(b) such other information relating to the charity or to its trustees or officers,

as may be prescribed by regulations made by the Secretary of State.

(2) Without prejudice to the generality of subsection (1) above, regulations under that subsection may make provision—

(a) for any such report as is mentioned in paragraph (a) of that subsection to be prepared in accordance with such principles as are specified or referred to in the regulations;
(b) enabling the Commissioners to dispense with any requirement prescribed by virtue of subsection (1)(b) above in the case of a particular charity or a particular class of charities, or in the case of a particular financial year of a charity or of any class of charities.

(3) Where in any financial year of a charity its gross income or total expenditure exceeds £10,000, the annual report required to be prepared under this section in respect of that year shall be transmitted to the Commissioners by the charity trustees—

(a) within ten months from the end of that year, or
(b) within such longer period as the Commissioners may for any special reason allow in the case of that report.

(3A) Where in any financial year of a charity neither its gross income nor its total expenditure exceeds £10,000, the annual report required to be prepared under this section in respect of that year shall, if the Commissioners so request, be transmitted to them by the charity trustees—

(a) in the case of a request made before the end of seven months from the end of the financial year to which the report relates, within ten months from the end of that year, and
(b) in the case of a request not so made, within three months from the date of the request,

or, in either case, within such longer period as the Commissioners may for any special reason allow in the case of that report.

(4) Subject to subsection (5) below, any annual report transmitted to the Commissioners under this section shall have attached to it the statement of accounts prepared for the financial year in question under section 42(1) above or (as the case may be) the account and statement so prepared under section 42(3) above, together with—

(a) where the accounts of the charity for that year have been audited under section 43 above, a copy of the report made by the auditor on that statement of accounts or (as the case may be) on that account and statement;
(b) where the accounts of the charity for that year have been examined under section 43 above, a copy of the report made by the independent examiner in respect of the examination carried out by him under that section.

(5) Subsection (4) above does not apply to a charity which is a company, and any annual report transmitted by the charity trustees of such a charity under this section shall instead have attached to it a copy of the charity's annual accounts prepared for the financial year in question under Part VII of the Companies Act 1985, together with a copy of any auditors' report or report made for the purposes of section 249A(2) of that Act on those accounts.

(6) Any annual report transmitted to the Commissioners under this section, together with the documents attached to it, shall be kept by the Commissioners for such period as they think fit.

(7) The charity trustees of a charity shall preserve, for at least six years from the end of the financial year to which it relates, any annual report prepared by them under subsection (1) above which they have not been required to transmit to the Commissioners.

(8) Subsection (4) of section 41 above shall apply in relation to the preservation of any such annual report as it applies in relation to the preservation of any accounting records (the references in subsection (3) of that section being read as references to subsection (7) above).

(9) The Secretary of State may by order amend subsection (3) or (3A) above by substituting a different sum for the time being specified there.

Note: Section shown as amended by the Deregulation and Contracting Out Act 1994, s 29(1)–(6); and the Companies Act 1985 (Audit Exemption) Regulations 1994 (SI 1994/1935), reg 4, Sch 1, Pt II, para 6.

46 Special provision as respects accounts and annual reports of exempt and other excepted charities

(1) Nothing in sections 41 to 45 above applies to any exempt charity; but the charity trustees of an exempt charity shall keep proper books of account with respect to the affairs of the charity, and if not required by or under the authority of any other Act to prepare periodical statements of account shall prepare consecutive statements of account consisting on each occasion of an income and expenditure account relating to a period of not more than fifteen months and a balance sheet relating to the end of that period.

(2) The books of accounts and statements of account relating to an exempt charity shall be preserved for a period of six years at least unless the charity ceases to exist and the Commissioners consent in writing to their being destroyed or otherwise disposed of.

(3) Nothing in sections 43 to 45 above applies to any charity which—

(a) falls within section 3(5)(c) above, and
(b) is not registered.

(4) Except in accordance with subsection (7) below, nothing in section 45 above applies to any charity (other than an exempt charity or a charity which falls within section 3(5)(c) above) which—

(a) is excepted by section 3(5) above, and
(b) is not registered.

(5) If requested to do so by the Commissioners, the charity trustees of any such charity as is mentioned in subsection (4) above shall prepare an annual report in respect of such financial year of the charity as is specified in the Commissioners' request.

(6) Any report prepared under subsection (5) above shall contain—

(a) such a report by the charity trustees on the activities of the charity during the year in question, and
(b) such other information relating to the charity or to its trustees or officers,

as may be prescribed by regulations made under section 45(1) above in relation to annual reports prepared under that provision.

(7) Subsections (3) to (6) of section 45 (as originally enacted) above shall apply to any report required to be prepared under subsection (5) above as if it were an annual report required to be prepared under subsection (1) of that section.

(8) Any reference in this section to a charity which falls within section 3(5)(c) above includes a reference to a charity which falls within that provision but is also excepted from registration by section 3(5)(b) above.

Note: Section shown as amended by the Deregulation and Contracting Out Act 1994, s 29(7).

47 Public inspection of annual reports etc

(1) Any annual report or other document kept by the Commissioners in pursuance of section 45(6) above shall be open to public inspection at all reasonable times—

(a) during the period for which it is so kept; or
(b) if the Commissioners so determine, during such lesser period as they may specify.

(2) Where any person—

(a) requests the charity trustees of a charity in writing to provide him with a copy of the charity's most recent accounts, and
(b) pays them such reasonable fee (if any) as they may require in respect of the costs of complying with the request,

those trustees shall comply with the request within the period of two months beginning with the date on which it is made.

(3) In subsection (2) above the reference to a charity's most recent accounts is—

(a) ...
(b) in the case of a charity other than one falling within paragraph (c) or (d) below, a reference to the statement of accounts or account and statement prepared in pursuance of section 42(1) or (3) above in respect of the last financial year of the charity in respect of which a statement of accounts or account and statement has or have been so prepared;
(c) in the case of a charity which is a company, a reference to the most recent annual accounts of the company prepared under Part VII of the Companies Act 1985 in relation to which any of the following conditions is satisfied—
  (i) they have been audited;
  (ii) a report required for the purposes of section 249A(2) of that Act has been made in respect of them; or
  (iii) they relate to a year in respect of which the company is exempt from audit by virtue of section 249A(1) of that Act; and
(d) in the case of an exempt charity, a reference to the accounts of the charity most recently audited in pursuance of any statutory or other requirement or, if its accounts are not required to be audited, the accounts most recently prepared in respect of the charity.

Note: Section shown as amended by the Deregulation and Contracting Out Act 1994, ss 39, 81(1), Sch 11, para 12, Sch 17; and the Companies Act 1985 (Audit Exemption) Regulations 1994 (SI 1994/1935), reg 4, Sch 1, Pt II, para 7.

48 Annual returns by registered charities

(1) Subject to subsection (1A) below, every registered charity shall prepare in respect of each of its financial years an annual return in such form, and containing such information, as may be prescribed by regulations made by the Commissioners.

(1A) Subsection (1) above shall not apply in relation to any financial year of a charity in which neither the gross income nor the total expenditure of the charity exceeds £10,000.

(2) Any such return shall be transmitted to the Commissioners by the date by which the charity trustees are, by virtue of section 45(3) above, required to transmit to them the annual report required to be prepared in respect of the financial year in question.

(3) The Commissioners may dispense with the requirements of subsection (1) above in the case of a particular charity or a particular class of charities, or in the case of a particular financial year of a charity or of any class of charities.

(4) The Secretary of State may by order amend subsection (1A) above by substituting a different sum for the sum for the time being specified there.

Note: Section shown as amended by the Deregulation and Contracting Out Act 1994, s 30.

49 Offences

Any person who, without reasonable excuse, is persistently in default in relation to any requirement imposed—

(a) by section 45(3) or (3A) above (taken with section 45(4) or (5), as the case may require), or
(b) by section 47(2) or 48(2) above,

shall be guilty of an offence and liable on summary conviction to a fine not exceeding level 4 on the standard scale.

Note: Section shown as amended by the Deregulation and Contracting Out Act 1994, s 29(8).

PART VII

INCORPORATION OF CHARITY TRUSTEES

50 Incorporation of trustees of a charity

(1) Where—

(a) the trustees of a charity, in accordance with section 52 below, apply to the Commissioners for a certificate of incorporation of the trustees as a body corporate, and
(b) the Commissioners consider that the incorporation of the trustees would be in the interests of the charity,

the Commissioners may grant such a certificate, subject to such conditions or directions as they think fit to insert in it.

(2) The Commissioners shall not, however, grant such a certificate in a case where the charity appears to them to be required to be registered under section 3 above but is not so registered.

(3) On the grant of such a certificate—

(a) the trustees of the charity shall become a body corporate by such name as is specified in the certificate; and
(b) (without prejudice to the operation of section 54 below) any relevant rights or liabilities of those trustees shall become rights or liabilities of that body.

(4) After their incorporation the trustees—

(a) may sue and be sued in their corporate name; and
(b) shall have the same powers, and be subject to the same restrictions and limitations, as respects the holding, acquisition and disposal of property for or in connection with the purposes of the charity as they had or were subject to while unincorporated;

and any relevant legal proceedings that might have been continued or commenced by or against the trustees may be continued or commenced by or against them in their corporate name.

(5) A body incorporated under this section need not have a common seal.

(6) In this section—

'relevant rights or liabilities' means rights or liabilities in connection with any property vesting in the body in question under section 51 below; and

'relevant legal proceedings' means legal proceedings in connection with any such property.

51 Estate to vest in body corporate

The certificate of incorporation shall vest in the body corporate all real and personal estate, of whatever nature or tenure, belonging to or held by any person or persons in trust for the charity, and thereupon any person or persons in whose name or names any stocks, funds or securities are standing in trust for the charity, shall transfer them into the name of the body corporate, except that the foregoing provisions shall not apply to property vested in the official custodian.

52 Applications for incorporation

(1) Every application to the Commissioners for a certificate of incorporation under this Part of this Act shall—

(a) be in writing and signed by the trustees of the charity concerned; and
(b) be accompanied by such documents or information as the Commissioners may require for the purpose of the application.

(2) The Commissioners may require—

(a) any statement contained in any such application, or
(b) any document or information supplied under subsection (1)(b) above,

to be verified in such manner as they may specify.

53 Nomination of trustees, and filling up vacancies

(1) Before a certificate of incorporation is granted under this Part of this Act, trustees of the charity must have been effectually appointed to the satisfaction of the Commissioners.

(2) Where a certificate of incorporation is granted vacancies in the number of the trustees of the charity shall from time to time be filled up so far as required by the constitution or settlement of the charity, or by any conditions or directions in the certificate, by such legal means as would have been available for the appointment of new trustees of the charity if no certificate of incorporation had been granted, or otherwise as required by such conditions or directions.

54 Liability of trustees and others, notwithstanding incorporation

After a certificate of incorporation has been granted under this Part of this Act all trustees of the charity, notwithstanding their incorporation, shall be chargeable for such property as shall come into their hands, and shall be answerable and accountable for their own acts, receipts, neglects, and defaults, and for the due administration of the charity and its property, in the same manner and to the same extent as if no such incorporation had been effected.

55 Certificate to be evidence of compliance with requirements for incorporation

A certificate of incorporation granted under this Part of this Act shall be conclusive evidence that all the preliminary requirements for incorporation under this Part of this

Act have been complied with, and the date of incorporation mentioned in the certificate shall be deemed to be the date at which incorporation has taken place.

56 Power of Commissioners to amend certificate of incorporation

(1) The Commissioners may amend a certificate of incorporation either on the application of the incorporated body to which it relates or of their own motion.

(2) Before making any such amendment of their own motion, the Commissioners shall by notice in writing—

(a) inform the trustees of the relevant charity of their proposals, and
(b) invite those trustees to make representations to them within a time specified in the notice, being not less than one month from the date of the notice.

(3) The Commissioners shall take into consideration any representations made by those trustees within the time so specified, and may then (without further notice) proceed with their proposals either without modification or with such modifications as appear to them to be desirable.

(4) The Commissioners may amend a certificate of incorporation either—

(a) by making an order specifying the amendment; or
(b) by issuing a new certificate of incorporation taking account of the amendment.

57 Records of applications and certificates

(1) The Commissioners shall keep a record of all applications for, and certificates of, incorporation under this Part of this Act and shall preserve all documents sent to them under this Part of this Act.

(2) Any person may inspect such documents, under the direction of the Commissioners, and any person may require a copy or extract of any such document to be certified by a certificate signed by the secretary of the Commissioners.

58 Enforcement of orders and directions

All conditions and directions inserted in any certificate of incorporation shall be binding upon and performed or observed by the trustees as trusts of the charity, and section 88 below shall apply to any trustee who fails to perform or observe any such condition or direction as it applies to a person guilty of disobedience to any such order of the Commissioners as is mentioned in that section.

59 Gifts to charity before incorporation to have same effect afterwards

After the incorporation of the trustees of any charity under this Part of this Act every donation, gift and disposition of property, real or personal, lawfully made before the incorporation but not having actually taken effect, or thereafter lawfully made, by deed, will or otherwise to or in favour of the charity, or the trustees of the charity, or otherwise for the purposes of the charity, shall take effect as if made to or in favour of the incorporated body or otherwise for the like purposes.

60 Execution of documents by incorporated body

(1) This section has effect as respects the execution of documents by an incorporated body.

(2) If an incorporated body has a common seal, a document may be executed by the body by the affixing of its common seal.

(3) Whether or not it has a common seal, a document may be executed by an incorporated body either—

(a) by being signed by a majority of the trustees of the relevant charity and expressed (in whatever form of words) to be executed by the body; or
(b) by being executed in pursuance of an authority given under subsection (4) below.

(4) For the purposes of subsection (3)(b) above the trustees of the relevant charity in the case of an incorporated body may, subject to the trusts of the charity, confer on any two or more of their number—

(a) a general authority, or
(b) an authority limited in such manner as the trustees think fit,

to execute in the name and on behalf of the body documents for giving effect to transactions to which the body is a party.

(5) An authority under subsection (4) above—

(a) shall suffice for any document if it is given in writing or by resolution of a meeting of the trustees of the relevant charity, notwithstanding the want of any formality that would be required in giving an authority apart from that subsection;
(b) may be given so as to make the powers conferred exercisable by any of the trustees, or may be restricted to named persons or in any other way;
(c) subject to any such restriction, and until it is revoked, shall, notwithstanding any change in the trustees of the relevant charity, have effect as a continuing authority given by the trustees from time to time of the charity and exercisable by such trustees.

(6) In any authority under subsection (4) above to execute a document in the name and on behalf of an incorporated body there shall, unless the contrary intention appears, be implied authority also to execute it for the body in the name and on behalf of the official custodian or of any other person, in any case in which the trustees could do so.

(7) A document duly executed by an incorporated body which makes it clear on its face that it is intended by the person or persons making it to be a deed has effect, upon delivery, as a deed; and it shall be presumed, unless a contrary intention is proved, to be delivered upon its being so executed.

(8) In favour of a purchaser a document shall be deemed to have been duly executed by such a body if it purports to be signed—

(a) by a majority of the trustees of the relevant charity, or
(b) by such of the trustees of the relevant charity as are authorised by the trustees of that charity to execute it in the name and on behalf of the body,

and, where the document makes it clear on its face that it is intended by the person or persons making it to be a deed, it shall be deemed to have been delivered upon its being executed.

For this purpose 'purchaser' means a purchaser in good faith for valuable consideration and includes a lessee, mortgagee or other person who for valuable consideration acquires an interest in property.

61 Power of Commissioners to dissolve incorporated body

(1) Where the Commissioners are satisfied—

(a) that an incorporated body has no assets or does not operate, or

(b) that the relevant charity in the case of an incorporated body has ceased to exist, or
(c) that the institution previously constituting, or treated by them as constituting, any such charity has ceased to be, or (as the case may be) was not at the time of the body's incorporation, a charity, or
(d) that the purposes of the relevant charity in the case of an incorporated body have been achieved so far as is possible or are in practice incapable of being achieved,

they may of their own motion make an order dissolving the body as from such date as is specified in the order.

(2) Where the Commissioners are satisfied, on the application of the trustees of the relevant charity in the case of an incorporated body, that it would be in the interests of the charity for that body to be dissolved, the Commissioners may make an order dissolving the body as from such date as is specified in the order.

(3) Subject to subsection (4) below, an order made under this section with respect to an incorporated body shall have the effect of vesting in the trustees of the relevant charity, in trust for that charity, all property for the time being vested—

(a) in the body, or
(b) in any other person (apart from the official custodian),

in trust for that charity.

(4) If the Commissioners so direct in the order—

(a) all or any specified part of that property shall, instead of vesting in the trustees of the relevant charity, vest—

(i) in a specified person as trustee for, or nominee of, that charity, or
(ii) in such persons (other than the trustees of the relevant charity) as may be specified;

(b) any specified investments, or any specified class or description of investments, held by any person in trust for the relevant charity shall be transferred—

(i) to the trustees of that charity, or
(ii) to any such person or persons as is or are mentioned in paragraph (a)(i) or (ii) above;

and for this purpose 'specified' means specified by the Commissioners in the order.

(5) Where an order to which this subsection applies is made with respect to an incorporated body—

(a) any rights or liabilities of the body shall become rights or liabilities of the trustees of the relevant charity; and
(b) any legal proceedings that might have been continued or commenced by or against the body may be continued or commenced by or against those trustees.

(6) Subsection (5) above applies to any order under this section by virtue of which—

(a) any property vested as mentioned in subsection (3) above is vested—

(i) in the trustees of the relevant charity, or
(ii) in any persons as trustee for, or nominee of, that charity; or

(b) any investments held by any person in trust for the relevant charity are required to be transferred—

(i) to the trustees of that charity, or

(ii) to any person as trustee for, or nominee of, that charity.

(7) Any order made by the Commissioners under this section may be varied or revoked by a further order so made.

62 Interpretation of Part VII

In this Part of this Act—

'incorporated body' means a body incorporated under section 50 above;
'the relevant charity', in relation to an incorporated body, means the charity the trustees of which have been incorporated as that body;
'the trustees', in relation to a charity, means the charity trustees.

PART VIII

CHARITABLE COMPANIES

63 Winding up

(1) Where a charity may be wound up by the High Court under the Insolvency Act 1986, a petition for it to be wound up under that Act by any court in England or Wales having jurisdiction may be presented by the Attorney General, as well as by any person authorised by that Act.

(2) Where a charity may be so wound up by the High Court, such a petition may also be presented by the Commissioners if, at any time after they have instituted an inquiry under section 8 above with respect to the charity, they are satisfied as mentioned in section 18(1)(a) or (b) above.

(3) Where a charitable company is dissolved, the Commissioners may make an application under section 651 of the Companies Act 1985 (power of court to declare dissolution of company void) for an order to be made under that section with respect to the company; and for this purpose subsection (1) of that section shall have effect in relation to a charitable company as if the reference to the liquidator of the company included a reference to the Commissioners.

(4) Where a charitable company's name has been struck off the register of companies under section 652 of the Companies Act 1985 (power of registrar to strike defunct company off register), the Commissioners may make an application under section 653(2) of that Act (objection to striking off by person aggrieved) for an order restoring the company's name to that register; and for this purpose section 653(2) shall have effect in relation to a charitable company as if the reference to any such person aggrieved as is there mentioned included a reference to the Commissioners.

(5) The powers exercisable by the Commissioners by virtue of this section shall be exercisable by them of their own motion, but shall be exercisable only with the agreement of the Attorney General on each occasion.

(6) In this section 'charitable company' means a company which is a charity.

64 Alteration of objects clause

(1) Where a charity is a company or other body corporate having power to alter the instruments establishing or regulating it as a body corporate, no exercise of that power which has the effect of the body ceasing to be a charity shall be valid so as to affect the application of—

(a) any property acquired under any disposition or agreement previously made otherwise than for full consideration in money or money's worth, or any property representing property so acquired,
(b) any property representing income which has accrued before the alteration is made, or
(c) the income from any such property as aforesaid.

(2) Where a charity is a company, any alteration by it—

(a) of the objects clause in its memorandum of association, or
(b) of any other provision in its memorandum of association, or any provision in its articles of association, which is a provision directing or restricting the manner in which property of the company may be used or applied,

is ineffective without the prior written consent of the Commissioners.

(3) Where a company has made any such alteration in accordance with subsection (2) above and—

(a) in connection with the alteration is required by virtue of—

(i) section 6(1) of the Companies Act 1985 (delivery of documents following alteration of objects), or
(ii) that provision as applied by section 17(3) of that Act (alteration of condition in memorandum which could have been contained in articles),

to deliver to the registrar of companies a printed copy of its memorandum, as altered, or

(b) is required by virtue of section 380(1) of that Act (registration etc of resolutions and agreements) to forward to the registrar a printed or other copy of the special resolution effecting the alteration,

the copy so delivered or forwarded by the company shall be accompanied by a copy of the Commissioner's consent.

(4) Section 6(3) of that Act (offences) shall apply to any default by a company in complying with subsection (3) above as it applies to any such default as is mentioned in that provision.

65 Invalidity of certain transactions

(1) Sections 35 and 35A of the Companies Act 1985 (capacity of company not limited by its memorandum; power of directors to bind company) do not apply to the acts of a company which is a charity except in favour of a person who—

(a) gives full consideration in money or money's worth in relation to the act in question, and
(b) does not know that the act is not permitted by the company's memorandum or, as the case may be, is beyond the powers of the directors,

or who does not know at the time the act is done that the company is a charity.

(2) However, where such a company purports to transfer or grant an interest in property, the fact that the act was not permitted by the company's memorandum or, as the case may be, that the directors in connection with the act exceeded any limitation on their powers under the company's constitution, does not affect the title of a person who subsequently acquires the property or any interest in it for full consideration without actual notice of any such circumstances affecting the validity of the company's act.

(3) In any proceedings arising out of subsection (1) above the burden of proving—

(a) that a person knew that an act was not permitted by the company's memorandum or was beyond the powers of the directors, or
(b) that a person knew that the company was a charity,

lies on the person making that allegation.

(4) Where a company is a charity, the ratification of an act under section 35(3) of the Companies Act 1985, or the ratification of a transaction to which section 322A of that Act applies (invalidity of certain transactions to which directors or their associates are parties), is ineffective without the prior written consent of the Commissioners.

66 Requirement of consent of Commissioners to certain acts

(1) Where a company is a charity—

(a) any approval given by the company for the purposes of any of the provisions of the Companies Act 1985 specified in subsection (2) below, and
(b) any affirmation by it for the purposes of section 322(2)(c) of that Act (affirmation of voidable arrangements under which assets are acquired by or from a director or person connected with him),

is ineffective without the prior written consent of the Commissioners.

(2) The provisions of the Companies Act 1985 referred to in subsection (1)(a) above are—

(a) section 312 (payment to director in respect of loss of office or retirement);
(b) section 313(1) (payment to director in respect of loss of office or retirement made in connection with transfer of undertaking or property of company);
(c) section 319(3) (incorporation in director's service contract of term whereby his employment will or may continue for a period of more than five years);
(d) section 320(1) (arrangement whereby assets are acquired by or from director or person connected with him);
(e) section 337(3)(a) (provision of funds to meet certain expenses incurred by director).

67 Name to appear on correspondence etc

Section 30(7) of the Companies Act 1985 (exemption from requirements relating to publication of name etc) shall not, in its application to any company which is a charity, have the effect of exempting the company from the requirements of section 349(1) of that Act (company's name to appear in its correspondence etc).

68 Status to appear on correspondence etc

(1) Where a company is a charity and its name does not include the word 'charity' or the word 'charitable' then, subject to subsection (1A), the fact that the company is a charity shall be stated in legible characters—

(a) in all business letters of the company,
(b) in all its notices and other official publications,
(c) in all bills of exchange, promissory notes, endorsements, cheques and orders for money or goods purporting to be signed on behalf of the company,
(d) in all conveyances purporting to be executed by the company, and
(e) in all bills rendered by it and in all its invoices, receipts, and letters of credit.

(1A) Where a company's name includes the word 'elusen' or the word 'elusennol' (the Welsh equivalents of the words 'charity' and 'charitable'), subsection (1) above shall not apply in relation to any document which is wholly in Welsh.

(1B) The statement required by subsection (1) above shall be in English, except that, in the case of a document which is otherwise wholly in Welsh, the statement may be in Welsh if it consists of or includes the word 'elusen' or the word 'elusennol'.

(2) In subsection (1)(d) above 'conveyance' means any instrument creating, transferring, varying or extinguishing an interest in land.

(3) Subsections (2) to (4) of section 349 of the Companies Act 1985 (offences in connection with failure to include required particulars in business letters etc) shall apply in relation to a contravention of subsection (1) above, taking the reference in subsection (3)(b) of that section to a bill of parcels as a reference to any such bill as is mentioned in subsection (1)(e) above.

Note: Section shown as amended by the Welsh Language Act 1993, ss 33, 35(1), Sch 2.

69 Investigation of accounts

(1) In the case of a charity which is a company the Commissioners may by order require that the condition and accounts of the charity for such period as they think fit shall be investigated and audited by an auditor appointed by them, being a person eligible for appointment as a company auditor under section 25 of the Companies Act 1989.

(2) An auditor acting under subsection (1) above—

(a) shall have a right of access to all books, accounts and documents relating to the charity which are in the possession or control of the charity trustees or to which the charity trustees have access;
(b) shall be entitled to require from any charity trustee, past or present, and from any past or present officer or employee of the charity such information and explanation as he thinks necessary for the performance of his duties;
(c) shall at the conclusion or during the progress of the audit make such reports to the Commissioners about the audit or about the accounts or affairs of the charity as he thinks the case requires, and shall send a copy of any such report to the charity trustees.

(3) The expenses of any audit under subsection (1) above, including the remuneration of the auditor, shall be paid by the Commissioners.

(4) If any person fails to afford an auditor any facility to which he is entitled under subsection (2) above the Commissioners may by order give to that person or to the charity trustees for the time being such directions as the Commissioners think appropriate for securing that the default is made good.

PART IX

MISCELLANEOUS

Powers of investment

70 Relaxation of restrictions on wider-range investments

(1) The Secretary of State may by order made with the consent of the Treasury—

(a) direct that, in the case of a trust fund consisting of property held by or in trust for a charity, any division of the fund in pursuance of section 2(1) of the Trustee Investments Act 1961 (trust funds to be divided so that wider-range and narrower-range investments are equal in value) shall be made so that the value of the wider-range part at the time of the division bears to the then value of the narrower-range part such proportion as is specified in the order;

(b) provide that, in its application in relation to such a trust fund, that Act shall have effect subject to such modifications so specified as the Secretary of State considers appropriate in consequence of, or in connection with, any such direction.

(2) Where, before the coming into force of an order under this section, a trust fund consisting of property held by or in trust for a charity has already been divided in pursuance of section 2(1) of that Act, the fund may, notwithstanding anything in that provision, be again divided (once only) in pursuance of that provision during the continuance in force of the order.

(3) No order shall be made under this section unless a draft of the order has been laid before and approved by a resolution of each House of Parliament.

(4) Expressions used in this section which are also used in the Trustee Investments Act 1961 have the same meaning as in that Act.

(5) (*Applies to Scotland only.*)

71 Extension of powers of investment

(1) The Secretary of State may by regulations made with the consent of the Treasury make, with respect to property held by or in trust for a charity, provision authorising a trustee to invest such property in any manner specified in the regulations, being a manner of investment not for the time being included in any Part of Schedule 1 to the Trustee Investments Act 1961.

(2) Regulations under this section may make such provision—

(a) regulating the investment of property in any manner authorised by virtue of subsection (1) above, and
(b) with respect to the variation and retention of investments so made,

as the Secretary of State considers appropriate.

(3) Such regulations may, in particular, make provision—

(a) imposing restrictions with respect to the proportion of the property held by or in trust for a charity which may be invested in any manner authorised by virtue of subsection (1) above, being either restrictions applying to investment in any such manner generally or restrictions applying to investment in any particular such manner;
(b) imposing the like requirements with respect to the obtaining and consideration of advice as are imposed by any of the provisions of section 6 of the Trustee Investments Act 1961 (duty of trustees in choosing investments).

(4) Any power of investment conferred by any regulations under this section—

(a) shall be in addition to, and not in derogation from, any power conferred otherwise than by such regulations; and
(b) shall not be limited by the trusts of a charity (in so far as they are not contained in any Act or instrument made under an enactment) unless it is excluded by those trusts in express terms;

but any such power shall only be exercisable by a trustee in so far as a contrary intention is not expressed in any Act or in any instrument made under an enactment and relating to the powers of the trustee.

(5) No regulations shall be made under this section unless a draft of the regulations has been laid before and approved by a resolution of each House of Parliament.

(6) In this section 'property'—

(a) in England and Wales, means real or personal property of any description, including money and things in action, but does not include an interest in expectancy; and
(b) (*applies to Scotland only*);

and any reference to property held by or in trust for a charity is a reference to property so held, whether it is for the time being in a state of investment or not.

(7) (*Applies to Scotland only.*)

Disqualification for acting as charity trustee

72 Persons disqualified for being trustees of a charity

(1) Subject to the following provisions of this section, a person shall be disqualified for being a charity trustee or trustee for a charity if—

(a) he has been convicted of any offence involving dishonesty or deception;
(b) he has been adjudged bankrupt or sequestration of his estate has been awarded and (in either case) he has not been discharged;
(c) he has made a composition or arrangement with, or granted a trust deed for, his creditors and has not been discharged in respect of it;
(d) he has been removed from the office of charity trustee or trustee for a charity by an order made—

(i) by the Commissioners under section 18(2)(i) above, or
(ii) by the Commissioners under section 20(1A)(i) of the Charities Act 1960 (power to act for protection of charities) or under section 20(1)(i) of that Act (as in force before the commencement of section 8 of the Charities Act 1992), or
(iii) by the High Court,

on the grounds of any misconduct or mismanagement in the administration of the charity for which he was responsible or to which he was privy, or which he by his conduct contributed to or facilitated;

(e) he has been removed, under section 7 of the Law Reform (Miscellaneous Provisions) (Scotland) Act 1990 (powers of Court of Session to deal with management of charities), from being concerned in the management or control of any body;
(f) he is subject to a disqualification order under the Company Directors Disqualification Act 1986 or to an order made under section 429(2)(b) of the Insolvency Act 1986 (failure to pay under county court administration order).

(2) In subsection (1) above—

(a) paragraph (a) applies whether the conviction occurred before or after the commencement of that subsection, but does not apply in relation to any conviction which is a spent conviction for the purposes of the Rehabilitation of Offenders Act 1974;
(b) paragraph (b) applies whether the adjudication of bankruptcy or the sequestration occurred before or after the commencement of that subsection;

(c) paragraph (c) applies whether the composition or arrangement was made, or the trust deed was granted, before or after the commencement of that subsection; and
(d) paragraphs (d) to (f) apply in relation to orders made and removals effected before or after the commencement of that subsection.

(3) Where (apart from this subsection) a person is disqualified under subsection (1)(b) above for being a charity trustee or trustee for any charity which is a company, he shall not be so disqualified if leave has been granted under section 11 of the Company Directors Disqualification Act 1986 (undischarged bankrupts) for him to act as director of the charity; and similarly a person shall not be disqualified under subsection (1)(f) above for being a charity trustee or trustee for such a charity if—

(a) in the case of a person subject to a disqualification order, leave under the order has been granted for him to act as director of the charity, or
(b) in the case of a person subject to an order under section 429(2)(b) of the Insolvency Act 1986, leave has been granted by the court which made the order for him to so act.

(4) The Commissioners may, on the application of any person disqualified under subsection (1) above, waive his disqualification either generally or in relation to a particular charity or a particular class of charities; but no such waiver may be granted in relation to any charity which is a company if—

(a) the person concerned is for the time being prohibited, by virtue of—

   (i) a disqualification order under the Company Directors Disqualification Act 1986, or
   (ii) section 11(1) or 12(2) of that Act (undischarged bankrupts; failure to pay under county court administration order),

from acting as director of the charity; and

(b) leave has not been granted for him to act as director of any other company.

(5) Any waiver under subsection (4) above shall be notified in writing to the person concerned.

(6) For the purposes of this section the Commissioners shall keep, in such manner as they think fit, a register of all persons who have been removed from office as mentioned in subsection (1)(d) above either—

(a) by an order of the Commissioners made before or after the commencement of subsection (1) above, or
(b) by an order of the High Court made after the commencement of section 45(1) of the Charities Act 1992;

and, where any person is so removed from office by an order of the High Court, the court shall notify the Commissioners of his removal.

(7) The entries in the register kept under subsection (6) above shall be available for public inspection in legible form at all reasonable times.

73 Persons acting as charity trustee while disqualified

(1) Subject to subsection (2) below, any person who acts as a charity trustee or trustee for a charity while he is disqualified for being such a trustee by virtue of section 72 above shall be guilty of an offence and liable—

(a) on summary conviction, to imprisonment for a term not exceeding six months or to a fine not exceeding the statutory maximum, or both;
(b) on conviction on indictment, to imprisonment for a term not exceeding two years or to a fine, or both.

(2) Subsection (1) above shall not apply where—

(a) the charity concerned is a company; and
(b) the disqualified person is disqualified by virtue only of paragraph (b) or (f) of section 72(1) above.

(3) Any acts done as charity trustee or trustee for a charity by a person disqualified for being such a trustee by virtue of section 72 above shall not be invalid by reason only of that disqualification.

(4) Where the Commissioners are satisfied—

(a) that any person has acted as charity trustee or trustee for a charity (other than an exempt charity) while disqualified for being such a trustee by virtue of section 72 above, and
(b) that, while so acting, he has received from the charity any sums by way of remuneration or expenses, or any benefit in kind, in connection with his acting as charity trustee or trustee for the charity,

they may by order direct him to repay to the charity the whole or part of any such sums, or (as the case may be) to pay to the charity the whole or part of the monetary value (as determined by them) of any such benefit.

(5) Subsection (4) above does not apply to any sums received by way of remuneration or expenses in respect of any time when the person concerned was not disqualified for being a charity trustee or trustee for the charity.

Small charities

74 Power to transfer all property, modify objects etc

(1) This section applies to a charity if—

(a) its gross income in its last financial year did not exceed £5,000, and
(b) it does not hold any land on trusts which stipulate that the land is to be used for the purposes, or any particular purposes, of the charity,

and it is neither an exempt charity nor a charitable company.

(2) Subject to the following provisions of this section, the charity trustees of a charity to which this section applies may resolve for the purposes of this section—

(a) that all the property of the charity should be transferred to such other charity as is specified in the resolution, being either a registered charity or a charity which is not required to be registered;
(b) that all the property of the charity should be divided, in such manner as is specified in the resolution, between such two or more other charities as are so specified, being in each case either a registered charity or a charity which is not required to be registered;
(c) that the trusts of the charity should be modified by replacing all or any of the purposes of the charity with such other purposes, being in law charitable, as are specified in the resolution;

(d) that any provision of the trusts of the charity—

(i) relating to any of the powers exercisable by the charity trustees in the administration of the charity, or

(ii) regulating the procedure to be followed in any respect in connection with its administration,

should be modified in such manner as is specified in the resolution.

(3) Any resolution passed under subsection (2) above must be passed by a majority of not less than two-thirds of such charity trustees as vote on the resolution.

(4) The charity trustees of a charity to which this section applies ('the transferor charity') shall not have power to pass a resolution under subsection (2)(a) or (b) above unless they are satisfied—

(a) that the existing purposes of the transferor charity have ceased to be conducive to a suitable and effective application of the charity's resources; and

(b) that the purposes of the charity or charities specified in the resolution are as similar in character to the purposes of the transferor charity as is reasonably practicable;

and before passing the resolution they must have received from the charity trustees of the charity, or (as the case may be) of each of the charities, specified in the resolution written confirmation that those trustees are willing to accept a transfer of property under this section.

(5) The charity trustees of any such charity shall not have power to pass a resolution under subsection (2)(c) above unless they are satisfied—

(a) that the existing purposes of the charity (or, as the case may be, such of them as it is proposed to replace) have ceased to be conducive to a suitable and effective application of the charity's resources; and

(b) that the purposes specified in the resolution are as similar in character to those existing purposes as is practical in the circumstances.

(6) Where charity trustees have passed a resolution under subsection (2) above, they shall—

(a) give public notice of the resolution in such manner as they think reasonable in the circumstances; and

(b) send a copy of the resolution to the Commissioners, together with a statement of their reasons for passing it.

(7) The Commissioners may, when considering the resolution, require the charity trustees to provide additional information or explanation—

(a) as to the circumstances in and by reference to which they have determined to act under this section, or

(b) relating to their compliance with this section in connection with the resolution;

and the Commissioners shall take into account any representations made to them by persons appearing to them to be interested in the charity where those representations are made within the period of six weeks beginning with the date when the Commissioners receive a copy of the resolution by virtue of subsection (6)(b) above.

(8) Where the Commissioners have so received a copy of a resolution from any charity trustees and it appears to them that the trustees have complied with this section in connection with the resolution, the Commissioners shall, within the period of three

months beginning with the date when they receive the copy of the resolution, notify the trustees in writing either—

(a) that the Commissioners concur with the resolution; or
(b) that they do not concur with it.

(9) Where the Commissioners so notify their concurrence with the resolution, then—

(a) if the resolution was passed under subsection (2)(a) or (b) above, the charity trustees shall arrange for all the property of the transferor charity to be transferred in accordance with the resolution and on terms that any property so transferred—

(i) shall be held and applied by the charity to which it is transferred ('the transferee charity') for the purposes of that charity, but
(ii) shall, as property of the transferee charity, nevertheless be subject to any restrictions on expenditure to which it is subject as property of the transferor charity,

and those trustees shall arrange for it to be so transferred by such date as may be specified in the notification; and

(b) if the resolution was passed under subsection (2)(c) or (d) above, the trusts of the charity shall be deemed, as from such date as may be specified in the notification, to have been modified in accordance with the terms of the resolution.

(10) For the purpose of enabling any property to be transferred to a charity under this section, the Commissioners shall have power, at the request of the charity trustees of that charity, to make orders vesting any property of the transferor charity—

(a) in the charity trustees of the first-mentioned charity or in any trustee for that charity, or
(b) in any other person nominated by those charity trustees to hold the property in trust for that charity.

(11) The Secretary of State may by order amend subsection (1) above by substituting a different sum for the sum for the time being specified there.

(12) In this section—

(a) 'charitable company' means a charity which is a company or other body corporate; and
(b) references to the transfer of property to a charity are references to its transfer—

(i) to the charity trustees, or
(ii) to any trustee for the charity, or
(iii) to a person nominated by the charity trustees to hold it in trust for the charity,

as the charity trustees may determine.

75 Power to spend capital

(1) This section applies to a charity if—

(a) it has a permanent endowment which does not consist of or comprise any land, and
(b) its gross income in its last financial year did not exceed £1,000,

and it is neither an exempt charity nor a charitable company.

(2) Where the charity trustees of a charity to which this section applies are of the opinion that the property of the charity is too small, in relation to its purposes, for any useful

purpose to be achieved by the expenditure of income alone, they may resolve for the purposes of this section that the charity ought to be freed from the restrictions with respect to expenditure of capital to which its permanent endowment is subject.

(3) Any resolution passed under subsection (2) above must be passed by a majority of not less than two-thirds of such charity trustees as vote on the resolution.

(4) Before passing such a resolution the charity trustees must consider whether any reasonable possibility exists of effecting a transfer or division of all the charity's property under section 74 above (disregarding any such transfer or division as would, in their opinion, impose on the charity an unacceptable burden of costs).

(5) Where charity trustees have passed a resolution under subsection (2) above, they shall—

- (a) give public notice of the resolution in such manner as they think reasonable in the circumstances; and
- (b) send a copy of the resolution to the Commissioners, together with a statement of their reasons for passing it.

(6) The Commissioners may, when considering the resolution, require the charity trustees to provide additional information or explanation—

- (a) as to the circumstances in and by reference to which they have determined to act under this section, or
- (b) relating to their compliance with this section in connection with the resolution;

and the Commissioners shall take into account any representations made to them by persons appearing to them to be interested in the charity where those representations are made within the period of six weeks beginning with the date when the Commissioners receive a copy of the resolution by virtue of subsection (5)(b) above.

(7) Where the Commissioners have so received a copy of a resolution from any charity trustees and it appears to them that the trustees have complied with this section in connection with the resolution, the Commissioners shall, within the period of three months beginning with the date when they receive the copy of the resolution, notify the trustees in writing either—

- (a) that the Commissioners concur with the resolution; or
- (b) that they do not concur with it.

(8) Where the Commissioners so notify their concurrence with the resolution, the charity trustees shall have, as from such date as may be specified in the notification, power by virtue of this section to expend any property of the charity without regard to any such restrictions as are mentioned in subsection (2) above.

(9) The Secretary of State may by order amend subsection (1) above by substituting a different sum for the sum for the time being specified there.

(10) In this section 'charitable company' means a charity which is a company or other body corporate.

Local charities

76 Local authority's index of local charities

(1) The council of a county or county borough or of a district or London borough and the Common Council of the City of London may maintain an index of local charities or of

any class of local charities in the council's area, and may publish information contained in the index, or summaries or extracts taken from it.

(2) A council proposing to establish or maintaining under this section an index of local charities or of any class of local charities shall, on request, be supplied by the Commissioners free of charge with copies of such entries in the register of charities as are relevant to the index or with particulars of any changes in the entries of which copies have been supplied before; and the Commissioners may arrange that they will without further request supply a council with particulars of any such changes.

(3) An index maintained under this section shall be open to public inspection at all reasonable times.

(4) A council may employ any voluntary organisation as their agent for the purposes of this section, on such terms and within such limits (if any) or in such cases as they may agree; and for this purpose 'voluntary organisation' means any body of which the activities are carried on otherwise than for profit, not being a public or local authority.

(5) A joint board discharging any of a council's functions shall have the same powers under this section as the council as respects local charities in the council's area which are established for purposes similar or complementary to any services provided by the board.

Note: Section shown as amended by the Local Government (Wales) Act 1994, s 66(6), Sch 16, para 101(1).

---

77 Reviews of local charities by local authority

(1) The council of a county or county borough or of a district or London borough and the Common Council of the City of London may, subject to the following provisions of this section, initiate, and carry out in co-operation with the charity trustees, a review of the working of any group of local charities with the same or similar purposes in the council's area, and may make to the Commissioners such report on the review and such recommendations arising from it as the council after consultation with the trustees think fit.

(2) A council having power to initiate reviews under this section may co-operate with other persons in any review by them of the working of local charities in the council's area (with or without other charities), or may join with other persons in initiating and carrying out such a review.

(3) No review initiated by a council under this section shall extend to any charity without the consent of the charity trustees, nor to any ecclesiastical charity.

(4) No review initiated under this section by the council of a district shall extend to the working in any county of a local charity established for purposes similar or complementary to any services provided by county councils unless the review so extends with the consent of the council of that county.

(4A) Subsection (4) above does not apply in relation to Wales.

(5) Subsections (4) and (5) of section 76 above shall apply for the purposes of this section as they apply for the purposes of that section.

Note: Section shown as amended by the Local Government (Wales) Act 1994, s 66(6), Sch 16, para 101(2).

78 Co-operation between charities, and between charities and local authorities

(1) Any local council and any joint board discharging any functions of such a council—

(a) may make, with any charity established for purposes similar or complementary to services provided by the council or board, arrangements for co-ordinating the activities of the council or board and those of the charity in the interests of persons who may benefit from those services or from the charity; and
(b) shall be at liberty to disclose to any such charity in the interests of those persons any information obtained in connection with the services provided by the council or board, whether or not arrangements have been made with the charity under this subsection.

In this subsection 'local council' means in relation to England, the council of a county, or of a district, London borough, or parish, and includes also the Common Council of the City of London and the Council of the Isles of Scilly and, in relation to Wales, the council of a county, county borough or community.

(2) Charity trustees shall, notwithstanding anything in the trusts of the charity, have power by virtue of this subsection to do all or any of the following things, where it appears to them likely to promote or make more effective the work of the charity, and may defray the expense of so doing out of any income or money applicable as income of the charity, that is to say—

(a) they may co-operate in any review undertaken under section 77 above or otherwise of the working of charities or any class of charities;
(b) they may make arrangements with an authority acting under subsection (1) above or with another charity for co-ordinating their activities and those of the authority or of the other charity;
(c) they may publish information of other charities with a view to bringing them to the notice of those for whose benefit they are intended.

Note: Section shown as amended by the Local Government (Wales) Act 1994, s 66(6), Sch 16, para 101(3).

79 Parochial charities

(1) Where trustees hold any property for the purposes of a public recreation ground, or of allotments (whether under inclosure Acts or otherwise), for the benefit of inhabitants of a parish having a parish council, or for other charitable purposes connected with such a parish, except for an ecclesiastical charity, they may with the approval of the Commissioners and with the consent of the parish council transfer the property to the parish council or to persons appointed by the parish council; and the council or their appointees shall hold the property on the same trusts and subject to the same conditions as the trustees did.

This subsection shall apply to property held for any public purpose as it applies to property held for charitable purposes.

(2) Where the charity trustees of a parochial charity in a parish, not being an ecclesiastical charity nor a charity founded within the preceding forty years, do not include persons elected by the local government electors, ratepayers or inhabitants of the parish or

appointed by the parish council or parish meeting, the parish council or parish meeting may appoint additional charity trustees, to such number as the Commissioners may allow; and if there is a sole charity trustee not elected or appointed as aforesaid of any such charity, the number of the charity trustees may, with the approval of the Commissioners, be increased to three of whom one may be nominated by the person holding the office of the sole trustee and one by the parish council or parish meeting.

(3) Where, under the trusts of a charity other than an ecclesiastical charity, the inhabitants of a rural parish (whether in vestry or not) or a select vestry were formerly (in 1894) entitled to appoint charity trustees for, or trustees or beneficiaries of, the charity, then—

(a) in a parish having a parish council, the appointment shall be made by the parish council or, in the case of beneficiaries, by persons appointed by the parish council; and
(b) in a parish not having a parish council, the appointment shall be made by the parish meeting.

(4) Where overseers as such or, except in the case of an ecclesiastical charity, churchwardens as such were formerly (in 1894) charity trustees of or trustees for a parochial charity in a rural parish, either alone or jointly with other persons, then instead of the former overseer or church warden trustees there shall be trustees (to a number not greater than that of the former overseer or churchwarden trustees) appointed by the parish council or, if there is no parish council, by the parish meeting.

(5) Where, outside Greater London (other than the outer London boroughs), overseers of a parish as such were formerly (in 1927) charity trustees of or trustees for any charity, either alone or jointly with other persons, then instead of the former overseer trustees there shall be trustees (to a number not greater than that of the former overseer trustees) appointed by the parish council or, if there is no parish council, by the parish meeting.

(6) In the case of an urban parish existing immediately before the passing of the Local Government Act 1972 which after 1 April 1974 is not comprised in a parish, the power of appointment under subsection (5) above shall be exercisable by the district council.

(7) In the application of the foregoing provisions of this section to Wales—

(a) for references in subsections (1) and (2) to a parish or a parish council there shall be substituted respectively references to a community or a community council;
(b) for references in subsections (3)(a) and (b) to a parish, a parish council or a parish meeting there shall be substituted respectively references to a community, a community council or the council of the county or (as the case may be) county borough;
(c) for references in subsections (4) and (5) to a parish council or a parish meeting there shall be substituted respectively references to a community council or the council of the county or (as the case may be) county borough.

(8) Any appointment of a charity trustee or trustee for a charity which is made by virtue of this section shall be for a term of four years, and a retiring trustee shall be eligible for re-appointment but—

(a) on an appointment under subsection (2) above, where no previous appointments have been made by virtue of that subsection or of the corresponding provision of the Local Government Act 1894 or the Charities Act 1960, and more than one trustee is appointed, half of those appointed (or as nearly as may be) shall be appointed for a term of two years; and
(b) an appointment made to fill a casual vacancy shall be for the remainder of the term of the previous appointment.

(9) This section shall not affect the trusteeship, control or management of any voluntary or grant-maintained school within the meaning of the Education Act 1996.

(10) The provisions of this section shall not extend to the Isles of Scilly, and shall have effect subject to any order (including any future order) made under any enactment relating to local government areas or the powers of local authorities.

(11) In this section the expression 'formerly (in 1894)' relates to the period immediately before the passing of the Local Government Act 1894, and the expression 'formerly (in 1927)' to the period immediately before 1 April 1927; and the word 'former' shall be construed accordingly.

Note: Section shown as amended by the Local Government (Wales) Act 1994, s 66(6), Sch 16, para 101(4); and the Education Act 1996, s 582(1), Sch 37, Pt I, para 119.

Scottish charities

80 Supervision by Commissioners of certain Scottish charities

(1) The following provisions of this Act, namely—

(a) sections 8 and 9,
(b) section 18 (except subsection (2)(ii)), and
(c) section 19,

shall have effect in relation to any recognised body which is managed or controlled wholly or mainly in or from England or Wales as they have effect in relation to a charity.

(2) Where—

(a) a recognised body is managed or controlled wholly or mainly in or from Scotland, but
(b) any person in England and Wales holds any property on behalf of the body or of any person concerned in its management or control,

then, if the Commissioners are satisfied as to the matters mentioned in subsection (3) below, they may make an order requiring the person holding the property not to part with it without their approval.

(3) The matters referred to in subsection (2) above are—

(a) that there has been any misconduct or mismanagement in the administration of the body; and
(b) that it is necessary or desirable to make an order under that subsection for the purpose of protecting the property of the body or securing a proper application of such property for the purposes of the body;

and the reference in that subsection to the Commissioners being satisfied as to those matters is a reference to their being so satisfied on the basis of such information as may be supplied to them by the Lord Advocate.

(4) Where—

(a) any person in England and Wales holds any property on behalf of a recognised body or of any person concerned in the management or control of such a body, and
(b) the Commissioners are satisfied (whether on the basis of such information as may be supplied to them by the Lord Advocate or otherwise)—

(i) that there has been any misconduct or mismanagement in the administration of the body, and
(ii) that it is necessary or desirable to make an order under this subsection for the purpose of protecting the property of the body or securing a proper application of such property for the purposes of the body,

the Commissioners may by order vest the property in such recognised body or charity as is specified in the order in accordance with subsection (5) below, or require any persons in whom the property is vested to transfer it to any such body or charity, or appoint any person to transfer the property to any such body or charity.

(5) The Commissioners may specify in an order under subsection (4) above such other recognised body or such charity as they consider appropriate, being a body or charity whose purposes are, in the opinion of the Commissioners, as similar in character to those of the body referred to in paragraph (a) of that subsection as is reasonably practicable; but the Commissioners shall not so specify any body or charity unless they have received—

(a) from the persons concerned in the management or control of the body, or
(b) from the charity trustees of the charity,

as the case may be, written confirmation that they are willing to accept the property.

(6) In this section 'recognised body' has the same meaning as in Part I of the Law Reform (Miscellaneous Provisions) (Scotland) Act 1990 (Scottish charities).

Administrative provisions about charities

81 Manner of giving notice of charity meetings, etc

(1) All notices which are required or authorised by the trusts of a charity to be given to a charity trustee, member or subscriber may be sent by post, and, if sent by post, may be addressed to any address given as his in the list of charity trustees, members or subscribers for the time being in use at the office or principle office of the charity.

(2) Where any such notice required to be given as aforesaid is given by post, it shall be deemed to have been given by the time at which the letter containing it would be delivered in the ordinary course of post.

(3) No notice required to be given as aforesaid of any meeting or election need be given to any charity trustee, member or subscriber, if in the list above mentioned he has no address in the United Kingdom.

82 Manner of executing instruments

(1) Charity trustees may, subject to the trusts of the charity, confer on any of their body (not being less than two in number) a general authority, or an authority limited in such manner as the trustees think fit, to execute in the names and on behalf of the trustees assurances or other deeds or instruments for giving effect to transactions to which the trustees are a party; and any deed or instrument executed in pursuance of an authority so given shall be of the same effect as if executed by the whole body.

(2) An authority under subsection (1) above—

(a) shall suffice for any deed or instrument if it is given in writing or by resolution of a meeting of the trustees, notwithstanding the want of any formality that would be required in giving an authority apart from that subsection;
(b) may be given so as to make the powers conferred exercisable by any of the trustees, or may be restricted to named persons or in any other way;

(c) subject to any such restriction, and until it is revoked, shall, notwithstanding any change in the charity trustees, have effect as a continuing authority given by the charity trustees from time to time of the charity and exercisable by such trustees.

(3) In any authority under this section to execute a deed or instrument in the names and on behalf of charity trustees there shall, unless the contrary intention appears, be implied authority also to execute it for them in the name and on behalf of the official custodian or of any other person, in any case in which the charity trustees could do so.

(4) Where a deed or instrument purports to be executed in pursuance of this section, then in favour of a person who (then or afterwards) in good faith acquires for money or money's worth an interest in or charge on property or the benefit of any covenant or agreement expressed to be entered into by the charity trustees, it shall be conclusively presumed to have been duly executed by virtue of this section.

(5) The powers conferred by this section shall be in addition to and not in derogation of any other powers.

83 Transfer and evidence of title to property vested in trustees

(1) Where, under the trusts of a charity, trustees of property held for the purposes of the charity may be appointed or discharged by resolution of a meeting of the charity trustees, members or other persons, a memorandum declaring a trustee to have been so appointed or discharged shall be sufficient evidence of that fact if the memorandum is signed either at the meeting by the person presiding or in some other manner directed by the meeting and is attested by two persons present at the meeting.

(2) A memorandum evidencing the appointment or discharge of a trustee under subsection (1) above, if executed as a deed, shall have the like operation under section 40 of the Trustee Act 1925 (which relates to vesting declarations as respects trust property in deeds appointing or discharging trustees) as if the appointment or discharge were effected by the deed.

(3) For the purposes of this section, where a document purports to have been signed and attested as mentioned in subsection (1) above, then on proof (whether by evidence or as a matter of presumption) of the signature the document shall be presumed to have been so signed and attested, unless the contrary is shown.

(4) This section shall apply to a memorandum made at any time, except that subsection (2) shall apply only to those made after the commencement of the Charities Act 1960.

(5) This section shall apply in relation to any institution to which the Literary and Scientific Institutions Act 1854 applies as it applies in relation to a charity.

PART X

SUPPLEMENTARY

84 Supply by Commissioners of copies of documents open to public inspection

The Commissioners shall, at the request of any person, furnish him with copies of, or extracts from, any document in their possession which is for the time being open to inspection under Parts II to VI of this Act.

85 Fees and other amounts payable to Commissioners

(1) The Secretary of State may by regulations require the payment to the Commissioners of such fees as may be prescribed by the regulations in respect of—

(a) the discharge by the Commissioners of such functions under the enactments relating to charities as may be so prescribed;
(b) the inspection of the register of charities or of other material kept by them under those enactments, or the furnishing of copies of or extracts from documents so kept.

(2) Regulations under this section may—

(a) confer, or provide for the conferring of, exemptions from liability to pay a prescribed fee;
(b) provide for the remission or refunding of a prescribed fee (in whole or in part) in circumstances prescribed by the regulations.

(3) Any regulations under this section which require the payment of a fee in respect of any matter for which no fee was previously payable shall not be made unless a draft of the regulations has been laid before and approved by a resolution of each House of Parliament.

(4) The Commissioners may impose charges of such amounts as they consider reasonable in respect of the supply of any publications produced by them.

(5) Any fees and other payments received by the Commissioners by virtue of this section shall be paid into the Consolidated Fund.

86 Regulations and orders

(1) Any regulations or order of the Secretary of State under this Act—

(a) shall be made by statutory instrument; and
(b) (subject to subsection (2) below) shall be subject to annulment in pursuance of a resolution of either House of Parliament.

(2) Subsection (1)(b) above does not apply—

(a) to an order under section 17(2), 70 or 99(2);
(b) to any regulations under section 71; or
(c) to any regulations to which section 85(3) applies.

(3) Any regulations of the Secretary of State or the Commissioners and any order of the Secretary of State under this Act may make—

(a) different provision for different cases; and
(b) such supplemental, incidental, consequential or transitional provision or savings as the Secretary of State or, as the case may be, the Commissioners consider appropriate.

(4) Before making any regulations under section 42, 44 or 45 above the Secretary of State shall consult such persons or bodies of persons as he considers appropriate.

87 Enforcement of requirements by order of Commissioners

(1) If a person fails to comply with any requirement imposed by or under this Act then (subject to subsection (2) below) the Commissioners may by order give him such directions as they consider appropriate for securing that the default is made good.

(2) Subsection (1) above does not apply to any such requirement if—

(a) a person who fails to comply with, or is persistently in default in relation to, the requirement is liable to any criminal penalty; or

(b) the requirement is imposed—

(i) by an order of the Commissioners to which section 88 below applies, or
(ii) by a direction of the Commissioners to which that section applies by virtue of section 90(2) below.

88 Enforcement of orders of Commissioners

A person guilty of disobedience—

(a) to an order of the Commissioners under section 9(1), 44(2), 61, 73 or 80 above; or
(b) to an order of the Commissioners under section 16 or 18 above requiring a transfer of property or payment to be called for or made; or
(c) to an order of the Commissioners requiring a default under this Act to be made good;

may on the application of the Commissioners to the High Court be dealt with as for disobedience to an order of the High Court.

89 Other provisions as to orders of Commissioners

(1) Any order made by the Commissioners under this Act may include such incidental or supplementary provisions as the Commissioners think expedient for carrying into effect the objects of the order, and where the Commissioners exercise any jurisdiction to make such an order on an application or reference to them, they may insert any such provisions in the order notwithstanding that the application or reference does not propose their insertion.

(2) Where the Commissioners make an order under this Act, then (without prejudice to the requirements of this Act where the order is subject to appeal) they may themselves give such public notice as they think fit of the making or contents of the order, or may require it to be given by any person on whose application the order is made or by any charity affected by the order.

(3) The Commissioners at any time within twelve months after they have made an order under any provision of this Act other than section 61 if they are satisfied that the order was made by mistake or on misrepresentation or otherwise than in conformity with this Act, may with or without any application or reference to them discharge the order in whole or in part, and subject or not to any savings or other transitional provisions.

(4) Except for the purposes of subsection (3) above or of an appeal under this Act, an order made by the Commissioners under this Act shall be deemed to have been duly and formally made and not be called in question on the ground only of irregularity or informality, but (subject to any further order) have effect according to its tenor.

90 Directions of the Commissioners

(1) Any direction given by the Commissioners under any provision contained in this Act—

(a) may be varied or revoked by a further direction given under that provision; and
(b) shall be given in writing.

(2) Sections 88 and 89(1), (2) and (4) above shall apply to any such directions as they apply to an order of the Commissioners.

(3) In subsection (1) above the reference to the Commissioners includes, in relation to a direction under subsection (3) of section 8 above, a reference to any person conducting an inquiry under that section.

(4) Nothing in this section shall be read as applying to any directions contained in an order made by the Commissioners under section 87(1) above.

91 Service of orders and directions

(1) This section applies to any order or direction made or given by the Commissioners under this Act.

(2) An order or direction to which this section applies may be served on a person (other than a body corporate)—

- (a) by delivering it to that person;
- (b) by leaving it at his last known address in the United Kingdom; or
- (c) by sending it by post to him at that address.

(3) An order or direction to which this section applies may be served on a body corporate by delivering it or sending it by post—

- (a) to the registered or principal office of the body in the United Kingdom, or
- (b) if it has no such office in the United Kingdom, to any place in the United Kingdom where it carries on business or conducts its activities (as the case may be).

(4) Any such order or direction may also be served on a person (including a body corporate) by sending it by post to that person at an address notified by that person to the Commissioners for the purposes of this subsection.

(5) In this section any reference to the Commissioners includes, in relation to a direction given under subsection (3) of section 8 above, a reference to any person conducting an inquiry under that section.

92 Appeals from Commissioners

(1) Provision shall be made by rules of court for regulating appeals to the High Court under this Act against orders or decisions of the Commissioners.

(2) On such an appeal the Attorney General shall be entitled to appear and be heard, and such other persons as the rules allow or as the court may direct.

93 Miscellaneous provisions as to evidence

(1) Where, in any proceedings to recover or compel payment of any rentcharge or other periodical payment claimed by or on behalf of a charity out of land or of the rents, profits or other income of land, otherwise than as rent incident to a reversion, it is shown that the rentcharge or other periodical payment has at any time been paid for twelve consecutive years to or for the benefit of the charity, that shall be prima facie evidence of the perpetual liability to it of the land or income, and no proof of its origin shall be necessary.

(2) In any proceedings, the following documents, that is to say,—

- (a) the printed copies of the reports of the Commissioners for enquiring concerning charities, 1818 to 1837, who were appointed under the Act 58 Geo 3 c 91 and subsequent Acts; and

(b) the printed copies of the reports which were made for various counties and county boroughs to the Charity Commissioners by their assistant commissioners and presented to the House of Commons as returns to orders of various dates beginning with 8 December 1890, and ending with 9 September 1909,

shall be admissible as evidence of the documents and facts stated in them.

(3) Evidence of any order, certificate or other document issued by the Commissioners may be given by means of a copy retained by them, or taken from a copy so retained, and certified to be a true copy by any officer of the Commissioners generally or specially authorised by them to act for this purpose; and a document purporting to be such a copy shall be received in evidence without proof of the official position, authority or handwriting of the person certifying it.

94 Restriction on institution of proceedings for certain offences

(1) No proceedings for an offence under this Act to which this section applies shall be instituted except by or with the consent of the Director of Public Prosecutions.

(2) This section applies to any offence under—

(a) section 5;
(b) section 11;
(c) section 18(14);
(d) section 49; or
(e) section 73(1).

95 Offences by bodies corporate

Where any offence under this Act is committed by a body corporate and is proved to have been committed with the consent or connivance of, or to be attributable to any neglect on the part of, any director, manager, secretary or other similar officer of the body corporate, or any person who was purporting to act in any such capacity, he as well as the body corporate shall be guilty of that offence and shall be liable to be proceeded against and punished accordingly.

In relation to a body corporate whose affairs are managed by its members, 'director' means a member of the body corporate.

96 Construction of references to a 'charity' or to particular classes of charity

(1) In this Act, except in so far as the context otherwise requires—

'charity' means any institution, corporate or not, which is established for charitable purposes and is subject to the control of the High Court in the exercise of the court's jurisdiction with respect to charities;

'ecclesiastical charity' has the same meaning as in the Local Government Act 1894;

'exempt charity' means (subject to section 24(8) above) a charity comprised in Schedule 2 to this Act;

'local charity' means, in relation to any area, a charity established for purposes which are by their nature or by the trusts of the charity directed wholly or mainly to the benefit of that area or of part of it;

'parochial charity' means, in relation to any parish or (in Wales) community, a charity the benefits of which are, or the separate distribution of the benefits of which is, confined to inhabitants of the parish or community, or of a single ancient ecclesiastical parish which included that parish or community or part of it, or of an area consisting of that parish or community with not more than four neighbouring parishes or communities.

(2) The expression 'charity' is not in this Act applicable—

(a) to any ecclesiastical corporation (that is to say, any corporation in the Church of England, whether sole or aggregate, which is established for spiritual purposes) in respect of the corporate property of the corporation, except to a corporation aggregate having some purposes which are not ecclesiastical in respect of its corporate property held for those purposes; or
(b) to any Diocesan Board of Finance within the meaning of the Endowments and Glebe Measure 1976 for any diocese in respect of the diocesan glebe land of that diocese within the meaning of that Measure; or
(c) to any trust of property for purposes for which the property has been consecrated.

(3) A charity shall be deemed for the purposes of this Act to have a permanent endowment unless all property held for the purposes of the charity may be expended for those purposes without distinction between capital and income, and in this Act 'permanent endowment' means, in relation to any charity, property held subject to a restriction on its being expended for the purposes of the charity.

(4) References in this Act to a charity whose income from all sources does not in aggregate amount to more than a specified amount shall be construed—

(a) by reference to the gross revenues of the charity, or
(b) if the Commissioners so determine, by reference to the amount which they estimate to be the likely amount of those revenues,

but without (in either case) bringing into account anything for the yearly value of land occupied by the charity apart from the pecuniary income (if any) received from that land; and any question as to the application of any such reference to a charity shall be determined by the Commissioners, whose decision shall be final.

(5) The Commissioners may direct that for all or any of the purposes of this Act an institution established for any special purposes of or in connection with a charity (being charitable purposes) shall be treated as forming part of that charity or as forming a distinct charity.

(6) The Commissioners may direct that for all or any of the purposes of this Act two or more charities having the same charity trustees shall be treated as a single charity.

Note: Section shown as amended by the Charities (Amendment) Act 1995, s 1.

---

97 General interpretation

(1) In this Act, except in so far as the context otherwise requires—

'charitable purposes' means purposes which are exclusively charitable according to the law of England and Wales;

'charity trustees' means the persons having the general control and management of the administration of a charity;

'the Commissioners' means the Charity Commissioners for England and Wales;

'company' means a company formed and registered under the Companies Act 1985 or to which the provisions of that Act apply as they apply to such a company;

'the court' means the High Court and, within the limits of its jurisdiction, any other court in England and Wales having a jurisdiction in respect of charities concurrent (within any limit of area or amount) with that of the High Court, and includes any judge or officer of the court exercising the jurisdiction of the court;

'financial year'—

(a) in relation to a charity which is a company, shall be construed in accordance with section 223 of the Companies Act 1985; and

(b) in relation to any other charity, shall be construed in accordance with regulations made by virtue of section 42(2) above;

but this definition is subject to the transitional provisions in section 99(4) below and Part II of Schedule 8 to this Act;

'gross income', in relation to charity, means its gross recorded income from all sources including special trusts;

'independent examiner', in relation to a charity, means such a person as is mentioned in section 43(3)(a) above;

'institution' includes any trust or undertaking;

'the official custodian' means the official custodian for charities;

'permanent endowment' shall be construed in accordance with section 96(3) above;

'the register' means the register of charities kept under section 3 above and 'registered' shall be construed accordingly;

'special trust' means property which is held and administered by or on behalf of a charity for any special purposes of the charity, and is so held and administered on separate trusts relating only to that property but a special trust shall not, by itself, constitute a charity for the purposes of Part VI of this Act;

'trusts' in relation to a charity, means the provisions establishing it as a charity and regulating its purposes and administration, whether those provisions take effect by way of trust or not, and in relation to other institutions has a corresponding meaning.

(2) In this Act, except in so far as the context otherwise requires, 'document' includes information recorded in any form, and, in relation to information recorded otherwise than in legible form—

(a) any reference to its production shall be construed as a reference to the furnishing of a copy of it in legible form; and

(b) any reference to the furnishing of a copy of, or extract from, it shall accordingly be construed as a reference to the furnishing of a copy of, or extract from, it in legible form.

(3) No vesting or transfer of any property in pursuance of any provision of Part IV or IX of this Act shall operate as a breach of a covenant or condition against alienation or give rise to a forfeiture.

98 Consequential amendments and repeals

(1) The enactments mentioned in Schedule 6 to this Act shall be amended as provided in that Schedule.

(2) The enactments mentioned in Schedule 7 to this Act are hereby repealed to the extent specified in the third column of the Schedule.

99 Commencement and transitional provisions

(1) Subject to subsection (2) below this Act shall come into force on 1st August 1993.

(2) Part VI, section 69 and paragraph 21(3) of Schedule 6 shall not come into force until

such day as the Secretary of State may by order appoint; and different days may be appointed for different provisions or different purposes.

(3) Until the coming into force of all the provisions mentioned in subsection (2) above the provisions mentioned in Part I of Schedule 8 to this Act shall continue in force notwithstanding their repeal.

(4) Part II of Schedule 8 to this Act shall have effect until the coming into force of the first regulations made by virtue of section 42(2) above for determining the financial year of a charity for the purposes of the provisions mentioned in that Part.

100 Short title and extent

(1) This Act may be cited as the Charities Act 1993.

(2) Subject to subsection (3) to (6) below, this Act extends only to England and Wales.

(3) Section 10 above and this section extend to the whole of the United Kingdom.

(4) Section 15(2) extends also to Northern Ireland.

(5) Sections 70 and 71 and so much of section 86 as relates to those sections extend also to Scotland.

(6) The amendments in Schedule 6 and the repeals in Schedule 7 have the same extent as the enactments to which they refer and section 98 above extends accordingly.

SCHEDULES

SCHEDULE 1

Section 1

CONSTITUTION ETC OF CHARITY COMMISSIONERS

1.—(1) There shall be a Chief Charity Commissioner and two other commissioners.

(2) Two at least of the commissioners shall be persons who have a seven year general qualification within the meaning of section 71 of the Courts and Legal Services Act 1990.

(3) The chief commissioner and the other commissioners shall be appointed by the Secretary of State, and shall be deemed for all purposes to be employed in the civil service of the Crown.

(4) There may be paid to each of the commissioners such salary and allowances as the Secretary of State may with the approval of the Treasury determine.

(5) If at any time it appears to the Secretary of State that there should be more than three commissioners, he may with the approval of the Treasury appoint not more than two additional commissioners.

2.—(1) The chief commissioner may, with the approval of the Treasury as to number and conditions of service, appoint such assistant commissioners and other officers and such employees as he thinks necessary for the proper discharge of the functions of the Commissioners and of the official custodian.

(2) There may be paid to officers and employees so appointed such salaries or remuneration as the Treasury may determine.

3.—(1) The Commissioners may use an official seal for the authentication of documents, and their seal shall be officially and judicially noticed.

(2) The Documentary Evidence Act 1868, as amended by the Documentary Evidence Act 1882, shall have effect as if in the Schedule to the Act of 1868 the Commissioners were included in the first column and any commissioner or assistant commissioner and any officer authorised to act on behalf of the Commissioners were mentioned in the second column.

(3) The Commissioners shall have power to regulate their own procedure and, subject to any such regulations and to any directions of the chief commissioner, any one commissioner or any assistant commissioner may act for and in the name of the Commissioners.

(4) Where the Commissioners act as a board, then—

- (a) if not more than four commissioners hold office for the time being, the quorum shall be two commissioners (of whom at least one must be a person having a qualification such as is mentioned in paragraph 1(2) above); and
- (b) if five commissioners so hold office, the quorum shall be three commissioners (of whom at least one must be a person having such a qualification);

and in the case of an equality of votes the chief commissioner or in his absence the commissioner presiding shall have a second or casting vote.

(5) The Commissioners shall have power to act notwithstanding any vacancy in their number.

(6) It is hereby declared that the power of a commissioner or assistant commissioner to act for and in the name of the Commissioners in accordance with sub-paragraph (3) above may, in particular, be exercised in relation to functions of the Commissioners under sections 8, 18, 19 and 63 of this Act, including functions under sections 8, 18 and 19 as applied by section 80(1).

4. Legal proceedings may be instituted by or against the Commissioners by the name of the Charity Commissioners for England and Wales, and shall not abate or be affected by any change in the persons who are the commissioners.

SCHEDULE 2

Sections 3 and 96

EXEMPT CHARITIES

The following institutions, so far as they are charities, are exempt charities within the meaning of this Act, that is to say—

- (a) any institution which, if the Charities Act 1960 had not been passed, would be exempted from the powers and jurisdiction, under the Charitable Trusts Acts 1853 to 1939, of the Commissioners or Minister of Education (apart from any power of the Commissioners or Minister to apply those Acts in whole or in part to charities otherwise exempt) by the terms of any enactment not contained in those Acts other than section 9 of the Places of Worship Registration Act 1855;
- (b) the universities of Oxford, Cambridge, London, Durham and Newcastle, the colleges and halls in the universities of Oxford, Cambridge, Durham and Newcastle, Queen Mary and Westfield College in the University of London and the colleges of Winchester and Eton;
- (c) any university, university college, or institution connected with a university or university college, which Her Majesty declares by Order in Council to be an exempt charity for the purposes of this Act;
- (d) a grant-maintained school;

(da) the Qualifications and Curriculum Authority;
(e) . . .;
(f) the Qualifications Curriculum and Assessment Authority for Wales;
(g) . . .;
(h) a higher education corporation;
(i) a successor company to a higher education corporation (within the meaning of section 129(5) of the Education Reform Act 1988) at a time when an institution conducted by the company is for the time being designated under that section;
(j) a further education corporation;
(k) the Board of Trustees of the Victoria and Albert Museum;
(l) the Board of Trustees of the Science Museum;
(m) the Board of Trustees of the Armouries;
(n) the Board of Trustees of the Royal Botanic Gardens, Kew;
(o) the Board of Trustees of the National Museum and Galleries on Merseyside;
(p) the trustees of the British Museum and the trustees of the National History Museum;
(q) the Board of Trustees of the National Gallery;
(r) the Board of Trustees of the Tate Gallery;
(s) the Board of Trustees of the National Portrait Gallery;
(t) the Board of Trustees of the Wallace Collection;
(u) the Trustees of the Imperial War Museum;
(v) the Trustees of the National Maritime Museum;
(w) any institution which is administered by or on behalf of an institution included above and is established for the general purposes of, or for any special purpose of or in connection with, the last-mentioned institution;
(x) the Church Commissioners and any institution which is administered by them;
(y) any registered society within the meaning of the Industrial and Provident Societies Act 1965 and any registered society or branch within the meaning of the Friendly Societies Act 1974;
(z) the Board of Governors of the Museum of London;
(za) the British Library Board;
(zb) the National Lottery Charities Board.

Note: Schedule shown as amended by the Education Act 1993: para (da) amended by s 307(1), Sch 19, para 175; para (f) is substituted by s 253(2), Sch 15, para 5; paras (e), (g) are repealed by the Education Act 1996, s 582(1), (2), Sch 37, Pt I, para 120, Sch 38, Pt I; paras (da), (f) are substituted by the Education Act 1997, s 57(1), Sch 7, para 7; and para (zb) is added by the National Lottery etc Act 1993, s 37(2), Sch 5, para 12.

SCHEDULE 3

Section 13

ENLARGEMENT OF AREAS OF LOCAL CHARITIES

Existing area	*Permissible enlargement*
1. Greater London	Any area comprising Greater London.
2. Any area in Greater London and not in, or partly in, the City of London.	(i) Any area in Greater London and not in, or partly in, the City of London; (ii) the area of Greater London exclusive of the City of London; (iii) any area comprising the area of Greater London, exclusive of the City of London; (iv) any area partly in Greater London and partly in any adjacent parish or parishes (civil or ecclesiastical), and not partly in the City of London.
3. A district	Any area comprising the district
3AA. Welsh county or county borough	Any area comprising that county or county borough.
4. Any area in a district	(i) Any area in the district; (ii) the district; (iii) any area comprising the district; (iv) any area partly in the district and partly in any adjacent district or in any adjacent Welsh county or county borough.
4A. Any area in a Welsh county or county borough	(i) Any area in the county or county borough; (ii) the county or county borough; (iii) any area comprising the county or county borough; (iv) any area partly in the county or county borough and partly in any adjacent Welsh county or county borough or in any adjacent district.
5. A parish (civil or ecclesiastical), or two or more parishes, or an area in a parish, or partly in each of two of more parishes.	Any area not extending beyond the parish or parishes comprising or adjacent to the area in column 1.
6. In Wales, a community, or two or more communities, or an area in a community, or partly in each of two or more communities.	Any area not extending beyond the community or communities comprising or adjacent to the area in column 1.

Note: Schedule shown as amended by the Local Government (Wales) Act 1994, s 66(6), Sch 16, para 101(5), (6).

SCHEDULE 4

Section 15

COURT'S JURISDICTION OVER CERTAIN CHARITIES GOVERNED BY OR UNDER STATUTE

1. The court may by virtue of section 15(3) of this Act exercise its jurisdiction with respect to charities—

(a) in relation to charities established or regulated by any provision of the Seamen's Fund Winding-up Act 1851 which is repealed by the Charities Act 1960;
(b) in relation to charities established or regulated by schemes under the Endowed Schools Act 1869 to 1948, or section 75 of the Elementary Education Act 1870 or by schemes given effect under section 2 of the Education Act 1973 or section 554 of the Education Act 1996;
(c) ...
(d) in relation to fuel allotments, that is to say, land which, by any enactment relating to inclosure or any instrument having effect under such an enactment, is vested in trustees upon trust that the land or the rents and profits of the land shall be used for the purpose of providing poor persons with fuel;
(e) in relation to charities established or regulated by any provision of the Municipal Corporations Act 1883 which is repealed by the Charities Act 1960 or by any scheme having effect under any such provision;
(f) in relation to charities regulated by schemes under the London Government Act 1899;
(g) in relation to charities established or regulated by orders or regulations under section 2 of the Regimental Charitable Funds Act 1935;
(h) in relation to charities regulated by section 79 of this Act, or by any such order as is mentioned in that section.

2. Notwithstanding anything in section 19 of the Commons Act 1876 a scheme for the administration of a fuel allotment (within the meaning of the foregoing paragraph) may provide—

(a) for the sale or letting of the allotments or any part thereof, for the discharge of the land sold or let from any restrictions as to the use thereof imposed by or under any enactment relating to inclosure and for the application of the sums payable to the trustees of the allotment in respect of the sale or lease; or
(b) for the exchange of the allotment or any part thereof for other land, for the discharge as aforesaid of the land given in exchange by the said trustees, and for the application of any money payable to the said trustees for equality of exchange; or
(c) for the use of the allotment or any part thereof for any purposes specified in the scheme.

Note: Schedule shown as amended by the Education Act 1996, s 582(1), Sch 37, Pt I, para 121; and the Statute Law (Repeals) Act 1993, s 1(1), Sch 1, Pt III.

SCHEDULE 5

Section 36(2)

MEANING OF 'CONNECTED PERSON' FOR PURPOSES OF SECTION 36(2)

1. In section 36(2) of this Act 'connected person', in relation to a charity, means—

(a) a charity trustee or trustee for the charity;
(b) a person who is the donor of any land to the charity (whether the gift was made on or after the establishment of the charity);
(c) a child, parent, grandchild, grandparent, brother or sister of any such trustee or donor;
(d) an officer, agent or employee of the charity;
(e) the spouse of any person falling within any of sub-paragraphs (a) to (d) above;
(f) an institution which is controlled—

 (i) by any person falling within any of sub-paragraphs (a) to (e) above, or
 (ii) by two or more such persons taken together; or

(g) a body corporate in which—

 (i) any connected person falling within any of sub-paragraphs (a) to (f) above has a substantial interest, or
 (ii) two or more such persons, taken together, have a substantial interest.

2.—(1) In paragraph 1(c) above 'child' includes a stepchild and an illegitimate child.

(2) For the purposes of paragraph 1(e) above a person living with another as that person's husband or wife shall be treated as that person's spouse.

3. For the purposes of paragraph 1(f) above a person controls an institution if he is able to secure that the affairs of the institution are conducted in accordance with his wishes.

4. (1) For the purposes of paragraph 1(g) above any such connected person as is there mentioned has a substantial interest in a body corporate if the person or institution in question—

(a) is interested in shares comprised in the equity share capital of that body of a nominal value of more than one-fifth of that share capital, or
(b) is entitled to exercise, or control the exercise of, more than one-fifth of the voting power at any general meeting of that body.

(2) The rules set out in Part I of Schedule 13 to the Companies Act 1985 (rules for interpretation of certain provisions of that Act) shall apply for the purposes of sub-paragraph (1) above as they apply for the purposes of section 346(4) of that Act ('connected persons' etc).

(3) In this paragraph 'equity share capital' and 'share' have the same meaning as in that Act.

SCHEDULE 6

Section 98(1)

CONSEQUENTIAL AMENDMENTS

The Places of Worship Registration Act 1855 (c 81)

1.—(1) Section 9 of the Places of Worship Registration Act 1855 shall be amended as follows.

(2) For 'subsection (4) of section four of the Charities Act 1960' there shall be substituted 'subsection (5) of section 3 of the Charities Act 1993'.

(3) At the end there shall be added—

> '(2) Section 89 of the said Act of 1993 (provisions as to orders under that Act) shall apply to any order under paragraph (b) above as it applies to orders under that Act.'

The Open Spaces Act 1906 (c 25)

2. At the end of section 4 of the Open Spaces Act 1906 there shall be added—

> '(4) Section 89 of the Charities Act 1993 (provisions as to orders under that Act) shall apply to any order of the Charity Commissioners under this section as it applies to orders made by them under that Act.'

The New Parishes Measure 1943 (No 1)

3.—(1) The New Parishes Measure 1943 shall be amended as follows.

(2) In subsection (1)(b) of section 14 for 'the Charities Act 1960' there shall be substituted 'the Charities Act 1993'.

(3) At the end of that section there shall be added—

> '(4) Section 89 of the Charities Act 1993 (provisions as to orders under that Act) shall apply to any order under section (1)(b) above as it applies to orders under that Act.'

(4) In section 31 for 'the Charities Act 1960' there shall be substituted 'the Charities Act 1993'.

The Clergy Pensions Measure 1961 (No 3)

4. In section 33 of the Clergy Pensions Measure 1961 for 'section 32 of the Charities Act 1992' and 'the Charities Act 1960' there shall be substituted respectively 'section 36 of the Charities Act 1993' and 'that Act'.

The Finance Act 1963 (c 25)

5. In section 65(2) of the Finance Act 1963 at the end of paragraph (a) there shall be added 'or to any common investment scheme under section 24 or any common deposit scheme under section 25 of the Charities Act 1993;'.

The Cathedrals Measure 1963 (No 2)

6.—(1) The Cathedrals Measure 1963 shall be amended as follows.

(2) In section 20(2)(iii) for 'section 32 of the Charities Act 1992' there shall be substituted 'section 36 of the Charities Act 1993'.

(3) In section 51 for 'the Charities Act 1960' there shall be substituted 'the Charities Act 1993'.

The Incumbents and Churchwardens (Trusts) Measure 1964 (No 2)

7. In section 1 of the Incumbents and Churchwardens (Trust) Measure 1964 for 'subsection (3) of section forty-five of the Charities Act 1960' there shall be substituted 'section 96(3) of the Charities Act 1993'.

The Leasehold Reform Act 1967 (c 88)

8. In section 23(4) of the Leasehold Reform Act 1967 for 'section 32 of the Charities Act 1992' there shall be substituted 'section 36 of the Charities Act 1993'.

The Greater London Council (General Powers) Act 1968 (c xxxix)

9. In section 43 of the Greater London Council (General Powers) Act 1968, in the definition of 'night café', for 'section 4 of the Charities Act 1960' and 'subsection (4) thereof' there shall be substituted respectively 'section 3 of the Charities Act 1993' and 'subsection (5) thereof'.

The Redundant Churches and other Religious Buildings Act 1969 (c 22)

10.—(1) The Redundant Churches and other Religious Buildings Act 1969 shall be amended as follows.

(2) In subsection (6) of section 4 for 'section 18 of the Charities Act 1960' there shall be substituted 'section 16 of the Charities Act 1993'.

(3) In subsection (7) of that section for 'subsection (4) of section 18 of that Act' there shall be substituted 'subsection (4) of section 16 of that Act'.

(4) In subsection (8) of that section for 'section 18 of the Charities Act 1960' and (where next occurring) 'section 18' there shall be substituted respectively 'section 16 of the Charities Act 1993' and 'section 16' and for 'section 21' there shall be substituted 'section 20'.

(5) In subsection (13) of that section for 'sections 45 and 46 of the Charities Act 1960' there shall be substituted 'sections 96 and 97 of the Charities Act 1993'.

(6) In section 7(2) for 'the Charities Act 1960' and 'section 23' there shall be substituted respectively 'the Charities Act 1993' and 'section 26'.

The Sharing of Church Buildings Act 1969 (c 38)

11.—(1) The Sharing of Church Buildings Act 1969 shall be amended as follows.

(2) In section 2(4) for 'the Charities Act 1960' there shall be substituted 'the Charities Act 1993'.

(3) In subsection (1) of section 8 for 'the Charities Act 1960' there shall be substituted 'the Charities Act 1993'.

(4) In subsection (2) of that section for 'section 45(2) of the Charities Act 1960' there shall be substituted 'section 96(2) of the Charities Act 1993'.

(5) In subsection (3) of that section for 'Section 32 of the Charities Act 1992' there shall be substituted 'Section 36 of the Charities Act 1993'.

The Local Government Act 1972 (c 70)

12.—(1) The Local Government Act 1972 shall be amended as follows.

(2) In sections 11(3)(c) and 29(3)(c) for 'section 37 of the Charities Act 1960' there shall be substituted 'section 79 of the Charities Act 1993'.

(3) In sections 123(6) and 127(4) for 'the Charities Act 1960' there shall be substituted 'the Charities Act 1993'.

(4) In section 131(3) for 'section 32 of the Charities Act 1992' and 'section 32(9)(a) of that Act' there shall be substituted respectively 'section 36 of the Charities Act 1993' and 'section 36(9)(a) of that Act'.

13. ...

The Theatres Trust Act 1976 (c 27)

14. In section 2(2)(d) of the Theatres Trust Act 1976 for 'sections 32 and 34 of the Charities Act 1992' there shall be substituted 'sections 36 and 38 of the Charities Act 1993'.

The Interpretation Act 1978 (c 30)

15. In Schedule 1 to the Interpretation Act 1978, in the definition of 'Charity Commissioners' for 'section 1 of the Charities Act 1960' there shall be substituted 'section 1 of the Charities Act 1993'.

The Reserve Forces Act 1980 (c 9)

16. ...

17. ...

The Pastoral Measure 1983 (No 1)

18.—(1) The Pastoral Measure 1983 shall be amended as follows.

(2) In section 55(1) for 'the Charities Act 1960' and 'section 45(2)(b)' there shall be substituted 'the Charities Act 1993' and 'section 96(2)(c)'.

(3) In section 63(3) for 'the Charities Act 1960' there shall be substituted 'the Charities Act 1993'.

(4) In section 87(1) for 'section 45 of the Charities Act 1960' there shall be substituted 'section 96 of the Charities Act 1993'.

(5) In paragraphs 11(6) and 16(1)(e) of Schedule 3 for 'section 18 of the Charities Act 1960' there shall be substituted 'section 16 of the Charities Act 1993'.

The Rates Act 1984 (c 33)

19. In section 3(9) of the Rates Act 1984 for 'section 4 of the Charities Act 1960' there shall be substituted 'section 3 of the Charities Act 1993'.

The Companies Act 1985 (c 6)

20.—(1) The Companies Act 1985 shall be amended as follows.

(2) In sections 35(4) and 35A(6) for 'section 30B(1) of the Charities Act 1960' there shall be substituted 'section 56(1) of the Charities Act 1993'.

(3) In section 209(1)(c) and paragraph 11(b) of Schedule 13 after 'the Charities Act 1960' there shall be inserted 'or section 24 or 25 of the Charities Act 1993'.

The Housing Associations Act 1985 (c 69)

21.—(1) The Housing Associations Act 1985 shall be amended as follows.

(2) In section 10(1) for 'sections 32 and 34 of the Charities Act 1992' there shall be substituted 'sections 36 and 38 of the Charities Act 1993'.

(3) . . .

(4) In section 35(2)(c) for 'section 32 of the Charities Act 1992' there shall be substituted 'section 36 of the Charities Act 1993'.

(5) In section 38—

(a) in paragraph (a) for 'the Charities Act 1960' there shall be substituted 'the Charities Act 1993';
(b) . . .

The Financial Services Act 1986 (c 60)

22. In section 45(1)(j) of the Financial Services Act 1986 after 'the Charities Act 1960' there shall be inserted ', section 24 or 25 of the Charities Act 1993'.

The Coal Industry Act 1987 (c 3)

23.—(1) In section 5 of the Coal Industry Act 1987 for subsection (8) there shall be substituted—

'(8) Sections 16(3), (9), (11) to (14), 17(1) to (5) and (7) and 20 of the Charities Act 1993 shall apply in relation to the powers of the Charity Commissioners and the making of schemes under this section as they apply in relation to their powers and the making of schemes under that Act and sections 89, 91 and 92 of that Act shall apply to orders and decisions under this section as they apply to orders and decisions under that Act.'

(2) In subsection (8A) of that section for 'section 29' (in both places) there shall be substituted 'section 17'.

The Reverter of Sites Act 1987 (c 15)

24. In section 4(4) of the Reverter of Sites Act 1987 for 'sections 40, 40A and 42 of the Charities Act 1960' there shall be substituted 'sections 89, 91 and 92 of the Charities Act 1993'.

The Income and Corporation Taxes Act 1988 (c 1)

25. In Schedule 20 to the Income and Corporation Taxes Act 1988—

(a) in paragraph 3 after 'the Charities Act 1960' there shall be inserted ', section 24 of the Charities Act 1993';
(b) in paragraph 3A after 'the Charities Act 1960' there shall be inserted 'or section 25 of the Charities Act 1993'.

The Courts and Legal Services Act 1990 (c 41)

26. In Schedule 11 to the Courts and Legal Services Act 1990, in the reference to a Charity Commissioner, for 'under the First Schedule to the Charities Act 1960' there shall be substituted 'as provided in Schedule 1 to the Charities Act 1993'.

The London Local Authorities Act 1990 (c vii)

27. In section 4 of the London Local Authorities Act 1990, in the definition of 'night café', for 'section 4 of the Charities Act 1960' and 'subsection (4) thereof' there shall be substituted respectively 'section 3 of the Charities Act 1993' and 'subsection (5) thereof'.

The London Local Authorities Act 1991 (c xiii)

28. In section 4 of the London Local Authorities Act 1991, in the definition of 'establishment for special treatment', for 'section 4 of the Charities Act 1960' and 'subsection (4) of that section' there shall be substituted respectively 'section 3 of the Charities Act 1993' and 'subsection (5) of that section'.

29. . . .

Other amendments

30. In the following provisions for 'the Charities Act 1960' there shall be substituted 'the Charities Act 1993'—

The National Health Service Reorganisation Act 1973 section 30(5).
The Consumer Credit Act 1974 section 189(1).
The Rent (Agriculture) Act 1976 section (5)(3)(f).
The Rent Act 1977 section 15(2)(b).
The National Health Service Act 1977 section 96(2).
The Dioceses Measure 1978 section 19(4).
The Ancient Monuments and Archaeological Areas Act 1979 section 49(3).
The Greater London Council (General Powers) Act 1984 section 10(2)(n).
The Local Government Act 1985 section 90(4).
The Housing Act 1985 sections 525 and 622.
The Landlord and Tenant Act 1987 section 60(1).
The Education Reform Act 1988 sections 128(5) and 192(11).
The Copyright Designs and Patents Act 1988 Schedule 6 paragraph 7.
The Housing Act 1988 Schedule 2 Part I Ground 6.
The University of Wales College of Cardiff Act 1988 section 9.
The Imperial College Act 1988 section 10.

Note: Schedule shown as amended by the Reserve Forces Act 1996, s 131(2), Sch 11; the Housing Act 1996 (Consequential Provisions) Order 1996, SI 1996/2325, art 4, Sch 1, Pt I; the Housing Grants, Construction and Regeneration Act 1996, s 147, Sch 3, Pt I; and the Housing Act 1996, s 227, Sch 19, Pt I.

SCHEDULE 7

Section 98(2)

REPEALS

Chapter	Short title	Extent of repeal
35 & 36 Vic c 24	The Charitable Trustees Incorporation Act 1872	The whole Act so far as unrepealed.
10 & 11 Geo 5 c 16	The Imperial War Museum Act 1920	Section 5.
24 & 25 Geo 5 c 43	The National Maritime Museum Act 1934	Section 7.
8 & 9 Eliz 2 c 58	The Charities Act 1960	The whole Act so far as unrepealed except— section 28(9) section 35(6) section 38(3) to (5) section 39(2) sections 48 and 49 Schedule 6.
1963 c 33	The London Government Act 1963	Section 81(9)(b) and (c).
1963 c xi	The Universities of Durham and Newcastle-upon-Tyne Act 1963	Section 10.
1965 c 17	The Museum of London Act 1965	Section 11.
1972 c 54	The British Library Act 1972	Section 4(2)
1972 c 70	The Local Government Act 1972	Section 210(9)
1973 c 16	The Education Act 1973	In section 2(7) the words from 'but' onwards. In Schedule 1, paragraph 1(1) and (3).
1976 No 4	The Endowments and Glebe Measure 1976	Section 44.
1983 c 47	The National Heritage Act 1983	In Schedule 5, paragraph 4.
1985 c 9	The Companies Consolidation (Consequential Provisions) Act 1985	In Schedule 2 the entry relating to the Charities Act 1960.
1985 c 20	The Charities Act 1985	Section 1.
1986 c 60	The Financial Services Act 1986	In Schedule 16, paragraph 1.
1988 c 40	The Education Reform Act 1988	In Schedule 12, paragraphs 9, 10, 63 and 64.
1989 c 40	The Companies Act 1989	Section 111.

Chapter	Short title	Extent of repeal
1989 c xiii	The Queen Mary and Westfield College Act 1989	Section 10.
1990 c 41	The Courts and Legal Services Act 1990	In Schedule 10, paragraph 14.
1992 c 13	The Further and Higher Education Act 1992	In Schedule 8, paragraph 69.
1992 c 41	The Charities Act 1992	The whole of Part I except—section 1(1) and (4) sections 29 and 30 section 36 sections 49 and 50 Section 75(b). Section 76(1)(a). In section 77, subsection (2)(a), (b) and (c) and in subsection (4) the figures 20, 22 and 23. Section 79(4) and (5). Schedules 1 to 4. In Schedule 6, paragraph 13(2). In Schedule 7, the entries relating to section 8 of the Charities Act 1960 and (so far as not in force at the date specified in section 99(1) of this Act) the Charities Act 1985.
1992 c 44	The Museums and Galleries Act 1992	In Schedule 8, paragraphs 4 and 10. In Schedule 9, the entry relating to the Charities Act 1960.

SCHEDULE 8

Section 99(3), (4)

TRANSITIONAL PROVISIONS

PART I

PROVISIONS APPLYING PENDING COMING INTO FORCE OF PART VI ETC

1. In the Charities Act 1960—

section 8
section 32
Part V so far as relevant to those sections.

2. In the Charities Act 1985

section 1
sections 6 and 7 so far as relevant to section 1.

PART II

PROVISIONS APPLYING PENDING COMING INTO FORCE OF 'FINANCIAL YEAR' REGULATIONS

Section 5

In section 5(1) of this Act 'financial year'—

(a) in relation to a charity which is a company, shall be construed in accordance with section 223 of the Companies Act 1985;
(b) in relation to any other charity, means any period in respect of which an income and expenditure account is required to be prepared whether under section 32 of the Charities Act 1960 or by or under the authority of any other Act, whether that period is a year or not.

Sections 74 and 75

In sections 74(1)(a) and 75(1)(b) of this Act 'financial year' means any period in respect of which an income and expenditure account is required to be prepared whether under section 32 of the Charities Act 1960 or by or under the authority of any other Act, whether that period is a year or not.

INCOME AND CORPORATION TAXES ACT 1988

CHAPTER VI
MISCELLANEOUS BUSINESSES AND BODIES

...

505 Charities: general

(1) Subject to subsections (2) and (3) below, the following exemptions shall be granted on a claim in that behalf to the Board—

(a) exemption from tax under Schedules A and D in respect of any profits or gains arising in respect of rents or other receipts from an estate, interest or right in or over any land (whether situated in the United Kingdom or elsewhere) to the extent that the profits or gains—

(i) arise in respect of rents or receipts from an estate, interest or right vested in any person for charitable purposes; and
(ii) are applied to charitable purposes only;

(b) ...;
(c) exemption—

(i) ...
(ii) from tax under Case III of Schedule D,
(iia) from tax under Case IV or V of Schedule D in respect of income equivalent to income chargeable under Case III of that Schedule but arising from securities or other possessions outside the United Kingdom,
(iib) from tax under Case V of Schedule D in respect of income consisting in any such dividend or other distribution of a company not resident in the United Kingdom as would be chargeable to tax under Schedule F if the company were so resident, and
(iii) from tax under Schedule F in respect of any distribution,

where the income in question forms part of the income of a charity, or is, according to rules or regulations established by Act of Parliament, charter, decree, deed of trust or will, applicable to charitable purposes only, and so far as it is applied to charitable purposes only;

(d) exemption from tax under Schedule D in respect of public revenue dividends on securities which are in the name of trustees, to the extent that the dividends are applicable and applied only for the repair of—

(i) any cathedral, college, church or chapel, or
(ii) any building used only for the purposes of divine worship;

(e) exemption from tax under Schedule D in respect of the profits of any trade carried on by a charity (whether in the United Kingdom or elsewhere), if the profits are applied solely to the purposes of the charity and either—

(i) the trade is exercised in the course of the actual carrying out of a primary purpose of the charity; or
(ii) the work in connection with the trade is mainly carried out by beneficiaries of the charity;

(f) exemption from tax under Schedule D in respect of profits accruing to a charity from a lottery if—

(i) the lottery is promoted and conducted in accordance with section 3 or 5 of the Lotteries and Amusements Act 1976 or Article 133 or 135 of the Betting, Gaming, Lotteries and Amusements (Northern Ireland) Order 1985; and
(ii) the profits are applied solely to the charity's purposes.

(1A) In subsection (1)(d) above 'public revenue dividends' means—

(a) income from securities which is payable out of the public revenue of the United Kingdom or Northern Ireland;
(b) income from securities issued by or on behalf of a government or a public or local authority in a country outside the United Kingdom.

(2) Any payment which—

(a) is received by a charity from another charity; and
(b) is not made for full consideration in money or money's worth; and
(c) is not chargeable to tax apart from this subsection; and
(d) is not, apart from this subsection, of a description which (on a claim) would be eligible for relief from tax by virtue of any provision of subsection (1) above;

shall be chargeable to tax under Case III of Schedule D but shall be eligible for relief from tax under subsection (1)(c) above as if it were an annual payment.

(3) If in any chargeable period of a charity—

(a) its relevant income and gains are not less than £10,000; and
(b) its relevant income and gains exceed the amount of its qualifying expenditure; and
(c) the charity incurs, or is treated as incurring, non-qualifying expenditure;

relief shall not be available under either subsection (1) above or section 256 of the 1992 Act for so much of the excess as does not exceed the non-qualifying expenditure incurred in that period.

(4) In relation to a chargeable period of less than 12 months, subsection (3) above shall have effect as if the amount specified in paragraph (a) of that subsection were proportionately reduced.

(5) In subsection (3) above 'relevant income and gains' means—

(a) income which apart from subsection (1) above would not be exempt from tax together with any income which is taxable notwithstanding that subsection; and
(b) gains which apart from section 256 of the 1992 Act would be chargeable gains together with any gains which are chargeable gains notwithstanding that section.

(6) Where by virtue of subsection (3) above there is an amount of a charity's relevant income and gains for which relief under subsection (1) above and section 256 of the 1992 Act is not available, the charity may, by notice to the Board, specify which items of its relevant income and gains are, in whole or in part, to be attributed to that amount, and, for this purpose, all covenanted payments to charity (within the meaning of section 347A(7) shall be treated as a single item; and if within 30 days of being required to do so by the Board, a charity does not give notice under this subsection, the items of its relevant income and gains which are to be attributed to the amount in question shall be such as the Board may determine.

(7) Where it appears to the Board that two or more charities acting in concert are engaged in transactions of which the main purpose or one of the main purposes is the avoidance of tax (whether by the charities or by any other person), the Board may by notice given to the charities provide that, for such chargeable periods as may be specified in the notice, subsection (3) above shall have effect in relation to them with the omission of paragraph (a).

(8) An appeal may be brought against a notice under subsection (7) above as if it were notice of the decision of the Board on a claim made by the charities concerned.

Note: Section shown as amended by the Finance Act 1996, ss 79(2), 146, 205, Sch 7, paras 19, 32, Sch 41, Pt V(2); the Finance Act 1988, s 148, Sch 14, Pt V; the Finance Act 1995, s 74, s 138, Sch 17, Pt II, para 7; the Taxation of Chargeable Gains Act 1992, s 290(1), Sch 10, para 14(1), (31).

---

506 Qualifying expenditure and non-qualifying expenditure

(1) In this section, section 505 and Schedule 20—

'charity' means any body of persons or trust established for charitable purposes only;
'qualifying expenditure', in relation to a chargeable period of a charity, means, subject to subsection (3) below, expenditure incurred in that period for charitable purposes only; and
'non-qualifying expenditure' means expenditure which is not qualifying expenditure.

(2) For the purposes of section 505 and subsection (1) above, where expenditure which is not actually incurred in a particular chargeable period properly falls to be charged against the income of that chargeable period as being referable to commitments (whether or not of a contractual nature) which the charity has entered into before or during that period, it shall be treated as incurred in that period.

(3) A payment made (or to be made) to a body situated outside the United Kingdom shall not be qualifying expenditure by virtue of this section unless the charity concerned has taken such steps as may be reasonable in the circumstances to ensure that the payment will be applied for charitable purposes.

(4) If in any chargeable period a charity—

(a) invests any of its funds in an investment which is not a qualifying investment, as defined in Part I of Schedule 20; or
(b) makes a loan (not being an investment) which is not a qualifying loan, as defined in Part II of that Schedule;

then, subject to subsection (5) below, the amount so invested or lent in that period shall be treated for the purposes of this section as being an amount of expenditure incurred by the charity, and, accordingly, as being non-qualifying expenditure.

(5) If, in any chargeable period, a charity which has in that period made an investment or loan falling within subsection (4) above—

(a) realises the whole or part of that investment; or
(b) is repaid the whole or part of that loan;

any further investment or lending in that period of the sum realised or repaid shall, to the extent that it does not exceed the sum originally invested or lent, be left out of account in determining the amount which, by virtue of subjection (4) above, is treated as non-qualifying expenditure incurred in that period.

(6) If the aggregate of the qualifying and non-qualifying expenditure incurred by a charity in any chargeable period exceeds the relevant income and gains of that period, Part III of Schedule 20 shall have effect to treat, in certain cases, some or all of that excess as non-qualifying expenditure incurred in earlier periods.

NATIONAL HEALTH SERVICE REORGANISATION ACT 1973

23 Winding-up of Hospital Endowments Fund

(1) The Hospital Endowments Fund shall be wound up by the Secretary of State, and the winding up shall be completed by 31st March 1974 or as soon after as is practicable.

(2) The Secretary of State shall by order provide for the distribution of the assets of the Hospital Endowments Fund among the following authorities and bodies, that is—

Regional Health Authorities,
Area Health Authorities, and
Special Trustees,

or among such as those authorities or trustees as are specified in the order, in such proportions or up to such amounts as may be so specified.

Note: Whole Act repealed, subject to a saving relating to s 44, by the Health Authorities Act 1995, ss 2(1), 4(1), 5(1), Sch 1, Pt III, para 98, Sch 2, para 12, Sch 3.

NATIONAL HEALTH SERVICE ACT 1977

1 Secretary of State's duty as to health service

(1) It is the Secretary of State's duty to continue the promotion in England and Wales of a comprehensive health service designed to secure improvement—

(a) in the physical and mental health of the people of those countries, and
(b) in the prevention, diagnosis and treatment of illness,

and for that purpose to provide or secure the effective provision of services in accordance with this Act.

(2) The service so provided shall be free of charge except in so far as the making and recovery of charges is expressly provided for by or under any enactment, whenever passed.

...

3 Services generally

(1) It is the Secretary of State's duty to provide throughout England and Wales, to such extent as he considers necessary to meet all reasonable requirements—

(a) hospital accommodation;
(b) other accommodation for the purpose of any service provided under this Act;
(c) medical, dental, nursing and ambulance services;
(d) such other facilities for the care of expectant and nursing mothers and young children as he considers are appropriate as part of the health service;
(e) such facilities for the prevention of illness, the care of persons suffering from illness and the after-care of persons who have suffered from illness as he considers are appropriate as part of the health service;
(f) such other services as are required for the diagnosis and treatment of illness.

(2) Where any hospital provided by the Secretary of State in accordance with this Act was a voluntary hospital transferred by virtue of the National Health Service Act 1946, and—

(a) the character and associations of that hospital before its transfer were such as to link it with a particular religious denomination, then
(b) regard shall be held in the general administration of the hospital to the preservation of that character and those associations.

(3) Nothing in section 2 above or in this section affects the provisions of Part II of this Act (which relates to arrangements with practitioners for the provision of medical, dental, ophthalmic and pharmaceutical services).

...

5 Other services

(1) It is the Secretary of State's duty—

(a) to provide for the medical inspection at appropriate intervals of pupils in attendance at schools maintained by local education authorities or at grant-maintained schools and for the medical treatment of such pupils;

(b) to arrange, to such extent as he considers necessary to meet all reasonable requirements in England and Wales, for the giving of advice on contraception, the medical examination of persons seeking advice on contraception, the treatment of such persons and the supply of contraceptive substances and appliances.

(1A) It is also the Secretary of State's duty to provide, to such extent as he considers necessary to meet all reasonable requirements—

(a) for the dental inspection of pupils in attendance at schools maintained by local education authorities or at grant-maintained schools;
(b) for the dental treatment of such pupils; and
(c) for the education of such pupils in dental health.

(1B) Schedule 1 to this Act shall have effect.

(2) The Secretary of State may—

(a) provide invalid carriages for persons appearing to him to be suffering from severe physical defect or disability and, at the request of such a person, may provide for him a vehicle other than an invalid carriage (and the additional provisions set out in Schedule 2 to this Act have effect in relation to this paragraph);
(b) arrange to provide accommodation and treatment outside Great Britain for persons suffering from respiratory tuberculosis;
(c) provide a microbiological service, which may include the provision of laboratories, for the control of the spread of infectious diseases and carry on such other activities as in his opinion can conveniently be carried on in conjunction with that service;
(d) conduct, or assist by grants or otherwise (without prejudice to the general powers and duties conferred on him under the Ministry of Health Act 1919) any person to conduct, research into any matters relating to the causation, prevention, diagnosis or treatment of illness, and into any such other matters connected with any service provided under this Act as he considers appropriate.

(2A) Charges may be made for services or materials supplied by virtue of paragraph (c) of subsection (2) above; and the powers conferred by that paragraph may be exercised both for the purposes of the health service and for other purposes.

(2B) The Secretary of State's functions may be performed outside England and Wales, in so far as they relate—

(a) to holidays for patients;
(b) to the transfer of patients to or from Scotland, Northern Ireland, the Isle of Man or the Channel Islands; or
(c) to the return of patients who have received treatment in England and Wales to countries or territories outside the British Islands.

(3) ...

(4) The Public Health Laboratory Service Board continues in being for the purpose of exercising such functions with respect to the powers conferred by paragraph (c) of subsection (2) above as the Secretary of State may determine.

(5) The Board shall continue to be constituted in accordance with Part I of Schedule 3 to this Act, and the additional provisions set out in Part II of that Schedule have effect in relation to the Board.

Note: Section shown as amended by the Health and Medicines Act 1988, ss 10(1), 25(2), Sch 3.

...

Trusts

90 Gifts on trust

A Health Authority or Special Health Authority has power to accept, hold and administer any property on trust for all or any purposes relating to the health service.

Note: Section shown as amended by the Health Authorities Act 1995, s 2(1), Sch 1, Pt I, paras 1, 42.

91 Private trusts for hospitals

(1) Where—

(a) the terms of a trust instrument authorise or require the trustees, whether immediately or in the future, to apply any part of the capital or income of the trust property for the purposes of any health service hospital, then
(b) the trust instrument shall be construed as authorising or (as the case may be) requiring the trustees to apply the trust property to the like extent, and at the like times, for the purpose of making payments, whether of capital or income, to the appropriate hospital authority.

(2) Any sum so paid to the appropriate hospital authority shall, so far as practicable, be applied by them for the purpose specified in the trust instrument.

(3) In this section 'the appropriate hospital authority' means—

(a) where special trustees are appointed for the hospital, those trustees;
(aa) where the hospital is owned and managed by an NHS trust and trustees have been appointed for the NHS trust, those trustees;
(ab) where the hospital is owned and managed by an NHS trust and neither paragraph (a) nor paragraph (aa) above applies, the NHS trust;
(b) in any other case, the Health Authority exercising functions on behalf of the Secretary of State in respect of the hospital.

(4) Nothing in this section applies to a trust for a special hospital, or to property transferred under section 24 of the National Health Service Reorganisation Act 1973.

Note: Section shown as amended by the National Health Service and Community Care Act 1990, ss 11(4), 66(2), Sch 10; and the Health Authorities Act 1995, s 2(1), Sch 1, Pt I, paras 1, 43.

92 Further transfers of trust property

(1) The Secretary of State may, having regard to any change or proposed change in the arrangements for the administration of a hospital or other establishment or facility or in the area or functions of any Health Authority or Special Health Authority, by order provide for the transfer of any trust property from any relevant health service body to any other relevant health service body.

(1A) In this section 'relevant health service body' means—

(a) a Health Authority;

(b) a Special Health Authority;
(c) an NHS trust;
(d) special trustees; or
(e) trustees for an NHS trust.

(2) If it appears to the Secretary of State at any time that all the functions of any special trustees should be discharged by one or more bodies which are relevant health service bodies by virtue of subsection (1A)(a) to (c) above then, whether or not there has been any such change as is mentioned in subsection (1) above, he may by order provide for the transfer of all trust property from the special trustees to the body or, in such proportions as may be specified in the order, to those bodies.

(3) Before so acting the Secretary of State shall consult the special trustees and other bodies concerned.

(4) Where by an order under this section, property is transferred to two or more bodies, it shall be apportioned by them in such proportions as they may agree or as may in default of agreement be determined by the Secretary of State, and the order may provide for the way in which the property is to be apportioned.

(5) Where property is so apportioned, the Secretary of State may by order make any consequential amendments of the trust instrument relating to the property.

(6) If it appears to the Secretary of State at any time that—

(a) the functions of any special trustees should be discharged by the trustees for an NHS trust, or
(b) the functions of the trustees for an NHS trust should be discharged by special trustees,

then, whether or not there has been any such change as is mentioned in subsection (1) above, he may, after consulting the special trustees and the trustees for the NHS trust, by order provide for the transfer of all trust property from or to the special trustees to or from the trustees for the NHS trust.

Note: Section shown as amended by the National Health Service and Community Care Act 1990, s 11(5); and the Health Authorities Act 1995, s 2(1), Sch 1, Pt I, paras 1, 41.

93 Trust property previously held for general hospital purposes

(1) This section applies—

(a) to property transferred under section 23 of the National Health Service Reorganisation Act 1973 (winding-up of hospital endowments funds), and
(b) to property transferred under section 24 of that Act (transfer of trust property from abolished authorities) which immediately before the day appointed for the purposes of that section was, in accordance with any provision contained in or made under section 7 of the National Health Service Act 1946, applicable for purposes relating to hospital services or relating to some form of research,

and this section continues to apply to the property after any further transfer under section 92 above.

(2) The person holding the property after the transfer or last transfer shall secure, so far as is reasonably practicable, that the objects of any original endowment, and the observance of any conditions attached to that endowment, including in particular conditions

intended to preserve the memory of any person or class of persons, are not prejudiced by this Part of this Act.

In this subsection 'original endowment' means a hospital endowment which was transferred under section 7 of that Act of 1946 and from which the property in question is derived.

(3) Subject to subsection (2) above, the property shall be held on trust for such purposes relating to hospital services (including research), or to any other part of the health service associated with any hospital, as the person holding the property thinks fit.

(4) Where the person holding the property is a body of special trustees, the power conferred by subsection (3) above shall be exercised as respects the hospitals for which they are appointed.

Note: Section shown as amended by the Health Authorities Act 1995, s 5(1), Sch 3.

---

94 Application of trust property: further provisions

(1) Any discretion given by a trust instrument to the trustees of property transferred under—

- (a) section 24 of the National Health Service Reorganisation Act 1973 (transfer of trust property from abolished authorities),
- (b) section 25 of that Act (transfer of trust property held for health services by local health authorities),
- (c) section 92 above.

shall be exercisable by the person to whom the property is so transferred and, subject to section 93 above and the following provisions of this section, the transfer shall not affect the trusts on which the property is held.

(2) Where—

- (a) property has been transferred under section 24 of that Act of 1973, and
- (b) any discretion is given by a trust instrument to the trustees to apply the property, or income arising from the property, to such hospital services (including research) as the trustees think fit without any restriction on the kinds of hospital services and without any restriction to one or more specified hospitals,

the discretion shall be enlarged so as to allow the application of the property or (as the case may be) of the income arising from the property, to such extent as the trustees think fit, for any other part of the health service associated with any hospital.

(3) Subsection (2) above shall apply on any subsequent transfer of the property under section 92 above.

95 Special trustees for a university or teaching hospital

(1) The bodies of trustees (in this Act referred to as special trustees) appointed by the Secretary of State under section 29 of the National Health Service Reorganisation Act 1973 or this section shall (subject to section 92 above) hold and administer the property transferred to them under that Act of 1973.

The special trustees so appointed are bodies of trustees appointed for the hospital or hospitals which, immediately before the day appointed for the purposes of section 29 of that Act of 1973, were controlled and managed by a University Hospital Management Committee or a Board of Governors, but excluding—

(a) a body on whose request an order was made under section 24(2) of that Act of 1973;
(b) a preserved Board within the meaning of section 15(6) of that Act of 1973.

(2) Special trustees have power to accept, hold and administer any property on trust for all or any purposes relating to hospital services (including research), or to any other part of the health service associated with hospitals, being a trust which is wholly or mainly for hospitals for which the special trustees are appointed.

(3) The number of trustees for any hospital or hospitals shall be such as the Secretary of State may from time to time determine after consultation with such persons as he considers appropriate.

(4) The term of office of any special trustees shall be fixed by the Secretary of State but a special trustee may be removed by the Secretary of State at any time during the special trustee's term of office.

Note: Section shown as amended by the Health Service Act 1980, ss 1, 2, Sch 1, Pt I, para 68.

---

96 Trusts: supplementary provisions

(1) Any provision in sections 90 to 95 above for the transfer of any property includes provision for the transfer of any rights and liabilities arising from that property.

(1A) Where any transfer of property by virtue of those sections is of, or includes,—

(a) land held on lease from a third party, that is to say, a person other than the Secretary of State, a Health Authority or Special Health Authority, or
(b) any other asset leased or hired from a third party or in which a third party has an interest,

the transfer shall be binding on the third party notwithstanding that, apart from this subsection, it would have required his consent or concurrence.

(2) Nothing in those sections shall affect any power of Her Majesty, the court (as defined in the Charities Act 1993) or any other person to alter the trusts of any charity.

(3) Nothing in section 12 of the Finance Act 1895 (which requires certain Acts and certain instruments relating to the vesting of property by virtue of an Act to be stamped as conveyances on sale) applies to section 90 to 95 above or to an order made in pursuance of any of those sections; and stamp duty shall not be payable on such an order.

Note: Section shown as amended by the National Health Service and Community Care Act 1990, s 11(6)(b), the Health Authorities Act 1995, s 2(1), Sch 1, Pt I, paras 1, 45; and the Charities Act 1993, s 98(1), Sch 6, para 30.

96A Power of health authorities, etc to raise money, etc, by appeals, collections, etc

(1) A Health Authority, Special Health Authority or NHS trust shall have power to engage in activities intended to stimulate the giving (whether on trust or otherwise) of money or other property to assist the authority or NHS trust in providing or improving any services or any facilities or accommodation which is or are or is or are to be provided as part of the health service or to assist them in connection with their functions with respect to research.

(2)...

(3) Subject to any directions of the Secretary of State excluding specified descriptions of activity, the activities authorised by this section include public appeals or collections and competitions, entertainments, bazaars, sales of produce or other goods and other similar activities and the activities may involve the use of land, premises or other property held by or for the benefit of the Health Authority, Special Health Authority or NHS trust exercising the power subject however to any restrictions on the purposes for which trust property may be used.

(4) Subject to the following provisions of this section, the Health Authority, Special Health Authority, or NHS trust at whose instance property is given in pursuance of this section shall, after defraying out of it any expenses incurred in obtaining it, hold, administer and apply the property on trust for or for the purpose for which it was given.

(5) Where property is given in pursuance of this section to or on trust for any purposes of a hospital for which special trustees have been appointed, the property may be held, administered and applied by the special trustees instead of by the body responsible for the hospital if that body and the special trustees agree; and in this subsection the body responsible for a hospital is,—

- (a) in the case of a hospital vested in a NHS trust, that trust; and
- (b) in any other case, the Health Authority exercising functions on behalf of the Secretary of State in respect of the hospital.

(5A) Where property is given in pursuance of this section on trust for any purposes of an NHS trust for which trustees have been appointed under section 11(1) of the National Health Service and Community Care Act 1990, then, if those trustees and the NHS trust agree, the property may be held, administered and applied by those trustees instead of by the NHS trust.

(6) Property given in pursuance of this section on trust may be transferred by order of the Secretary of State under section 92 above in the same circumstances as other trust property may be transferred under that section, and sections 94 and 96 above shall apply as they apply to other trust property transferred under the said section 92.

(7) Where property held by a Health Authority, Special Health Authority or NHS trust under this section is more than sufficient to enable the purpose for which it was given to be fulfilled the excess shall be applicable, in default of any provision for its application made by the trust or other instrument under or in accordance with which the property comprising the excess was given, for such purposes connected with any of the functions of the Health Authority, Special Health Authority or NHS trust as the Health Authority, Special Health Authority or NHS trust think fit.

(8) Where property held by a Health Authority, Special Health Authority or NHS trust under this section is insufficient to enable the purpose for which it was given to be fulfilled then—

- (a) the Health Authority, Special Health Authority or NHS trust may apply so much of the capital or income at their disposal as is needed to enable the purpose to be fulfilled subject, however, in the case of trust property, to any restrictions on the purpose for which the trust property may be applied and, in the case of money paid or payable by the Secretary of State under section 97 below, to any directions he may give; but
- (b) where the capital or income applicable under paragraph (a) above is insufficient or is not applied to enable the purpose to be fulfilled, the property so held by the Health Authority, Special Health Authority or NHS trust shall be applicable, in

default of any provision for its application made by the trust or other instrument under or in accordance with which the property was given, for such purposes connected with any of the functions of the Health Authority, Special Health Authority or NHS trust as the authority or trust think fit.

(9) Where under subsection (7) or (8) above property becomes applicable for purposes other than that for which it was given the authority, NHS trust or Board shall have regard to the desirability of applying the property for a purpose similar to that for which it was given.

(10) In this section 'special trustees' has the same meaning as in section 95 above and references to the purposes for which trust property may be used or applied are to be taken, in the case of trust property which has been transferred under section 92 above, to include references to those purposes as enlarged by section 94 above.

Note: Section shown as amended by the Health Services Act 1980, s 5(1) and the National Health Service and Community Care Act 1990, s 5, Sch 2, Pt III, para 23; and the Health Authorities Act 1995, ss 2(1), 5(1), Sch 1, Pt I, paras 1, 46, Sch 3.

TRUSTEE INVESTMENTS ACT 1961

(9 & 10 Eliz 2 c 62)

ARRANGEMENT OF SECTIONS

An Act to make fresh provision with respect to investment by trustees and persons having the investment powers of trustees, and by local authorities, and for purposes connected therewith [3 August 1961]

Northern Ireland. This Act applies to the extent mentioned in s 17(2) post.

1 New powers of investment of trustees

(1) A trustee may invest any property in his hands, whether at the time in a state of investment or not, in any manner specified in Part I or II of the First Schedule to this Act or, subject to the next following section, in any manner specified in Part III of that Schedule, and may also from time to time vary any such investments.

(2) The supplemental provisions contained in Part IV of that Schedule shall have effect for the interpretation and for restricting the operation of the said Parts I to III.

(3) No provision relating to the powers of the trustee contained in any instrument (not being an enactment or an instrument made under an enactment) made before the passing of this Act shall limit the powers conferred by this section, but those powers are exerciseable only in so far as a contrary intention is not expressed in any Act or instrument made under an enactment, whenever passed or made, and so relating or in any other instrument so relating which is made after the passing of this Act.

For the purposes of this subsection any rule of the law of Scotland whereby a testamentary writing may be deemed to be made on a date other than that on which it was actually executed shall be disregarded.

(4) In this Act 'narrower-range investment' means an investment falling within Part I or II of the First Schedule to this Act and 'wider-range investment' means an investment falling within Part III of that Schedule.

2 Restrictions on wider-range investment

(1) A trustee shall not have power by virtue of the foregoing section to make or retain any wider-range investment unless the trust fund has been divided into two parts (hereinafter referred to as the narrower-range part and the wider-range part), the parts being, subject to the provisions of this Act, equal in value at the time of the division; and where such a division has been made no subsequent division of the same fund shall be made for the purposes of this section, and no property shall be transferred from one part of the fund to the other unless either—

(a) the transfer is authorised or required by the following provisions of this Act, or
(b) a compensating transfer is made at the same time.

In this section 'compensating transfer', in relation to any transferred property, means a transfer in the opposite direction of property of equal value.

(2) Property belonging to the narrower-range part of a trust fund shall not by virtue of the foregoing section be invested except in narrower-range investments, and any property invested in any other manner which is or becomes comprised in that part of the trust fund shall either be transferred to the wider-range part of the fund, with a compensating transfer, or be reinvested in narrower range investments as soon as may be.

(3) Where any property accrues to a trust fund after the fund has been divided in pursuance of subsection (1) of this section, then—

(a) if the property accrues to the trustee as owner or former owner of property comprised in either part of the fund, it shall be treated as belonging to that part of the fund;
(b) in any other case, the trustee shall secure, by apportionment of the accruing property or the transfer of property from one part of the fund to the other, or both, that the value of each part of the fund is increased by the same amount.

Where a trustee acquires property in consideration of a money payment the acquisition of the property shall be treated for the purposes of this section as investment and not as the accrual of property to the trust fund, notwithstanding that the amount of the consideration is less than the value of the property acquired; and paragraph (a) of this subsection shall not include the case of a dividend or interest becoming part of a trust fund.

(4) Where in the exercise of any power or duty of a trustee property falls to be taken out of the trust fund, nothing in this section shall restrict his discretion as to the choice of property to be taken out.

3 Relationship between Act and other powers of investment

(1) The powers conferred by section one of this Act are in addition to and not in derogation from any power conferred otherwise than by this Act of investment or postponing conversion exerciseable by a trustee (hereinafter referred to as a 'special power').

(2) Any special power (however expressed) to invest property in any investment for the time being authorised by law for the investment of trust property, being a power

conferred on a trustee before the passing of this Act or conferred on him under any enactment passed before the passing of this Act, shall have effect as a power to invest property in like manner and subject to the like provisions as under the foregoing provisions of this Act.

(3) In relation to property, including wider-range but not including narrower-range investments,—

(a) which a trustee is authorised to hold apart from—

  (i) the provisions of section one of this Act or any of the provisions of Part I of the Trustee Act 1925, or any of the provisions of the Trusts (Scotland) Act 1921, or
  (ii) any such power to invest in authorised investments as is mentioned in the foregoing subsection, or

(b) which became part of a trust fund in consequence of the exercise by the trustee, as owner of property falling within this subsection, of any power conferred by subsection (3) or (4) of section ten of the Trustee Act 1925, or paragraph (o) or (p) of subsection (1) of section four of the Trusts (Scotland) Act 1921,

the foregoing section shall have effect subject to the modifications set out in the Second Schedule to this Act.

(4) The foregoing subsection shall not apply where the powers of the trustee to invest or postpone conversion have been conferred or varied—

(a) by an order of any court made within the period of ten years ending with the passing of this Act, or
(b) by any enactment passed, or instrument having effect under an enactment made, within that period, being an enactment or instrument relating specifically to the trusts in question; or
(c) by an enactment contained in a local Act of the present Session;

but the provisions of the Third Schedule to this Act shall have effect in a case falling within this subsection.

4 Interpretation of references to trust property and trust funds

(1) In this Act 'property' includes real or personal property of any description, including money and things in action:

Provided that it does not include an interest in expectancy, but the falling into possession of such an interest, or the receipt of proceeds of the sale thereof, shall be treated for the purposes of this Act as an accrual of property to the trust fund.

(2) So much of the property in the hands of a trustee shall for the purposes of this Act constitute one trust fund as is held on trusts which (as respects the beneficiaries or their respective interests or the purposes of the trust or as respects the powers of the trustee) are not identical with those on which any other property in his hands is held.

(3) Where property is taken out of a trust fund by way of appropriation so as to form a separate fund, and at the time of the appropriation the trust fund had (as to the whole or a part thereof) been divided in pursuance of subsection (1) of section two of this Act, or that subsection as modified by the Second Schedule to this Act, then if the separate fund is so divided the narrower-range and wider-range parts of the separate fund may be constituted so as either to be equal, or to bear to each other the same proportion as the two corresponding parts of the fund out of which it was so appropriated (the values of those

parts of those funds being ascertained as at the time of appropriation), or some intermediate proportion.

(4) (*Applies to Scotland only.*)

5 Certain valuations to be conclusive for purposes of division of trust fund

(1) If for the purposes of section two or four of this Act or the Second Schedule thereto a trustee obtains, from a person reasonably believed by the trustee to be qualified to make it, a valuation in writing of any property, the valuation shall be conclusive in determining whether the division of the trust fund in pursuance of subsection (1) of the said section two, or any transfer or apportionment of property under that section or the said Second Schedule, has been duly made.

(2) The foregoing subsection applies to any such valuation notwithstanding that it is made by a person in the course of his employment as an officer or servant.

6 Duty of trustees in choosing investments

(1) In the exercise of his powers of investment a trustee shall have regard—

(a) to the need for diversification of investments of the trust, in so far as is appropriate to the circumstances of the trust;
(b) to the suitability to the trust of investments of the description of investment proposed and of the investment proposed as an investment of that description.

(2) Before exercising any power conferred by section one of this Act to invest in a manner specified in Part II or III of the First Schedule to this Act, or before investing in any such manner in the exercise of a power falling within subsection (2) of section three of this Act, a trustee shall obtain and consider proper advice on the question whether the investment is satisfactory having regard to the matters mentioned in paragraphs (a) and (b) of the foregoing subsection.

(3) A trustee retaining any investment made in the exercise of such a power and in such a manner as aforesaid shall determine at what intervals the circumstances, and in particular the nature of the investment, make it desirable to obtain such advice as aforesaid, and shall obtain and consider such advice accordingly.

(4) For the purposes of the two foregoing subsections, proper advice is the advice of a person who is reasonably believed by the trustee to be qualified by his ability in and practical experience of financial matters; and such advice may be given by a person notwithstanding that he gives it in the course of his employment as an officer or servant.

(5) A trustee shall not be treated as having complied with subsection (2) or (3) of this section unless the advice was given or has been subsequently confirmed in writing.

(6) Subsections (2) and (3) of this section shall not apply to one of two or more trustees where he is the person giving the advice required by this section to his co-trustee or co-trustees, and shall not apply where powers of a trustee are lawfully exercised by an officer or servant competent under subsection (4) of this section to give proper advice.

(7) Without prejudice to section eight of the Trustee Act 1925, or section thirty, of the Trusts (Scotland) Act 1921 (which relate to valuation, and the proportion of the value to be lent, where a trustee lends on the security of property) the advice required by this section shall not include, in the case of a loan on the security of freehold or leasehold property in England and Wales or Northern Ireland or on heritable security in Scotland, advice on the suitability of the particular loan.

7 Application of ss 1–6 to persons, other than trustees, having trustee investment powers

(1) Where any persons, not being trustees, have a statutory power of making investments which is or includes power—

(a) to make the like investments as are authorised by section one of the Trustee Act 1925, or section ten of the Trusts (Scotland) Act 1921, or
(b) to make the like investments as trustees are for the time being by law authorised to make,

however the power is expressed, the foregoing provisions of this Act shall with the necessary modifications apply in relation to them as if they were trustees:

Provided that property belonging to a Consolidated Loans Fund or any other fund applicable wholly or partly for the redemption of debt shall not by virtue of the foregoing provisions of this Act be invested or held invested in any manner specified in paragraph 6 of Part II of the First Schedule to this Act or in wider-range investments.

(2) Where, in the exercise of powers conferred by any enactment, an authority to which paragraph 9 of Part II of the First Schedule to this Act applies uses money belonging to any fund for a purpose for which the authority has power to borrow, the foregoing provisions of this Act, as applied by the foregoing subsection, shall apply as if there were comprised in the fund (in addition to the actual content thereof) property, being narrower-range investments, having a value equal to so much of the said money as for the time being has not been repaid to the fund, and accordingly any repayment of such money to the fund shall not be treated for the said purposes as the accrual of property to the fund:

Provided that nothing in this subsection shall be taken to require compliance with any of the provisions of section six of this Act in relation to the exercise of such powers as aforesaid.

(3) In this section 'Consolidated Loans Fund' means a fund established under section fifty-five of the Local Government Act 1958, and includes a loans fund established under Schedule 3 to the Local Government (Scotland) Act 1975 and 'statutory power' means a power conferred by an enactment passed before the passing of this Act or by any instrument made under any such enactment.

Note: Section shown as amended by the Local Government and Planning (Scotland) Act 1982, s 66(1), Sch 3, para 4.

---

8 Application of ss 1–6 in special cases

(1) In relation to persons to whom this section applies—

(a) notwithstanding anything in subsection (3) of section one of this Act, no provision of any enactment passed, or instrument having effect under an enactment and made, before the passing of this Act shall limit the powers conferred by the said section one;
(b) subsection (1) of the foregoing section shall apply where the power of making investments therein mentioned is or includes a power to make some only of the investments mentioned in paragraph (a) or (b) of that subsection.

(2) This section applies to—

(a) the persons for the time being authorised to invest funds of the Duchy of Lancaster;

(b) any persons specified in an order made by the Treasury by statutory instrument, being persons (whether trustees or not) whose power to make investments is conferred by or under any enactment contained in a local or private Act.

(3) An order of the Treasury made under the foregoing subsection may provide that the provisions of sections one to six of this Act (other than the provisions of subsection (3) of section one) shall, in their application to any persons specified therein, have effect subject to such exceptions and modifications as may be specified.

9 Supplementary provisions as to investments

(1) (Omitted.)
(2) It is hereby declared that the power to subscribe for securities conferred by subsection (4) of the said section ten includes power to retain them for any period for which the trustee has power to retain the holding in respect of which the right to subscribe for the securities was offered, but subject to any conditions subject to which the trustee has that power.

Note: Section 9(1) inserts s 10(3)(bb) into the Trustee Act 1925.

10 *(Applies to Scotland only.)*

11 Local Authority investment schemes

(1) Without prejudice to powers conferred by or under any other enactment any authority to which this section applies may invest property held by the authority in accordance with a scheme submitted to the Treasury by any association of local authorities and approved by the Treasury as enabling investments to be made collectively without in substance extending the scope of powers of investment.

(2) A scheme under this section may apply to a specified authority or to a specified class of authorities, may make different provisions as respects different authorities or different classes of authorities or as respects different descriptions of property or property held for different purposes, and may impose restrictions on the extent to which the power controlled by the foregoing subsection shall be exerciseable.

(3) In approving a scheme under this section, the Treasury may direct that the Financial Services Act 1986 shall not apply to dealings undertaken or documents issued for the purposes of the scheme, or to such dealings or documents of such descriptions as may be specified in the direction.

(4) The authorities to which this section applies are—

(a) in England and Wales the council of a county, a county borough, a borough, a district, or a parish, the Common Council of the City of London, the Broads Authority, a National Park Authority, a police authority established under section 3 of the Police Act 1996, the Service Authority for the National Crime Squad, a joint authority established by Part IV of the Local Government Act 1985 and the Council of the Isles of Scilly;
(b) in Scotland, a local authority within the meaning of the Local Government (Scotland) Act 1947;

(c) in any part of Great Britain, a joint board or joint committee constituted to discharge or advise on the discharge of the functions of any two or more of the authorities mentioned in the foregoing paragraphs (including a joint committee established by those authorities acting in combination in accordance with regulations made under section 7 of the Superannuation Act 1972;

(d) in Northern Ireland a district council established under the Local Government Act (Northern Ireland) 1972 and the Northern Ireland Local Government Officers' Superannuation Committee established under the Local Government (Superannuation) Act (Northern Ireland) 1950.

(e) in any part of the United Kingdom, the Service Authority for the National Criminal Intelligence Service.

Note: Section shown as amended by the Local Government Act 1985, s 102(2), Sch 17 (repealing words inserted by the Greater London Council (General Powers) Act 1967, s 10(1)); the London Government Act 1963, s 93(1), Sch 18, Pt II; the Financial Services Act 1986, s 212(2), Sch 16, para 2(a); the Local Government Act 1972, s 272(1), Sch 30; the Local Government Act 1985, s 84, Sch 14, Pt II, para 38; the Education Reform Act 1988, s 237(2), Sch 13, Pt 1; the Water Act 1989, s 190(1), Sch 25, para 29(1) (having previously been amended by the Water Resources Act 1963, s 136(1), Sch 13, para 16); the Norfolk and Suffolk Broads Act 1988, s 21, Sch 6, para 3; the Police and Magistrates' Courts Act 1994, s 43, Sch 4, Pt II, para 46; the Local Government Act 1985, s 84, Sch 14, Pt II, para 38 and s 102(2) of, and Sch 17 to, the 1985 Act; the Superannuation Act 1972, s 29(1), Sch 6, para 40; the Transfer of Functions (Local Government, etc) (Northern Ireland) Order 1973, SR & O (NI) 1973/256, art 3, Sch 2; the Environment Act 1995, s 78, Sch 10, para 5; the Police Act 1996, s 103(1), Sch 7, Pt I, paras 1(1), 2(a); the Police Act 1997, s 134(1), Sch 9, para 4; and the Local Government (Wales) Act 1994, s 66(6), Sch 16, para 19(1).

---

12 Power to confer additional powers of investment

(1) Her Majesty may by Order in Council extend the powers of investment conferred by section one of this Act by adding to Part I, Part II or Part III of the First Schedule to this Act any manner of investment specified in the Order.

(2) Any Order under this section shall be subject to annulment in pursuance of a resolution of either House of Parliament.

13 Power to modify provisions as to division of trust fund

(1) The Treasury may by order made by statutory instrument direct that, subject to subsection (3) of section four of this Act, any division of a trust fund made in pursuance of subsection (1) of section two of this Act during the continuance in force of the order shall be made so that the value of the wider-range part at the time of the division bears to the then value of the narrower-range part such proportion, greater than one but not greater than three to one, as may be prescribed by the order; and in this Act 'the prescribed proportion' means the proportion for the time being prescribed under this subsection.

(2) A fund which has been divided in pursuance of subsection (1) of section two of this Act before the coming into operation of an order under the foregoing subsection may notwithstanding anything in that subsection be again divided (once only) in pursuance of the said subsection (1) during the continuance in force of the order.

(3) If an order is made under subsection (1) of this section, then as from the coming into operation of the order—

(a) paragraph (b) of subsection (3) of section two of this Act and subparagraph (b) of paragraph 3 of the Second Schedule thereto shall have effect with the substitution, for the words from 'each' to the end, of the words 'the wider-range part of the fund is increased by an amount which bears the prescribed proportion to the amount by which the value of the narrower-range part of the fund is increased';

(b) subsection (3) of section four of this Act shall have effect as if for the words 'so as either' to 'each other' there were substituted the words 'so as to bear to each other either the prescribed proportion or'.

(4) An order under this section may be revoked by a subsequent order thereunder prescribing a greater proportion.

(5) An order under this section shall not have effect unless approved by a resolution of each House of Parliament.

14 (*Applies to Scotland only.*)

15 Saving for powers of court

The enlargement of the investment powers of trustees by this Act shall not lessen any power of a court to confer wider powers of investment on trustees, or affect the extent to which any such power is to be exercised.

16 Minor and consequential amendments and repeals

(1) The provisions of the Fourth Schedule to this Act (which contain minor amendments and amendments consequential on the foregoing provisions of this Act) shall have effect.

(2) . . .

Note: Section shown as amended by the Statute Law (Repeals) Act 1974.

17 Short title, extent and construction

(1) This Act may be cited as the Trustee Investments Act 1961.

(2) Sections eleven and sixteen of this Act shall extend to Northern Ireland, but except as aforesaid and except so far as any other provisions of the Act apply by virtue of subsection (1) of section one of the Trustee Act (Northern Ireland) 1958, or any other enactment of the Parliament of Northern Ireland, to trusts the execution of which is governed by the law in force in Northern Ireland, this Act does not apply to such trusts.

(3) So much of section sixteen of this Act as relates to the National Savings Bank shall extend to the Isle of Man and the Channel Islands.

(4) Except where the context otherwise requires, in this Act, in its application to trusts the execution of which is governed by the law in force in England and Wales, expressions have the same meaning as in the Trustee Act 1925.

(5) (*Applies to Scotland only.*)

Note: Section shown as amended by the Post Office Act 1969, ss 94, 114, Sch 6, Pt III; and the Trustee Savings Banks Act 1985, ss 4(3), 7(3), Sch 4.

SCHEDULES

FIRST SCHEDULE

Section 1

MANNER OF INVESTMENT

PART I

NARROWER-RANGE INVESTMENTS NOT REQUIRING ADVICE

1. In Defence Bonds, National Savings Certificates Ulster Savings Certificates, Ulster Development Bonds, National Development Bonds, British Savings Bonds, National Savings Income Bonds National Savings Deposit Bonds, National Savings Indexed-Income Bonds, National Savings Capital Bonds, National Savings FIRST Option Bonds, National Savings Pensioners Guaranteed Income Bonds.

2. In deposits in the National Savings Bank, . . . and deposits in a bank or department thereof certified under subsection (3) of section nine of the Finance Act 1956.

Note: Paragraphs shown as amended by the Trustee Investments (Additional Powers) (No 2) Order 1962, SI 1962/2611; the Trustee Investment (Additional Powers) Order 1964, SI 1964/703; the Trustee Investments (Additional Powers) Order 1968, SI 1968/470; the Trustee Investment (Additional Powers) Order 1982, SI 1982/1086; the Trustee Investments (Additional Powers) (No 2) Order 1983, SI 1983/1525; the Trustee Investments (Additional Powers) Order 1985, SI 1985/1780; the Trustee Investments (Additional Powers) Order 1988, SI 1988/2254; the Trustee Investments (Additional Powers) Order 1992, SI 1992/1738; the Trustee Investments (Additional Powers) Order 1994, SI 1994/265; the Post Office Act 1969, ss 94, 114, Sch 6, Pt III; and the Trustee Savings Banks Act 1976, s 36(2), Sch 6.

PART II

NARROWER-RANGE INVESTMENTS REQUIRING ADVICE

1. In securities issued by Her Majesty's Government in the United Kingdom, the Government of Northern Ireland or the Government of the Isle of Man, not being securities falling within Part I of this Schedule and being fixed-interest securities registered in the United Kingdom or the Isle of Man, Treasury Bills or Tax Reserve Certificates or any variable interest securities issued by Her Majesty's Government in the United Kingdom and registered in the United Kingdom.

2. In any securities the payment of interest on which is guaranteed by Her Majesty's Government in the United Kingdom or the Government of Northern Ireland.

3. In fixed-interest securities issued in the United Kingdom by any public authority or nationalised industry or undertaking in the United Kingdom.

4. In fixed-interest securities issued in the United Kingdom by the government of any overseas territory within the Commonwealth or by any public or local authority within such a territory, being securities registered in the United Kingdom.

References in this paragraph to an overseas territory or to the government of such a territory shall be construed as if they occurred in the Overseas Service Act 1958.

4A. In securities issued in the United Kingdom by the government of an overseas territory within the Commonwealth or by any public or local authority within such a territory, being securities registered in the United Kingdom and in respect of which the rate of interest is variable by reference to one or more of the following:—

(a) the Bank of England's minimum lending rate;
(b) the average rate of discount on allotment on 91-day Treasury bills;
(c) a yield on 91-day Treasury bills;
(d) a London sterling inter-bank offered rate;
(e) a London sterling certificate of deposit rate.

References in this paragraph to an overseas territory or to the government of such a territory shall be construed as if they occurred in the Overseas Service Act 1958.

5. In fixed-interest securities issued in the United Kingdom by the African Development Bank, the Asian Development Bank, the Caribbean Development Bank, the European Bank for Reconstruction and Development, the International Finance Corporation, the International Monetary Fund or by the International Bank for Reconstruction and Development, being securities registered in the United Kingdom.

In fixed-interest securities issued in the United Kingdom by the Inter-American Development Bank,

In fixed interest securities issued in the United Kingdom by the European Atomic Energy Community, the European Economic Community, the European Investment Bank or by the European Coal and Steel Community, being securities registered in the United Kingdom.

5A. In securities issued in the United Kingdom by

(i) the International Bank for Reconstruction and Development or by the European Investment Bank or by the European Coal and Steel Community, being securities registered in the United Kingdom or
(ii) the Inter-American Development Bank

being securities in respect of which the rate of interest is variable by reference to one or more of the following:—

(a) the Bank of England's minimum lending rate;
(b) the average rate of discount on allotment on 91-day Treasury bills;
(c) a yield on 91-day Treasury bills;
(d) a London sterling inter-bank offered rate;
(e) a London sterling certificate of deposit rate.

5B. In securities issued in the United Kingdom by the African Development Bank, the Asian Development Bank, the Caribbean Development Bank, the European Atomic Energy Community, the European Bank of Reconstruction and Development, the European Economic Community, the International Finance Corporation or by the International Monetary Fund, being securities registered in the United Kingdom and in respect of which the rate of interest is variable by reference to one or more of the following:—

(a) The average rate of discount on allotment on 91-day Treasury Bills;
(b) a yield on 91-day Treasury Bills;
(c) a London sterling inter-bank offered rate;
(d) a London sterling certificate of deposit rate.

6. In debentures issued in the United Kingdom by a company incorporated in the United Kingdom, being debentures registered in the United Kingdom.

7. In stock of the Bank of Ireland.

In Bank of Ireland 7 per cent Loan Stock 1968/91.

8. . . .

9. In loans to any authority to which this paragraph applies charged on all or any of the revenues of the authority or on a fund into which all or any of those revenues are payable, in any fixed-interest securities issued in the United Kingdom by any such authority for the purpose of borrowing money so charged, and in deposits with any such authority by way of temporary loan made on the giving of a receipt for the loan by the treasurer or other similar officer of the authority and on the giving of an undertaking by the authority that, if requested to charge the loan as aforesaid, it will either comply with the request or repay the loan.

This paragraph applies to the following authorities, that is to say—

(a) any local authority in the United Kingdom;
(b) any authority all the members of which are appointed or elected by one or more local authorities in the United Kingdom;
(c) any authority the majority of the members of which are appointed or elected by one or more local authorities in the United Kingdom, being an authority which by virtue of any enactment has power to issue a precept to a local authority in England and Wales, or a requisition to a local authority in Scotland, or to the expenses of which, by virtue of any enactment, a local authority in the United Kingdom is or can be required to contribute;
(d) the Receiver for the Metropolitan Police District or a police authority established under s 3 of the Police Act 1996;
(da) the Service Authority for the National Criminal Intelligence Service or the Service Authority for the National Crime Squad;
(e) the Belfast City and District Water Commissioners.
(f) the Great Ouse Water Authority.
(g) any district council in Northern Ireland.
(h) . . .
(i) any residuary body established by section 57 of the Local Government Act 1985.

9A. In any securities issued in the United Kingdom by any authority to which paragraph 9 applies for the purpose of borrowing money charged on all or any of the revenues of the authority or on a fund into which all or any of those revenues are payable and being securities in respect of which the rate of interest is variable by reference to one or more of the following:—

(a) the Bank of England's minimum lending rate;
(b) the average rate of discount on allotment on 91-day Treasury bills;
(c) a yield on 91-day Treasury bills;
(d) a London sterling inter-bank offered rate;

(e) a London sterling certificate of deposit rate.

10. In debentures or in the guaranteed or preference stock of any incorporated company, being statutory water undertakers within the meaning of the Water Act 1945, or any corresponding enactment in force in Northern Ireland, and having during each of the ten years immediately preceding the calendar year in which the investment was made paid a dividend of not less than five per cent on its ordinary shares.

10A. In any units of a gilt unit trust scheme.

References in this Schedule to a gilt unit trust scheme are references to a collective investment scheme—

(a) which is an authorised unit trust scheme within the meaning of the Financial Services Act 1986, a recognised scheme within the meaning of that Act or a UCITS; and
(b) whose objective is to invest not less than 90% of the property of the scheme in loan stock, bonds and other instruments creating or acknowledging indebtedness which are transferable and which are issued or guaranteed by—

    (i) the government of the United Kingdom or of any other country or territory elsewhere,
    (ii) by a local authority in the United Kingdom or in a relevant state, or
    (iii) by an international organisation the members of which include the United Kingdom or a relevant state;

and, in respect of the remainder of the property of the scheme, whose objective is to invest in any instrument falling within any of paragraphs 1 to 3, 5 or 6 of Schedule 1 to the Financial Services Act 1986.

11. . . .

12. In deposits with a building society within the meaning of the Building Societies Act 1986.

13. In mortgages of freehold property in England and Wales or Northern Ireland and of leasehold property in those countries of which the unexpired term at the time of investment is not less than sixty years, and in loans on heritable security in Scotland.

14. In perpetual rent-charges charged on land in England and Wales or Northern Ireland and fee-farm rents (not being rent-charges) issuing out of such land, and in feu-duties or ground annuals in Scotland.

15. In Certificates of Tax Deposit.

16. In fixed-interest or variable interest securities issued by the government of a relevant state.

17. In any securities the payment of interest on which is guaranteed by the government of a relevant state.

18. In fixed-interest securities issued in any relevant state by any public authority or nationalised industry or undertaking in that state.

19. In fixed-interest or variable interest securities issued in a relevant state by the government of any overseas territory within the Commonwealth or by any public or local authority within such a territory.

References in this paragraph to an overseas territory or to the government of such a territory shall be construed as if they occurred in the Overseas Development and Co-operation Act 1980.

20. In the fixed-interest or variable interest securities issued in a relevant state by—

(a) the African Development Bank;
(b) the Asian Development Bank;
(c) the Caribbean Development Bank;
(d) the International Finance Corporation;
(e) the International Monetary Fund;
(f) the International Bank for Reconstruction and Development;
(g) the Inter-American Development Bank;
(h) the European Atomic Energy Community;
(i) the European Bank for Reconstruction and Development;
(j) the European Economic Community;
(k) the European Investment Bank; or
(l) the European Coal and Steel Community.

21. In debentures issued in any relevant state by a company incorporated in that state.

22. In loans to any authority to which this paragraph applies secured on all or any of the revenues of the authority or on a fund into which all or any of those revenues are payable, in fixed-interest or variable interest securities issued in a relevant state by any such authority in that state for the purpose of borrowing money so secured, and in deposits with any authority to which this paragraph applies by way of temporary loan made on the giving of a receipt for the loan by the treasurer or other similar officer of the authority and on the giving of an undertaking by the authority that, if requested to charge the loan as aforesaid, it will either comply with the request or repay the loan.

This paragraph applies to the following authorities, that is to say—

(a) any local authority in a relevant state; or
(b) any local authority all the members of which are appointed or elected by one or more local authorities in any such state.

23. In deposits with a mutual investment society whose head office is located in a relevant state.

24. In loans secured on any interest in property in a relevant state which corresponds to an interest in property falling within paragraph 13 of this Part of this Schedule.

Note: Paragraphs shown as amended by the Trustee Investments (Additional Powers) Order 1977, SI 1977/831; the Trustee Investments (Additional Powers) (No 2) Order 1977, SI 1977/1878; the Trustee Investments (Additional Powers) Order 1983, SI 1983/772; the Trustee Investments (Additional Powers) Order 1991, SI 1991/999; the Trustee Investments (Additional Powers) (No 2) Order 1964, SI 1964/1404; the Trustee Investments (Additional Powers) Order 1972, SI 1972/1818; the Trustee Investments (Additional Powers) Order 1966, SI 1966/401; the Agriculture and Forestry (Financial Provisions) Act 1991, s 1(1), (5), Schedule, Pt IV; the Police and Magistrates' Courts Act 1994, s 43, Sch 4, Pt II, para 47; the Trustee Investments (Additional Powers) Order 1962, SI 1962/658; the Trustee Investments (Additional Powers) Order 1973, SI 1973/1332; the Trustee Investments (Additional Powers) Order 1986, SI 1986/601; the Education Reform Act 1988, s 237(2), Sch 13, Pt I; the Trustee Investments (Additional Powers) (No 2) Order 1994, SI 1994/1908, art 2(1); the Trustee Savings Banks Act 1976, s 36(2), Sch 6; the Building Societies Act 1986, s 120(1), Sch 18, Pt I, para 4(2); the Trustee Investments (Additional Powers) Order 1975, SI 1975/1710; the Trustee Investments (Additional Powers) (No 2) Order 1994, SI 1994/1908, art 2(2); the Water Act 1989, s 190(1), Sch 25, para 29(2), (3), Vol 49, title Water (Pt I); the Police Act 1996, s 103(1), Sch 7, Pt I, paras 1(1), 2(a); the Trustee Investments (Additional Powers) Order 1995, SI 1995/768, art 3; and the Police Act 1997, s 134(1), Sch 9, para 5.

PART III

WIDER-RANGE INVESTMENTS

1. In any securities issued in the United Kingdom by a company incorporated in the United Kingdom, being securities registered in the United Kingdom and not being securities falling within Part II of this Schedule.

2. In shares in a building society within the meaning of the Building Societies Act 1986.

2A. In any shares in an investment company with variable capital within the meaning of the Open-Ended Investment Companies (Investment Companies with Variable Capital) Regulations 1996.

3. In any units of an authorised unit trust scheme within the meaning of the Financial Services Act 1986.

4. In any securities issued in any relevant state by a company incorporated in that state or by any unincorporated body constituted under the law of that state, not being (in either case) securities falling within Part II of this Schedule or paragraph 6 of this part of this Schedule.

5. In shares in a mutual investment society whose head office is located in a relevant state.

6. In any units of a collective investment scheme which is—

(a) a recognised scheme within the meaning of the Financial Services Act 1986 which is constituted in a relevant state; or
(b) a UCITS;

and which does not fall within Part II of this Schedule.

Note: Paragraphs shown as amended by the Building Societies Act 1986, s 120(1), Sch 18, Pt I, para 4(3); the Financial Services Act 1986, s 212(2), Sch 16, para 2(b); the Trustee Investments (Additional Powers) (No 2) Order 1994, SI 1994/1908, art 2(3); and the Open-Ended Investment Companies (Investment Companies with Variable Capital) Regulations 1996.

PART IV

SUPPLEMENTAL

1. The securities mentioned in Parts I to III of this Schedule do not include any securities where the holder can be required to accept repayment of the principal, or the payment of any interest, otherwise than in sterling, in the currency of a relevant state or in the european currency unit (as defined in article 1 of Council Regulation No 3180/78/EEC).

2. The securities mentioned in paragraphs 1 to 8 of Part II, other than Treasury Bills or Tax Reserve Certificates, securities issued before the passing of this Act by the Government of the Isle of Man, securities falling within paragraph 4 of the said Part II issued before the

passing of this Act or securities falling within paragraph 9 of that Part, and the securities mentioned in paragraph 1 of Part III of this Schedule, do not include—

(a) securities the price of which is not quoted on a recognised investment exchange within the meaning of the Financial Services Act 1986 or on an investment exchange which constitutes the principal or only market established in a relevant state on which securities admitted to official listing are dealt in or traded;
(b) shares or debenture stock not fully paid up (except shares or debenture stock which by the terms of issue are required to be fully paid up within nine months of the date of issue).

2A. The securities mentioned in paragraphs 16 to 21 of Part II of this Schedule, other than securities traded on a relevant money market or securities falling within paragraph 22 of Part II of this Schedule, and the securities mentioned in paragraph 4 of Part III of this Schedule do not include—

(a) securities the price for which is not quoted on a recognised investment exchange within the meaning of the Financial Services Act 1986 or on an investment exchange which constitutes the principal or only market established in a relevant state on which securities admitted to official listing are dealt in or traded;
(b) shares or debenture stock not fully paid up (except shares or debenture stock which by the terms of issue are required to be fully paid up within nine months of the date of issue or shares issued with no nominal value).

3. The securities mentioned in paragraph 6 and 21 of Part II and paragraph 1 or 4 of Part III of this Schedule do not include—

(a) shares or debentures of an incorporated company of which the total issued and paid up share capital is less than one million pounds;
(ab) shares or debentures of an incorporated company of which the total issued and paid up share capital at any time on the business day before the investment is made is less than the equivalent of one million pounds in the currency of a relevant state (at the exchange rate prevailing in the United Kingdom at the close of business on the day before the investment is made);
(b) shares or debentures of an incorporated company which has not in each of the five years immediately preceding the calendar year in which the investment is made paid a dividend on all the shares issued by the company, excluding any shares issued after the dividend was declared and any shares which by their terms of issue did not rank for the dividend for that year.

For the purposes of sub-paragraph (b) of this paragraph a company formed—

(i) to take over the business of another company or other companies, or
(ii) to acquire the securities of, or control of, another company or other companies,

or for either of those purposes and for other purposes shall be deemed to have paid a dividend as mentioned in that sub-paragraph in any year in which such a dividend has been paid by the other company or all the other companies, as the case may be.

For the purposes of sub-paragraph (b) of this paragraph in relation to investment in shares or debentures of a successor company within the meaning of the Electricity (Northern Ireland) Order 1992 the company shall be deemed to have paid a dividend as mentioned in that sub-paragraph—

(iii) in every year preceding the calender year in which the transfer date within the meaning of Part III of that Order of 1992 falls (the first investment year) which is included in the relevant five years; and

(iv) in the first investment year, if that year is included in the relevant five years and that company does not in fact pay such a dividend in that year; and

'the relevant five years' means the five years immediately preceding the year in which the investment in question is made or proposed to be made.

4. In this Schedule, unless the context otherwise requires, the following expressions have the meanings hereby respectively assigned to them, that is to say—

'debenture' includes debenture stock and bonds, whether constituting a charge on assets or not, and loan stock or notes;
'enactment' includes an enactment of the Parliament of Northern Ireland;
'fixed-interest securities' means securities which under their terms of issue bear a fixed rate of interest;
'local authority' in relation to the United Kingdom, means any of the following authorities—

(a) in England and Wales, the council of a county, a . . . borough . . . an urban or rural district or a parish, the Common Council of the City of London, the Greater London Council and the Council of the Isles of Scilly;
(b) in Scotland, a local authority within the meaning of the Local Government (Scotland) Act 1947;
(c) . . .

. . . . .

'mutual investment society' means a credit institution which operates on mutual principles and which is authorised by the appropriate supervisory authority of a relevant state;
'relevant money market' means a money market which is supervised by the central bank, or a government agency, of a relevant state;
'relevant state' means Austria, Finland, Iceland, Liechtenstein, Norway, Sweden or a member state other than the United Kingdom;
'securities' includes shares, debentures, units within paragraph 3 or 6 of Part III of this Schedule Treasury Bills and Tax Reserve Certificates;
'shares' includes stock;
'Treasury Bills' includes bills issued by Her Majesty's Government in the United Kingdom and Northern Ireland Treasury Bills.

5. It is hereby declared that in this Schedule 'mortgage', in relation to freehold or leasehold property in Northern Ireland, includes a registered charge which, by virtue of subsection (4) of section forty of the Local Registration of Title (Ireland) Act 1891, or any other enactment, operates as a mortgage by deed.

6. In relation to the United Kingdom, References in this Schedule to an incorporated company are references to a company incorporated by or under any enactment and include references to a body of persons established for the purpose of trading for profit and incorporated by Royal Charter.

6A. References in this Schedule to a UCITS are references to a collective investment scheme which is constituted in a relevant state and which complies with the conditions necessary for it to enjoy the rights conferred by the Council Directive 85/611/EEC co-ordinating the laws, regulations and administrative provisions relating to undertakings for collective investment in transferable securities; and section 86(8) of the Financial Services Act 1986 (meaning of 'constituted in a member state') shall apply for the purposes of this paragraph as it applies for the purposes of that section but as if for references in that section to a member state there were substituted references to a relevant state.

7. . . .

Note: Paragraphs shown as amended by the Trustee Investments (Additional Powers) (No 2) Order 1994, SI 1994/1908, arts 3(1)–(5), (7), (8); the Financial Services Act 1986, s 212(2), Sch 16, para 2(c); the Electricity (Northern Ireland Consequential Amendments) Order 1992, SI 1992/232, art 4; the Building Societies Act 1986, s 120(2), Sch 19, Pt I; the London Government Act 1963, ss 83(1), 93(1), Sch 17, para 25, Sch 18, Pt II; the Local Government Act 1972, s 272(1), Sch 30, the SL(R) Act 1981; the Trustee Savings Banks Act 1976, s 36(2), Sch 6; the Trustee Investments (Additional Powers) (No 2) Order 1994, SI 1994/1908, arts 3(1), (6)(a), (b); the National Loans Act 1968, s 24(2), Sch 6, Pt I; the Local Government (Wales) Act 1994, s 66(6), Sch 16, para 19(2); and the Trustee Investments (Additional Powers) Order 1995, SI 1995/768, art 2.

SECOND SCHEDULE

Section 3

MODIFICATION OF S 2 IN RELATION TO PROPERTY FALLING WITHIN S 3(3)

1. In this Schedule 'special-range property' means property falling within subsection (3) of section three of this Act.

2.—(1) Where a trust fund includes special-range property, subsection (1) of section two of this Act shall have effect as if references to the trust fund were references to so much thereof as does not consist of special-range property, and the special-range property shall be carried to a separate part of the fund.

(2) Any property which—

(a) being property belonging to the narrower-range or wider-range part of a trust fund, is converted into special-range property, or
(b) being special-range property, accrues to a trust fund after the division of the fund or part thereof in pursuance of subsection (1) of section two of this Act or of that subsection as modified by sub-paragraph (1) of this paragraph,

shall be carried to such a separate part of the fund as aforesaid; and subsections (2) and (3) of the said section two shall have effect subject to this sub-paragraph.

3. Where property carried to such a separate part as aforesaid is converted into property other than special-range property,—

(a) it shall be transferred to the narrower-range part of the fund or the wider-range part of the fund or apportioned between them, and
(b) any transfer of property from one of those parts to the other shall be made which is necessary to secure that the value of each of those parts of the fund is increased by the same amount.

THIRD SCHEDULE

Section 3

PROVISIONS SUPPLEMENTARY TO S 3(4)

1. Where in a case falling within subsection (4) of section three of this Act, property belonging to the narrower-range part of a trust fund—

(a) is invested otherwise than in a narrower-range investment, or
(b) being so invested, is retained and not transferred or as soon as may be reinvested as mentioned in subsection (2) of section two of this Act.

then, so long as the property continues so invested and comprised in the narrower-range part of the fund, section one of this Act shall not authorise the making or retention of any wider-range investment.

2. Section four of the Trustee Act 1925, or section thirty-three of the Trusts (Scotland) Act, 1921 (which relieve a trustee from liability for retaining an investment which has ceased to be authorised), shall not apply where an investment ceased to be authorised in consequence of the foregoing paragraph.

FOURTH SCHEDULE

Section 16

MINOR AND CONSEQUENTIAL AMENDMENTS

1.—(1) References in the Trustee Act 1925, except in subsection (2) of section sixty-nine of that Act, to section one of that Act or to provisions which include that section shall be construed respectively as references to section one of this Act and as including references to section one of this Act.

(2) References in the Trusts (Scotland) Act 1921, to section ten or eleven of that Act, or to provisions which include either of those sections, shall be construed respectively as references to section one of this Act and as including references to that section.

2–6 . . .

Note: Paragraphs shown as amended by the Water Act 1989, s 190(3), Sch 27, Pt II; the National Savings Bank Act 1971, s 28, Sch 2; the Housing (Consequential Provisions) Act 1985, s 3, Sch I, Pt I; and the Statute Law (Repeals) Act 1974.

THE CHARITIES (TRUSTEE INVESTMENTS ACT 1961) ORDER 1995 (SI 1995/1902)

1 This Order may be cited as the Charities (Trustee Investments Act 1961) Order 1995 and shall come into force on the fourteenth day after the day on which it is made.

2 It is hereby directed that, in the case of a trust fund consisting of property held by or in trust for a charity, any division of the fund in pursuance of section 2(1) of the Trustee Investments Act 1961 shall be made so that the value of the wider-range part at the time of the division bears to the then value of the narrower-range part the proportion of three to one.

3—(1) The Trustee Investments Act 1961 shall, in its application in relation to a trust fund consisting of property held by or in trust for a charity, have effect subject to the modifications specified in the following paragraphs of this article, being modifications which the Secretary of State considers appropriate in consequence of, or in connection with, the direction contained in article 2 of this Order.

(2) Paragraph (b) of section 2(3) and sub-paragraph (b) of paragraph 3 of the Second Schedule shall have effect as if for the words from 'each' to the end there were substituted the words 'the wider-range part of the fund is increased by an amount which bears the specified proportion to the amount by which the value of the narrower-range part of the fund is increased'.

(3) Section 4(3) shall have effect as if for the words 'so as either to be equal, or to bear to each other' there were substituted the words 'so as to bear to each other either the specified proportion or'.

(4) Section 17 shall have effect as if at the end there were added the following subsection—

> '(6) In this Act, "the specified proportion" means the proportion specified in article 2 of the Charities (Trustee Investments Act 1961) Order 1995'.

Appendix 2

FORMS AND CONTRACTS

MODEL CLAUSES

The clauses set out below can be inserted in the objects clause of the Charity Law Association's model Deed of Trust or Memorandum & Articles of Association:

1. *General charitable purposes*

   The [Trustee/Trustees *enter exact details*] shall hold the trust fund upon trust to apply the income and at the [Trustee/Trustees *enter exact details*] discretion, capital for such charitable purpose or purposes [for the relief of sickness *or enter details of other specific purposes*] relating to the National Health Service for the benefit of the public at [*enter name of hospital or other institution*].

2. *Specific charitable purposes*

   The following clauses are set out as examples of specific charitable purposes:

   2.1 *Research*
   To advance the education of the public by conducting or promoting scientific or medical research into the causes and treatment of persons suffering from [*enter specific details*] and to disseminate the useful results thereof to the public.

   2.2 *Hospital amenities/equipment*
   To preserve and protect the good health of patients at [*enter name of hospital or other institution*] through the provision of [*enter details such as library facilities, videos, CD players etc*] [*or enter details of equipment such as body scanners, x-ray machines etc*].

   2.3 *Therapeutic treatment*
   To preserve and protect the good health of patients at [*enter name of hospital or other institution*] through the meditative and therapeutic effects of plain chant.

   2.4 *Education*
   To advance the education of members of the [*enter details of profession such as medical/nursing etc*] profession in [*enter details of subject area of study*] with a view to enhancing professional standards and developing a body of knowledge for the benefit of the public.

The Trustee/Trustees will either be a health service body or an independent Trustee/ Trustees of a separately run charity.

TRUST DEED FOR A CHARITABLE TRUST

Charitable Trust Deed

THIS DECLARATION OF TRUST is made __________ *[date]* by the First Trustees

____

____

____

____

____

[Full names and residential addresses of all of the First Trustees.]

WITNESSES AS FOLLOWS

1. INTRODUCTION

1.1 The First Trustees hold ______________ *[details]* on the trusts declared in this Deed ('the **Trust**')

1.2 Further money or property may be paid or transferred to the **Trustees** for the Trust

1.3 ____

______________________________________ [any other explanatory statement]

2. NAME & OBJECTS

2.1 The Name of the Trust is ______________ *[name]* (or any other name chosen by resolution of the Trustees)

2.2 The objects of the Trust are ______________________________

____

____

____

____

[OBJECTS] (the '**Objects**')

2.3 The Trustees must use the income [and may use the capital] of the Trust in promoting the Objects

3. POWERS

The Trustees have the following powers, which may be exercised only in promoting the Objects:

3.1 To promote or carry out research

3.2 To provide advice

3.3 To publish or distribute information

3.4 To co-operate with other bodies

3.5 To support, administer or set up other charities

3.6 To raise funds (but not by means of **taxable trading**)

3.7 To borrow money and give security for loans (but only in accordance with the restrictions imposed by the Charities Act 1993)

3.8 To acquire or hire property of any kind

3.9 To let or dispose of property of any kind (but only in accordance with the restrictions imposed by the Charities Act 1993)

3.10 To make grants or loans of money and to give guarantees

3.11 To set aside funds for special purposes or as reserves against future expenditure

3.12 To deposit or invest funds in any lawful manner (but to invest only after obtaining advice from a **financial expert** and having regard to the suitability of investments and the need for diversification)

3.13 To delegate the management of investments to a financial expert, but only on terms that:

3.13.1 the investment policy is recorded **in writing** for the financial expert by the Trustees

3.13.2 every transaction is reported promptly to the Trustees

3.13.3 the performance of the investments is reviewed regularly with the Trustees

3.13.4 the Trustees are entitled to cancel the delegation arrangement at any time

3.13.5 the investment policy and the delegation arrangement are reviewed at least once a **year**

3.13.6 all payments due to the financial expert are on a scale or at a level which is agreed in advance and are notified promptly to the Trustees on receipt

3.13.7 the financial expert must not do anything outside the powers of the Trustees

3.14 To insure the property of the Trust against any foreseeable risk and take out other insurance policies to protect the Trust when required

3.15 To insure the Trustees against the costs of a successful defence to a criminal prosecution brought against them as **charity trustees** or against personal liability incurred in respect of any act or omission which is or is alleged to be a breach of trust or breach of duty (unless the Trustee concerned knew that, or was reckless whether, the act or omission was a breach of trust or breach of duty)

3.16 To pay reasonable fees to any nominee or **holding trustee**

3.17 Subject to clause 6.3 to employ paid or unpaid agents, staff or advisers

3.18 To enter into contracts to provide services to or on behalf of other bodies

3.19 To pay the costs of forming the Trust

3.20 To do anything else within the law which promotes or helps to promote the Objects

4. THE TRUSTEES

4.1 The Trustees as the charity trustees have control of the Trust and its property and funds

4.2 The full number of Trustees is ________ *[number]* individuals ________________ *[add special qualification if any is to be required]*

4.3 Subject to clause 4.7 the First Trustees are entitled to hold office for life

OR

Subject to clause 4.7 the First Trustees shall each hold office for the following periods:

________________________________ *[Trustee's name]* ________ *[No. of] years*

________________________________ *[Trustee's name]* ________ *[No. of] years*

________________________________ *[Trustee's name]* ________ *[No. of] years*

________________________________ *[Trustee's name]* ________ *[No. of] years*

4.4 Future Trustees must be appointed [for terms of office of ________ *[number]* years] by resolution of the Trustees

[4.5 A retiring Trustee who is competent to act may be re-appointed at the end of his/her term of office [but a Trustee shall not eligible for re-appointment until ________ *[period]* after the end of ________ *[number]* consecutive terms of office]

4.6 Every future Trustee must sign a declaration of willingness to act as a Trustee of the Trust before he or she is eligible to vote at any meeting of the Trustees

4.7 A Trustee automatically ceases to be a Trustee if he or she:

4.7.1 is disqualified under the Charities Act 1993 from acting as a charity trustee or trustee for a charity

4.7.2 is incapable, whether mentally or physically, of managing his or her own affairs

4.7.3 is absent from ________ *[number]* consecutive meetings of the Trustees

4.7.4 resigns by **written** notice to the Trustees (but only if at least two Trustees will remain in office)

[4.7.5 ceases to be ________________ *[specially qualified]*]

[4.7.6 is removed by a resolution passed by all the other Trustees after inviting the views of the Trustee concerned and considering the matter in the light of any such views]

4.8 A retiring Trustee is entitled to an indemnity from the continuing Trustees at the expense of the Trust in respect of any liabilities properly incurred during his or her trusteeship

4.9 A technical defect in the appointment of a Trustee of which the Trustees are unaware at the time does not invalidate decisions taken by the Trustees

5. PROCEEDINGS OF TRUSTEES

5.1 The Trustees must hold at least ________ *[number]* meetings each year

5.2 A quorum at a meeting is ________ *[number]* Trustees

[5.3 A meeting may be held either in person or by suitable electronic means agreed by the Trustees in which all participants may communicate with all the other participants]

5.4 The [**Chairman**] of the Trustees or (if the Chairman is unable or unwilling to do so) some other Trustee chosen by them presides at each meeting

5.5 Except where otherwise provided in this Deed, every issue may be determined by a simple majority of the votes cast at a meeting of the Trustees but a resolution which is in writing and signed by all the Trustees is as valid as a resolution passed at a meeting and for this purpose the resolution may be contained in more than one document and will be treated as passed on the date of the last signature

5.6 Except for the chairman of the meeting, who has a second or casting vote, every Trustee has one vote on each issue

5.7 The Trustees have the following powers in the administration of the Trust:

5.7.1 to appoint a Chairman, Treasurer and other honorary officers

5.7.2 to delegate any of their functions to committees consisting of two or more persons appointed by them [(but at least ________ *[number]* member(s) of every committee must be a Trustee)] and all proceedings of committees must be reported promptly to the Trustees

5.7.3 to make rules consistent with this Deed to govern proceedings at their meetings and at meetings of committees

5.7.4 to make regulations consistent with this Deed to govern the use and application of the [income] [property and funds] of the Trust including regulations about the operation of bank accounts and the commitment of funds

6. PROPERTY & FUNDS

6.1 Any Trustee who possesses specialist skills or knowledge, and any a firm or company of which such a Trustee is a member or employee, may charge and be paid reasonable fees for work carried out for the Trust on the instructions of the other Trustees (but only if the procedure prescribed by clause 6.3 is followed in selecting the Trustee, firm or company and setting the amount of the fees and provided that this provision may not apply to more than one half of the Trustees in any one financial year)

6.2 No Trustee may receive from the Trust any payment of money or other **material benefit** (whether direct or indirect) except

6.2.1 under clauses 3.15 (indemnity insurance) and 6.1 (fees)

6.2.2 reimbursement of reasonable out-of-pocket expenses (including hotel and travel costs) actually incurred in the administration of the Trust

6.2.3 interest at a reasonable rate on money lent to the Trust

6.2.4 a reasonable rent or hiring fee for property let or hired to the Trust

6.2.5 an indemnity in respect of any liabilities incurred in or about the administration of the Trust (including the costs of a successful defence to criminal proceedings)

6.2.6 in exceptional cases, other payments or benefits (but only with the written approval of the **Commission** in advance)

6.3 Whenever a Trustee has a personal interest in a matter to be discussed at a meeting of the Trustees or any committee, the Trustee concerned must:

6.3.1 declare an interest before discussion on the matter begins

6.3.2 withdraw from the meeting for that item unless expressly invited to remain in order to provide information

6.3.3 not be counted in the quorum during that part of the meeting

6.3.4 withdraw during the vote and have no vote on the matter

6.4 Funds which are not required for immediate use or which will be required for use at a future date must be placed on deposit or invested in accordance with clause 3.12 until needed

6.5 Investments and other property of the Trust may be held:

6.5.1 in the names of the Trustees (or in the name of the trustee body if incorporated under the Charities Act 1993)

6.5.2 in the name of a nominee (being a corporate body registered or having an established place of business in England and Wales) under the control of the Trustees or of a financial expert acting on their instructions

6.5.3 in the name of a **trust corporation** as a holding trustee for the Trust which must be appointed (and may be removed) by deed executed by the Trustees

6.5.4 in the case of land, by the Official Custodian for Charities under an order of the Commissioners or the Court

7. RECORDS & ACCOUNTS

7.1 The Trustees must comply with the requirements of the Charities Act 1993 relating to the keeping of financial records, the audit or independent examination of the accounts and the preparation and transmission to the Commission of:

7.1.1 annual reports

7.1.2 annual returns

7.1.3 annual statements of account

7.2 The Trustees must maintain proper records of:

7.2.1 all proceedings at meetings of the Trustees

7.2.2 all reports of committees

7.2.3 all professional advice obtained

7.3 Financial records, annual reports and statements of account relating to the Trust must be available for inspection by any Trustee

7.4 A copy of the latest available statement of account must be supplied to any person who makes a written request and pays the Trustees' reasonable costs (as required by the Charities Act 1993)

[8. AMENDMENTS

This Deed may be amended by supplemental deed on a resolution passed by ________ *[percentage]* of the Trustees but no amendment is valid if it would make a **fundamental change** to the Objects or to this clause or destroy the charitable status of the Trust. No amendment may be made to clauses 6.2, 6.3 or 6.4 without the prior written consent of the Commission]

[9. AMALGAMATION

9.1 The Trustees may at any time on a resolution passed by at least ________ *[percentage]* of the Trustees transfer the assets and liabilities of the Trust to another charity established for exclusively charitable purposes within, the same as or similar to the Objects ____

____ *[add any special qualification]*

9.2 On a transfer under clause 9.1 the Trustees must ensure that all necessary steps are taken as to:

9.2.1 the transfer of land and other property

9.2.2 the novation of contracts of employment and transfer of any pension rights

9.2.3 the trusteeship of any property held for special purposes]

[10. DISSOLUTION

10.1 The Trustees may at any time decide by resolution passed by at least ________ *[percentage]* of the Trustees that the Trust is to be dissolved. The Trustees will then be responsible for the orderly winding up of the Trust's affairs

10.2 After making provision for all outstanding liabilities of the Trust, the Trustees must apply the remaining property and funds in one or more of the following ways:

10.2.1 by transfer to one or more other bodies established for exclusively charitable purposes within, the same as or similar to the Objects

10.2.2 directly for the Objects or charitable purposes within or similar to the Objects

10.2.3 in such other manner consistent with charitable status as the Commission approve in writing in advance

10.3 A final report and statement of account relating to the Trust must be sent to the Commission]

11. INTERPRETATION

In this Deed

11.1 The following expressions have the following meanings:

['area of benefit' means ___________ *[geographical area]*]

['beneficiaries' means ___________ *[qualifications of beneficiaries]*]

'the Chairman' means the person appointed by the Trustees to preside at their meetings

'charity trustees' has the meaning prescribed by section 97(1) of the Charities Act 1993

'the Commission' means the Charity Commissioners for England and Wales

'financial expert' means an individual, company or firm who is an authorised person or an exempted person within the meaning of the Financial Services Act 1986

['fundamental change' means such a change as would not have been within the reasonable contemplation of a person making a donation to the Trust]

'holding trustee' means an individual or corporate body responsible for holding the title to property but not authorised to make any decisions relating to its use, investment or disposal

'independent examiner' has the meaning prescribed by section 43(3)(a) of the Charities Act 1993

'material benefit' means a benefit which may not be financial but has a monetary value

'the Objects' means the charitable objects of the Trust set out in clause 2

'taxable trading' means carrying on a trade or business on a continuing basis for the principal purpose of raising funds and not for the purpose of actually carrying out the Objects

'the Trust' means the charity created by this Deed

'trust corporation' has the meaning prescribed by section 205(1)(xxviii) of the Law of Property Act 1925 but does not include the Public Trustee

'Trustee' means a charity trustee of the Trust

'written' or 'in writing' refers to a legible document on paper [not] including a fax message

'year' means calendar year

11.2 References to an Act of Parliament are references to the Acts as amended or re-enacted from time to time and to any subordinate legislation made under it

IN WITNESS of the above the parties have executed this Deed

SIGNED AS A DEED BY

[Name of Trustee]	*[Signature of Trustee]*

in the presence of:

[Name, address and occupation of Witness]	*[Signature of Witness]*

SIGNED AS A DEED BY

[Name of Trustee]	*[Signature of Trustee]*

in the presence of:

[Name, address and occupation of Witness]	*[Signature of Witness]*

SIGNED AS A DEED BY

[Name of Trustee]	*[Signature of Trustee]*

in the presence of:

[Name, address and occupation of Witness]	*[Signature of Witness]*

[Repeat for each of the Trustees]

MEMORANDUM & ARTICLES OF ASSOCIATION FOR A CHARITABLE COMPANY

COMPANIES ACTS 1985 & 1989

COMPANY LIMITED BY GUARANTEE AND NOT HAVING A SHARE CAPITAL

MEMORANDUM OF ASSOCIATION OF

____ *[Name]*

1. NAME

The name of the Company is ____

____ *[Name]* (**'the Charity'**)

2. REGISTERED OFFICE

The registered office of the Charity is to be in England and Wales

3. OBJECTS

The objects of the Charity are ____

____

____

____

____ *[Objects]* (**'the Objects'**)

4. POWERS

The Charity has the following powers, which may be exercised only in promoting the Objects:

4.1 To promote or carry out research

4.2 To provide advice

4.3 To publish or distribute information

4.4 To co-operate with other bodies

4.5 To support, administer or set up other charities

4.6 To raise funds (but not by means of **taxable trading**)

4.7 To borrow money and give security for loans (but only in accordance with the restrictions imposed by the Charities Act 1993)

4.8 To acquire or hire property of any kind

4.9 To let or dispose of property of any kind (but only in accordance with the restrictions imposed by the Charities Act 1993)

4.10 To make grants or loans of money and to give guarantees

4.11 To set aside funds for special purposes or as reserves against future expenditure

4.12 To deposit or invest funds in any manner (but to invest only after obtaining advice from a **financial expert** and having regard to the suitability of investments and the need for diversification)

4.13 To delegate the management of investments to a financial expert, but only on terms that:

4.13.1 the investment policy is set down **in writing** for the financial expert by the **Trustees**

4.13.2 every transaction is reported promptly to the Trustees

4.13.3 the performance of the investments is reviewed regularly with the Trustees

4.13.4 the Trustees are entitled to cancel the delegation arrangement at any time

4.13.5 the investment policy and the delegation arrangement are reviewed at least once a **year**

4.13.6 all payments due to the financial expert are on a scale or at a level which is agreed in advance and are notified promptly to the Trustees on receipt

4.13.7 the financial expert must not do anything outside the powers of the Trustees

4.14 To arrange for investments or other property of the Charity to be held in the name of a nominee (being a corporate body registered or having an established place of business in England and Wales) under the control of the Trustees or of a financial expert acting under their instructions and to pay any reasonable fee required

4.15 To insure the property of the Charity against any foreseeable risk and take out other insurance policies to protect the Charity when required

4.16 To insure the Trustees against the costs of a successful defence to a criminal prosecution brought against them as charity trustees or against personal liability incurred in respect of any act or omission which is or is alleged to be a breach of trust or breach of duty, unless the **Trustee** concerned knew that, or was reckless whether, the act or omission was a breach of trust or breach of duty

4.17 Subject to clause 5, to employ paid or unpaid agents, staff or advisers

4.18 To enter into contracts to provide services to or on behalf of other bodies

4.19 To establish subsidiary companies to assist or act as agents for the Charity

4.20 To pay the costs of forming the Charity

4.21 To do anything else within the law which promotes or helps to promote the Objects

5. BENEFITS TO MEMBERS AND TRUSTEES

5.1 The property and funds of the Charity must be used only for promoting the Objects and do not belong to the **members** of the Charity but

5.1.1 members who are not Trustees may be employed by or enter into contracts with the Charity and received reasonable payment for goods or services supplied

5.1.2 members (including Trustees) may be paid interest at a reasonable rate on money lent to the Charity

5.1.3 members (including Trustees) may be paid a reasonable rent or hiring fee for property let or hired to the Charity

5.1.4 individual members who are not trustees but who are beneficiaries may receive charitable benefits in that capacity

5.2 A Trustee must not receive any payment of money or other **material benefit** (whether direct or indirect) from the Charity except

5.2.1 as mentioned in clauses 4.16, 5.1.2, 5.1.3 or 5.3

5.2.2 reimbursement of reasonable out-of-pocket expenses (including hotel and travel costs) actually incurred in running the Charity

5.2.3 an indemnity in respect of any liabilities properly incurred in running the Charity (including the costs of a successful defence to criminal proceedings)

5.2.4 payment to any company in which a Trustee has no more than a 1 per cent shareholding

5.2.5 in exceptional cases, other payments or benefits (but only with the written approval of the **Commission** in advance)

5.3 Any Trustee (or any firm or company of which a Trustee is a member) may enter into a contract with the Charity to supply goods or services in return for a payment or other material benefit but only if

5.3.1 the goods or services are actually required by the Charity

5.3.2 the nature and level of the remuneration is no more than is reasonable in relation to the value of the goods or services and is set in accordance with the procedure in clause 5.4

5.3.3 no more than one half of the Trustees are subject to such a contract in any financial year

5.4 Whenever a Trustee has a personal interest in a matter to be discussed at a meeting of the Trustees or a committee the Trustee concerned must:

5.4.1 declare an interest at or before discussion begins on the matter

5.4.2 withdraw from the meeting for that item unless expressly invited to remain in order to provide information

5.4.3 not be counted in the quorum for that part of the meeting

5.4.4 withdraw during the vote and have no vote on the matter

5.5 This clause may not be amended without the prior written consent of the **Commission**

6. LIMITED LIABILITY

The liability of members is limited

7. GUARANTEE

Every member promises, if the Charity is dissolved while he, she or it remains a member or within 12 months afterwards, to pay up to [£1] towards the costs of dissolution and the liabilities incurred by the Charity while the contributor was a member

8. DISSOLUTION

8.1 If the Charity is dissolved the assets (if any) remaining after provision has been made for all its liabilities must be applied in one or more of the following ways:

8.1.1 by transfer to one or more other bodies established for exclusively charitable purposes within, the same as or similar to the Objects

8.1.2 directly for the Objects or charitable purposes within or similar to the Objects

8.1.3 in such other manner consistent with charitable status as the Commission approve in writing in advance

8.2 A final report and statement of account must be sent to the Commission

9. INTERPRETATION

9.1 Words and expressions defined in the Articles have the same meanings in this Memorandum.

9.2 References to an Act of Parliament are references to the Act as amended or re-enacted from time to time and to any subordinate legislation made under it

We wish to be formed into a company under this Memorandum of Association

NAMES & ADDRESSES OF SUBSCRIBERS	SIGNATURES OF SUBSCRIBERS
[List the full name and residential address of each of the subscribers]	*[Signature of each of the subscribers]*

Date ________________________ *[Date]*

Witness to the above signatures

____

____

____

________________________	________________________
[Name, address and occupation of witness]	*[Signature of witness]*

COMPANIES ACTS 1985 & 1989

COMPANY LIMITED BY GUARANTEE AND NOT HAVING A SHARE CAPITAL

ARTICLES OF ASSOCIATION OF

____ *[Name]*

1. MEMBERSHIP

1.1 The number of members with which the company proposes to be registered is unlimited

1.2 The Charity must maintain a register of members

1.3 **Membership** of the Charity is open to any individual [or organisation] interested in promoting the Objects who

1.3.1 applies to the Charity in the form required by the Trustees

1.3.2 is approved by the Trustees

and

1.3.3 signs the Register of members or consents in writing to become a member [either personally or (in the case of a member organisation) through an **authorised representative**]

1.4 The Trustees may establish different classes of membership and prescribe their respective privileges and duties and set the amounts of any subscriptions

1.5 Membership is terminated if the member concerned

1.5.1 gives written notice of resignation to the Charity

1.5.2 dies [or (in the case of an organisation) ceases to exist]

1.5.3 is six **months** in arrears in paying the relevant subscription (if any) (but in such a case the member may be reinstated on payment of the amount due)

or

1.5.4 is removed from membership by resolution of the Trustees on the ground that in their reasonable opinion the member's continued membership is harmful to the Charity (but only after notifying the member in writing and considering the matter in the light of any written representations which the member concerned puts forward within 14 **clear days** after receiving notice)

1.6 Membership of the Charity is not transferable

2. GENERAL MEETINGS

2.1 Members are entitled to attend general meetings [either] personally [or (in the case of a member organisation) by an authorised representative]. General meetings are called on at least clear 21 days' written notice specifying the business to be discussed

2.2 There is a quorum at a general meeting if the number of members [or authorised representatives] personally present is at least ______ *[number]* or ______ *[percentage]* of the members if greater)

2.3 The [**Chairman**] or (if the Chairman is unable or unwilling to do so) some other member elected by those present presides at a general meeting

2.4 Except where otherwise provided by the **Act**, every issue is decided by a majority of the votes cast

2.5 Except for the chairman of the meeting, who has a second or casting vote, every member present in person [(or through an authorised representative)] has one vote on each issue

2.6 A written resolution signed by all those entitled to vote at a general meeting is as valid as a resolution actually passed at a general meeting (and for this purpose the written resolution may be set out in more than one document and will be treated as passed on the date of the last signature)

2.7 The Charity must hold an **AGM** in every year which all members are entitled to attend. The first AGM may be held within 18 months after the Charity's incorporation

2.8 At an AGM the members:

2.8.1 receive the accounts of the Charity for the previous financial year

2.8.2 receive the Trustees' report on the Charity's activities since the previous AGM

2.8.3 accept the retirement of those Trustees who wish to retire or who are retiring by rotation

2.8.4 elect persons to be Trustees to fill the vacancies arising

2.8.5 appoint auditors for the Charity

2.8.6 may confer on any individual (with his or her consent) the honorary title of Patron, President or Vice-President of the Charity

and

2.8.7 discuss and determine any issues of policy or deal with any other business put before them

2.9 Any general meeting which is not an AGM is an **EGM**

2.10 An EGM may be called at any time by the Trustees and must be called within 28 days on a written request from at least ______ *[number]* members

THE TRUSTEES

3.1 The Trustees as **charity trustees** have control of the Charity and its property and funds

3.2 The Trustees when complete consist of at least [three] and not more than ______ *[number]* individuals, [all of whom must be members *[add any special qualification]*]

3.3 The subscribers to the Memorandum are the first Trustees of the Charity

3.4 Every Trustee must sign a declaration of willingness to act as a charity trustee of the Charity before he or she is eligible to vote at any meeting of the Trustees

3.5 One third (or the number nearest one third) of the Trustees must retire at each AGM, those longest in office retiring first and the choice between any of equal service being made by drawing lots

3.6 A Trustee's term of office automatically terminates if he or she:

3.6.1 is disqualified under the Charities Act 1993 from acting as a charity trustee

3.6.2 is incapable, whether mentally or physically, of managing his or her own affairs

3.6.3 is absent from ________ *[number]* consecutive meetings of the Trustees

3.6.4 ceases to be a member [(but such a person may be reinstated by resolution passed by all the other Trustees on resuming membership of the Charity before the next AGM)]

3.6.5 resigns by written notice to the Trustees (but only if at least two Trustees will remain in office)

3.6.6 is removed by resolution passed by at least ________ *[number or percentage]* of the members present and voting at a general meeting after the meeting has invited the views of the Trustee concerned and considered the matter in the light of any such views]

or

[3.6.7 ceases to ________________________________ *[have the required qualification]*]

3.7 The Trustees may at any time co-opt any person duly qualified to be appointed as a Trustee to fill a vacancy in their number or as an additional Trustee, but a co-opted Trustee holds office only until the next AGM

3.8 A technical defect in the appointment of a Trustee of which the Trustees are unaware at the time does not invalidate decisions taken at a meeting

4. PROCEEDINGS OF TRUSTEES

4.1 The Trustees must hold at least ________ *[number]* meetings each year

4.2 A quorum at a meeting of the Trustees is ________ *[number]* Trustees

[4.3 A meeting of the Trustees may be held either in person or by suitable electronic means agreed by the Trustees in which all participants may communicate with all the other participants]

4.4 The Chairman or (if the Chairman is unable or unwilling to do so) some other Trustee chosen by the Trustees present presides at each meeting

4.5 Every issue may be determined by a simple majority of the votes cast at a meeting but a written resolution signed by all the Trustees is as valid as a resolution passed at a meeting (and for this purpose the resolution may be contained in more than one document and will be treated as passed on the date of the last signature)

4.6 Except for the chairman of the meeting, who has a second or casting vote, every Trustee has one vote on each issue

4.7 A procedural defect of which the Trustees are unaware at the time does not invalidate decisions taken at a meeting

5. POWERS OF TRUSTEES

The Trustees have the following powers in the administration of the Charity

5.1 to appoint (and remove) any member (who may be a Trustee) to act as Secretary to the Charity in accordance with the Act

5.2 to appoint a Chairman, Treasurer and other honorary officers from among their number

5.3 to delegate any of their functions to committees consisting of two or more individuals appointed by them (but at least ________ *[number]* member of every committee must be a Trustee and all proceedings of committees must be reported promptly to the Trustees)

5.4 to make Standing Orders consistent with the **Memorandum, these Articles** and the Act) to govern proceedings at general meetings

5.5 to make Rules consistent with the Memorandum, these Articles and the Act to govern proceedings at their meetings and at meetings of committees

5.6 to make Regulations consistent with the Memorandum, these Articles and the Act to govern the administration of the Charity and the use of its seal (if any)

5.7 to establish procedures to assist the resolution of disputes within the Charity

5.8 to exercise any powers of the Charity which are not reserved to a general meeting

6. RECORDS & ACCOUNTS

6.1 The Trustees must comply with the requirements of the Act and of the Charities Act 1993 as to keeping financial records, the audit of accounts and the preparation and transmission to the Registrar of Companies and the Commission of:

6.1.1 annual reports

6.1.2 annual returns

6.1.3 annual statements of account

6.2 The Trustees must keep proper records of

6.2.1 all proceedings at general meeting

6.2.2 all proceedings at meetings of the Trustees

6.2.3 all reports of committees and

6.2.4 all professional advice obtained

6.3 Accounting records relating to the Charity must be made available for inspection by any Trustee at any reasonable time during normal office hours and may be made available for inspection by members who are not Trustees if the Trustees so decide

6.4 A copy of the Charity's latest available statement of account must be supplied on request to any Trustee or member, or to any other person who makes a written request and pays the Charity's reasonable costs, within two months

7. NOTICES

7.1 Notices under these Articles may be sent by hand, or by post or by suitable electronic means or (where applicable to members generally) may be published in any suitable journal or [national] newspaper [circulating in area of benefit] or any newsletter distributed by the Charity

7.2 The only address at which a member is entitled to receive notices is the address shown in the register of members

7.3 Any notice given in accordance with these Articles is to be treated for all purposes as having been received

7.3.1 24 hours after being sent by electronic means or delivered by hand to the relevant address

7.3.2 two clear days after being sent by first class post to that address

7.3.3 three clear days after being sent by second class or overseas post to that address

7.3.4 on the date of publication of a newspaper containing the notice

7.3.5 on being handed to the member [(or, in the case of a member organisation, its authorised representative)] personally or, if earlier,

7.3.6 as soon as the member acknowledges actual receipt

7.4 A technical defect in the giving of notice of which the Trustees are unaware at the time does not invalidate decisions taken at a meeting

8. DISSOLUTION

The provisions of the Memorandum relating to dissolution of the Charity take effect as though repeated here

9. INTERPRETATION

In the Memorandum and in the Articles:

9.1 ['beneficiaries' means ______________________________

____

____

____

______________________________ *[qualifications of beneficiaries]*]

'The Act' means the Companies Act 1985

'AGM' means an annual general meeting of the Charity

['area of benefit' means ______________________________ *[geographical area]*]

'these Articles' means these articles of association

['authorised representative' means an individual who is authorised by a member organisation to act on its behalf at meetings of the Charity and whose name is given to the Secretary]

'Chairman' means the chairman of the Trustees

'the Charity' means the company governed by these Articles

'charity trustee' has the meaning prescribed by section 97(1) of the Charities Act 1993

'clear day' means 24 hours from midnight following the relevant event

'the Commission' means the Charity Commissioners for England and Wales

'EGM' means an extraordinary general meeting of the Charity

'financial expert' means an individual, company or firm who is an authorised person or an exempted person with the meaning of the Financial Services Act 1986

'material benefit' means a benefit which may not be financial but has a monetary value

'member' and 'membership' refer to membership of the Charity

'Memorandum' means the Charity's Memorandum of Association

'month' means calendar month

'the Objects' means the Objects of the Charity as defined in clause 3 of the Memorandum

'Secretary' means the Secretary of the Charity

'taxable trading' means carrying on a trade or business on a continuing basis for the principal purpose of raising funds and not for the purpose of actually carrying out the Objects

'Trustee' means a director of the Charity and 'Trustees' means all of the directors

'written' or 'in writing' refers to a legible document on paper [not] including a fax message

'year' means calendar year

9.2 Expressions defined in the Act have the same meaning

9.3 References to an Act of Parliament are to the Act as amended or re-enacted from time to time and to any subordinate legislation made under it

NAMES & ADDRESSES OF SUBSCRIBERS	SIGNATURES OF SUBSCRIBERS
[List the full name and residential address of each of the subscribers]	*[Signature of each of the subscribers]*

Date ________________ *[Date]*

Witness to the above signatures

____

____

____

________________ ________________

[Name, address and occupation of witness] *[Signature of witness]*

STANDARD FORM OF CONTRACT FOR COMMERCIAL PARTICIPATORS

[To be typed on headed notepaper of charity]

(Subject to contract – to be deleted upon signature)

To:

For the attention of:

Dear Sirs

We set out below the terms agreed by us (the 'Agreement') by which we [*name of charity*], a registered charity, charity number [*charity number*], (the 'Charity') will participate with you (the 'Commercial Participator') in a promotion linking the Commercial Participator's name with a fund-raising scheme for the Charity to be run in connection with [*enter details of the fund-raising event*] to be jointly run by the Charity and the Commercial Participator (the 'Promotion').

1.1 The Promotion will be run from [*day*] [*month*] 1998 to [*day*] [*month*] 1998 (the 'Contract Period') and will invite members of the Charity to attend the Promotion which will be organised and presented by the Commercial Participator who will charge each such member a fee for attending the Promotion (the 'Consideration').

1.2 From the Consideration paid by a member of the Charity to the Commercial Participator, the Commercial Participator will donate to the Charity [*percentage*] of the net profit (which shall mean the total income received from the Promotion less the expenses incurred in organising the Promotion except where the Promotion is provided in conjunction with other charities ([*name of charities*]) then the net profit shall be donated to each of the charities on a pro rata basis in proportion to the number of members who attend the Promotion from each of the charities.

1.3 Within ten calendar days after the end of each calendar month, the Commercial Participator shall provide the Charity with a statement of sums payable to the Charity in respect of that month and shall issue the Charity with a payment in accordance with Regulation 6(2)(a)(i) of (ii) Charities Institutions (Fund-Raising) Regulations 1994.

1.4 The Agreement shall subsist for the Contract Period set out in Clause 1.1 subject to either part serving no less than [*specify*] notice in writing of termination of the Agreement to expire before the end of the Contract Period.

1.5 Full details and the copy of the Promotion, approved by both parties, are attached as Exhibit A.

2.1 Subject to these terms, the Charity agrees that the Commercial Participator shall have the exclusive right during the Contract Period:

(A) to hold out the Promotion and its name in the United Kingdom as having the recognition and support of the Charity; and

(B) to use the Charity's logo (which the Charity owns) as reproduced in Exhibit B and the Charity's name on and in connection with the Promotion on all merchandising, promotional and advertising material which is connected or associated with the Promotion (the 'Promotional Material').

2.2 For the purpose of this Agreement, recognition and support includes any indication that the Commercial Participator is in any way associated with or recognised by or in any other way connected with the Charity.

2.3 The Charity agrees to provide the Commercial Participator with all reasonable co-operation and assistance (but without being obliged to incur any costs) as the Commercial Participator may request, to enable the Commercial Participator to derive maximum benefit from its association with the Charity. Reasonable co-operation and assistance shall include advertising the Promotion in the Charity's newsletters and other internal circulars (where appropriate) and shall include the provision of the name and addresses of the Charity's members.

2.4 The Charity undertakes to the Commercial Participator not to authorise any other person, firm, association, body or company to hold itself out in relation to any similar promotion during the Contract Period as being in any way associated with or having the recognition and support of the Charity.

3. All artwork and copy for the Promotion and Promotional Material must receive prior written consent of the Charity before printing, such consent not to be unreasonably withheld or delayed.

4. In return for the rights granted and derived under the Agreement, the Commercial Participator shall pay the Charity £1 and make a donation in accordance with the terms of Clause 1.2 of the Agreement.

5. The Commercial Participator shall be entitled to retain the balance of any net profit from the Promotion once the donation has been made to the Charity in accordance with the terms of Clause 1.2 of the Agreement.

6. In the course of the Agreement, each party may become aware of aspects of the other's marketing plans and other commercially sensitive or secret information and agrees not to use or disclose this or any of the other's confidential information to any third party without the other's permission. Copyright in all material produced by the Charity shall remain in the Charity. The Commercial Participator shall not use, for its own purposes, nor acquire nor seek to acquire nor represent in any way that it is entitled to any of the Charity's intellectual property rights which shall remain the Charity's property. These obligations shall continue to be in force even after the end of the Contract Period.

7. Any modification of this Agreement shall be effective only if agreed in writing and signed by both parties hereto and the intention to amend the Agreement is clearly expressed.

8. The Commercial Participator shall, on request and all reasonable times, make available to the Charity any books, documents or other records (however kept) which relate to the Charity and which are kept for the purpose of the Agreement.

9. Except as provided by Clause 2.1 of this Agreement, the Commercial Participator shall have no rights in the name of the Charity or the service marks or in the goodwill associated therewith and the Commercial Participator hereby acknowledges that except as expressly provided in the Agreement, it shall not acquire any rights in respect thereof and that all such rights and goodwill are, and shall remain, vested in the Charity.

10. On termination of the Agreement, the Commercial Participator shall either return or destroy any documents with the Charity's logo or name on them.

11. This Agreement is subject to English law and both parties agree to be bound by the non-exclusive jurisdiction of the English Court.

Please sign the attached copy of this letter to indicate your acceptance of the above terms.

Yours sincerely

....
For and on behalf of the Charity
[to be signed by the Honorary Treasurer or, in his or her absence, by another officer of the Committee of the Charity]

....
For and on behalf of the Commercial Participator

STANDARD FORM OF AGREEMENT BETWEEN [CHARITY] AND [FUNDRAISING CONSULTANT]

THIS AGREEMENT is made the day of 19__
BETWEEN [Name of Charity] whose office is at [Address] (hereinafter called 'the Charity') of the one part and [Name of Fundraising Consultant] of [Address] (hereinafter called the Fundraising Consultant) of the other part.

WHEREAS the Charity wishes to raise funds for its charitable purposes [and to launch an Appeal][1]

NOW IT IS HEREBY AGREED AND DECLARED as follows:

1 This Agreement shall commence on the day of 19__ and shall continue for a period of [Duration]. Thereafter, subject to paragraph 2 hereof, this Agreement may be determined by either party giving not less than [ ] months previous notice in writing to the other expiring on any date. Such determination to be without prejudice to any right of action or remedy of either party against the other subsisting at the time of determination.

2 Either party may at any time determine this Agreement by giving the other [ ] months notice in writing and the Charity may, in the event of any breach by the Fundraising Consultant of this Agreement, determine the same without notice.

3 Subject to such special instructions and variations as may be agreed in writing the Fundraising Consultant will provide advice/services in respect of the following.[2]

4 The Fundraising Consultant shall require all donors and prospective donors to draw cheques and other like promissory notes in favour of the Charity.

5 All cash cheques and donations of whatever kind received by the Fundraising Consultant pursuant to this Agreement shall forthwith [as soon as practicable] be handed over to the Charity which shall keep accurate records thereof (such records to be open to inspection by the Fundraising Consultant on reasonable notice).[3]

6 All reasonable subsistence, travelling and other expenses incurred by the Fundraising Consultant in the execution of its obligations under this Agreement (as varied) will be reimbursed in full within [ ] days upon receipt of written submissions by the Fundraising Consultant to the Charity.

7 The Copyright for all purposes in all artwork, copy and any other work capable of being subject to copyright produced or created by the Fundraising Consultant at the specific request of the Charity shall vest in the Charity.

All such artwork copy and other work held by the Fundraising Consultant will be submitted to the Charity within 30 working days of the termination of this Agreement.

8 The Fundraising Consultant will not without the written consent of the Charity during or after the currency of the Agreement disclose any confidential information relating to the Charity which is acquired as a result of the Fundraising Consultant's involvement with the Charity. Provided always that the Fundraising Consultant shall be at liberty to use as it thinks fit any general marketing intelligence obtained in pursuance of this Agreement.[4,5]

9 The Fundraising Consultant agrees to abide by the Code or Codes of Practice issued from time to time by the Institute of Charity Fundraising Managers.[6]

10 Any Notice may be served by either party upon the other by sending it through the post in a pre-paid envelope addressed to such other party at its last known address and any Notice so sent shall be deemed to have been received within [ ] days of posting.[7]

11 In consideration of the provision by the Fundraising Consultant of the said advice/services the Charity will pay to the Fundraising Consultant a fee of [amount/method of calculation/dates of payment].[8]

12 This Agreement shall be governed by and construed in accordance with the Laws of England.

13 If any difference shall arise between the Charity and the Fundraising Consultant touching the meaning of this Agreement or any of the rights and liabilities hereunder the same shall be referred to a single person appointed in default of Agreement between the parties and on the application of either party by the President for the time being of the Law Society of England and Wales and the decision of such parties (who shall act as an expert and not as an arbitrator) shall be final and binding on the parties.

AS WITNESS the hands of the parties hereto

[Signatures of both parties (or their authorised representatives)].

NOTES

1 It is important to define clearly the precise boundaries of the proposed Consultant's duties. An indication of some of the possible areas of work is given in Footnote 2. If at the same time the Consultant is to be asked to launch specific Appeals (perhaps working to different departmental heads) then this should be explicitly stated in the Agreement or become the subject of an additional one.

2 Fundraising Consultants are contracted to undertake various different types of advisory and/or actual fundraising activities on behalf of charities and your attention is drawn to clauses 2, 5, 7, 8 and 13 in the accompanying guidelines. A clear indication both of the areas of work to be undertaken and the content and nature of that work should be included within any Agreement. Minimum/maximum staff and time commitments for both Charity and Consultant should be identified, as should the nature of any support services to be offered by the charity both directly (administrative/secretarial) or indirectly (attendance at meetings etc).

The following provides an indication of some areas of activity often required, any such list cannot be exhaustive as individual Agreements will vary according to particular need.

	Possible areas of specific Fundraising Activity		Possible areas of Support and Advice
a	Overall strategy	a	Staff Recruitment
b	Soliciting donations	b	Staff Development
c	Sponsoring and gifts in kind	c	Management Systems
d	Promotional Schemes	d	Development of appropriate literature
e	Deeds of Covenant	e	Tax, legal and commercial management
f	Payroll Giving	f	Budgetary management
g	Corporate Giving	g	Research services
h	Trust Giving		
i	Special Events		
j	Advertising		
k	Lotteries		
l	Promotion of Legacies		
m	Trading		

It is equally important that the lines of responsibility are clearly defined. Who will undertake the work within the Fundraising Consultancy and to whom will they report within the Charity?

3 If it so wishes, a Charity could add a clause introducing a penalty clause regarding the late payment of monies to them. Such a clause might be expressed as a payment of interest on the sum overdue c alculted at X% over base rate.

However, it should be noted that Charities are likely to incur considerable difficulties in recovering any such additional payments at law and any consequent loss of goodwill from the introduction of such a clause must be borne in mind.

4 It is clear that what constitutes 'confidential information' and 'general marketing intelligence' might in some circumstances provide a bone of contention between Client and Consultant.

No definitive guidance can be given as this will depend upon the precise nature of the duties undertaken by the Consultant. In general however, where information is acquired for the client from published or other gleanable sources (eg directories, newspaper clippings or other published material) this might properly be considered 'general marketing intelligence'. Where information is the product of particular comments and commitments given in private meetings on behalf of the Client and specific to that Charity these might be regarded as 'confidential information' to that client.

5 The issue of whether the Charity or the Fundraising Consultant is required to register under the Data Protection Act (1984) is entirely dependent on who is exercising *control* over the *content* and *use* of the personal data.

Control means having the power to decide what information about an individual is to be recorded, whether the information should be added to, amended or deleted, and to what use the information may be put either by the data user or others.

Illustrative examples of relationships similar to charity and fundraising consultant can be found in Guideline 2, section 10, of the series of Guidelines published by The Data Protection Registrar, Springfield House, Water Lane, Wilmslow, Cheshire SK9 5AX.

6 Members of the Institute of Charity Fundraising Managers, including Fundraising Consultants, are committed to the Institute's Code of Conduct and various specific Codes of Practice. Copies of these are available from the ICFM, 208 Market Towers, 1 Nine Elms Lane, London SW8 5NQ.

7 The duration of any contractual relationship will naturally be a matter for negotiation. Clients and Consultants should be wary not to enter into agreements that will tie either party beyond the scope of the consultancy need of the charity.

There is no reason why such an agreement should not include an initial probationary period together with successive renewal clauses limited to specific time spans.

8 It is of great importance that the method and amount of payment is clearly defined in any agreement. Concern has been expressed regarding the various methods of payment that might be employed.

In particular, the payment of consultancy fees on a commission alone basis has been discouraged in successive Charity Commission and public reports due to its association with malpractice in fundraising. There might well be exceptional circumstances where this form of arrangement remains the only option, but where it is entered into it should only be done so under the clearest provision of time and rate of payment and the identification of specific tasks to be undertaken.

For a fuller discussion of the merits/demerits of the various methods of payment you are strongly advised to consult the 1986 'NCVO Malpractice in Fundraising for Charity' Report clauses 5.10–5.24 (obtainable from the NCVO, 26 Bedford Square, London WC1B 3HU).

SPECIMEN COMMUNITY CARE CONTRACT

Grants under care in the community arrangements

Title of Project:	Morton House
Managing Authority:	Morton House (A Company Limited by Guarantee with Charitable Status)
Company Number:	2798323
Charity Number:	942314
Source of Finance:	Health Authority Grant/Income Generation

A. Details of scheme

1. *Summary of Objectives and Benefits*

To rent from the Health Authority premises in 132 Brompton Road for the purpose of providing opportunities for employment, sheltered work and training for people with mental health problems who are resident in the area covered by Glazebrook Health Authority. Through the provision of work, the scheme will perform a rehabilitative function, giving its clients a sense of self-worth and developing everyday living skills. The scheme will provide a service to people with mental health problems living in the community and will initially serve primarily to facilitate the re-settlement of patients currently resident in Stroud Hospital. The scheme will also provide benefits in terms of integration with the community at large.

2. *Details of residential or other places to be provided*

The scheme will provide a variety of non-residential work-based activities on a scale sufficient to meet the needs of that proportion of the 52 adults re-settled from Stroud who have expressed or subsequently express a desire for work activity. In addition, the scheme may provide work-based activities for other people with mental health problems for whom Glazebrook Health Authority has a responsibility if it can be shown that the needs of ex-Stroud clients are being met.

3. *Organisation and management arrangements*

The scheme will be managed by Morton House, a company limited by guarantee with charitable status. The company will employ staff, procure such materials as are necessary and provide day-to-day management and maintenance of the building. The scheme will function as a number of separate specialised elements. Some will form an integral part of Morton House and be accountable to its Management Committee; others will be tenants, having a contractual arrangement with Morton House but managed independently. This approach is designed to incorporate flexibility and a variety of philosophical approaches.

4. *Purpose of the grant*

i) The grant will enable the rental of the building at 132 Brompton Road, (under a separate tenancy agreement) the employment of staff and the deployment of resources to provide employment, sheltered work and training to people with mental health problems, subject to an agreed Operational Policy. Morton House may also generate additional income through commercial activities and securing grants and fees from other bodies.

ii) Use of Health Authority grant for purposes not specified in paragraph 1 will be subject to Glazebrook Health Authority approval.

iii) Morton House will not be in breach of any of the terms of Circular HN(86)11 nor will it cause Glazebrook Health Authority to be in breach of such terms and it will supply all information reasonably requested by Glazebrook Health Authority for the purposes of ensuring that such terms are and continue to be satisfied.

iv) Internal property management will be subject to a separate tenancy agreement.

5. *Start date of scheme*

Full funding for this scheme starts on 1st June 1990.

6. *Mechanism for service monitoring*

Morton House will make available to the Health Authority such information as is required to monitor the progress of the scheme. The criteria against which the scheme will be evaluated will be based on the agreed Operational Policy. Annual audited accounts will be made available by Morton House as the basis for monitoring of financial performance.

7. *Proposed review date*

The scheme will be formally reviewed after 6 months and future funding determined by the outcome.

B. Grant funding requirements

1. CAPITAL	TOTAL	YEAR 1 1987/88 (£)	YEAR 2 1988/89 (£)	YEAR 3 1989/90 (£)
Total cost	0	0	0	0
Funded by Glazebrook H.A.	0	0	0	0
Funded by Morton House	0	0	0	0
Other	0	0	0	0
Costs as at 1st April 1990				

2. REVENUE	YEAR 1 1990/91 (£)	YEAR 2 1991/92 (£)	YEAR 3 1992/93 (£)
Revenue		198,071	
Income		0	
Net total		198,071	
Funded by Glazebrook H.A.		198,071	
Funded by Morton House		0	
Other		0	
Costs as at 1990/91 prices			

3. *Funding arrangements for future years*

Grant payments will be made to the Health Authority on a quarterly basis on receipt of a written request from Morton House. Annual Uplift for inflation will be linked to prices inflation rates prescribed by NE Thames Regional Health Authority.

Any other changes will be negotiated in the context of the operational policy and annual review outcomes. Future income levels will be taken into account, and are likely to result in a reduction of the Health Authority grant.

C. Conditions of grants

General conditions

1. The attached memorandum of agreement is to be completed for each scheme under the terms of Circular HN(86)11 in relation to payments for the purpose of enabling people in hospital to be discharged and supplied with accommodation and for services provided by local authorities or other bodies to whom payments may be made.

2. A revised memorandum should be completed to record variations in the agreed conditions.

3. No scheme can proceed without completion of a memorandum of agreement.

4. The health authority making a payment shall be responsible for ensuring as far as practicable the efficient and effective use of the financial resources involved.

5. The health authority must be satisfied that the purpose for which the payment is to be made relates to the movement of people at present in hospital into accommodation of care provided by local authorities or other bodies.

6. Payments to meet the full revenue cost or part of the revenue cost of a project made from the health authority's main allocation of funds may be made until such time as alternative arrangements are made by central government for financing the revenue costs of such projects.

7. If the services provided by the body receiving the payment in respect of the project are reduced, the payment shall be reduced accordingly.

8(1). Where any payment is made towards the cost of acquiring land or other property or of executing works for the purposes of any functions specified in section 28A(2) then if the body receiving the payment either:

(a) disposes of, or

(b) uses for purposes other then the functions specified in section 28A(2),

the whole or any part of the land or other property so acquired or in respect of which works were executed such body shall repay to the health authority an amount equal to that portion of the open market value of such land or other property (or part thereof as the case may be) as is attributable to the expenditure of the payment.

8(2). For the purposes of paragraph (1) the open market value shall be assessed by the District Valuer and the apportionment of the part of such value attributable to the expenditure of the payment shall be made by the District Treasurer. Such value shall be assessed and such apportionment shall be made at the date at which disposal is completed or alternative use commences as the case may be. Disposal shall include a disposal by way of sale, assignment, the creation of any lease or tenancy, surrender or merger.

9. Paragraph 8 shall not apply when a payment is made towards the cost of acquiring premises for the purpose of rental and a tenant subsequently exercises a right to buy the premises.

10. The local authority or voluntary organisation (for expenditure totalling more than £10,000 in any one year) or other body shall submit an annual voucher, in the form specified by the Secretary of State for Social Services, to the health authority stating expenditure incurred in accordance wih the memorandum of agreement.

Specific conditions

1. Glazebrook Health Authority will provide at least 6 months notice of any reduction in the value of the annual grant except:
   a) if Morton House is in breach of the terms of the Memorandum of Agreement;
   b) insofar as Morton House may be expected to carry a proportionate share of any overall reductions in Glazebrook Health Authority's expenditure on mental health services.
2. Morton House will consult Glazebrook Health Authority before:
   a) putting forward proposals to amend its Memorandum and Articles of Association;
   b) altering the number of nominees to its Management Committee from other bodies as specified in paragraph 24 of the Articles of Association.
3. The Morton House Management Committee shall appoint from among its members an Honorary Treasurer who, on behalf of the Committee, shall ensure that proper accounts are kept and that there are appropriate arrangements for controlling expenditure. Apportionment of the part of such value attributable to the expenditure of the payment shall be made by the District Treasurer. Such value shall be assessed and such apportionment shall be made at the date at which disposal is completed or alternative use commences as the case may be. Disposal shall include a disposal by way of sale, assignment, the creation of any lease or tenancy, surrender or merger.

Appendix 3

BIBLIOGRAPHY

'A Legal Health Check', *Top 1,000 Charities Guide 1996* (Barings Asset Management)

An Illustrated History of the Royal Free Hospital L A Amidon (The Special Trustees of the Royal Free Hospital, 1996)

Aneurin Bevan Vol 2, M Foot (Davis-Poynter, 1973)

Barings Asset Management – Top 3,000 Charities 1997, The Guide to UK Charities (CaritasData, 1997)

Barings Asset Management – Top 3,000 Charities 1998, The Guide to UK Charities (CaritasData, 1998)

'Breaking the Deadlock at Bhopal', *Legal Business* 49, November 1994

CC8 *Internal Financial Controls for Charities* (Charity Commission, 1996)

CC19 *Charities' Reserves* (Charity Commission, 1997)

CC35 *Charities and Trading* (Charity Commission, 1997)

CC49 *Charities and Insurance* (Charity Commission, 1996)

CS2 *Trading by Charities* (Inland Revenue, 1995)

Charities, Trusts and Social Welfare M Chesterman (Weidenfeld & Nicholson, 1979)

Charities: Law and Practice 2nd edn, E Cairns (Sweet & Maxwell, 1997)

'Charity and the NHS – use or abuse', *Private Client Business*, Vol 5, A Paines (Sweet & Maxwell, 1994)

Charity Commission Report 7, 1994

Charity Law A to Z: Key Questions Answered J Claricoat and H Phillips (Jordans, 1995)

Charity Trends, 11th edn (Charities Aid Foundation, 1988)

Community Care and the Law L Clements (LAG, 1996)

Community Care for Older People: Rights, Remedies and Finance M Richards (Jordans, 1996)

Decisions of the Charity Commissioners Vol 3, April (HMSO, 1994)

Drug Injuries and the Pursuit of Compensation P R Ferguson (Sweet & Maxwell, 1996)

Efficiency Scrutiny of the Supervision of Charities (HMSO, 1988) under the Chairmanship of Sir Philip Woodfield

English Philanthropy 1660–1960 D Owen (Oxford University Press, 1965)

'From Vision to System: The Maturing of the Hospice Movement', *Death Rites – Law and Ethics at the End of Life* R Lee and D Morgan (eds) (Routledge, 1994)

Health Services in London – A Strategic Review (The Stationery Office, 1998)

History of the Law of Charity 1532–1827 G Jones (Cambridge University Press, 1969)

'Hospital Endowments – Casualties of Tomlinson?', *NGO Finance Magazine*, 12 February 1993, B Sage

Medical Law Texts with Materials I Kennedy and A Grubb (Butterworths, 1994)

Hanbury and Martin: Modern Equity, J E Martin (Sweet & Maxwell, 1997)

NHS Charitable Funds: A Guide (Charity Commission, November 1994)

Philanthropy and the Hospitals of London: The Kings Fund 1897–1990 F K Prochaska (Clarendon Press, 1992)

Public, Private or Community – What Next for the NHS? C Ham (Demos, 1996)

Statistics of Middle Class Expenditure (British Library of Political and Economic Science) Pamphlet HD6/D267

'Thalidomide Victims Given "£3.75m Bail Out"' *The Independent* 4 May 1995

'The AIDS Scandal', *Economic Affairs*, Vol 11, No 4 (Institute of Economic Affairs, June 1991)

The Corrosion of Charity R Whelan (Institute of Economic Affairs, 1996)

The Gift of Health M Lattimer (Directory of Social Change, 1996)

The Independent, 27 May 1996

The Independent, 6 March 1997

The Independent, 11 May 1998

The Law and Practice Relating to Charities 2nd edn, H Picara (Butterworths, 1995)

The Modern Rise of Population and the Role of Medicine: Dream, Mirage or Nemesis? (Nuffield Provincial Hospital Trust, 1976)

The New NHS. Modern. Dependable (The Stationery Office, 1997)

The Times, 23 August 1997

Tolley's Value Added Tax, 1997–98 R Wareham and A Dolton

'Trusting to a Corporate Solution', *NGO Finance Magazine*, Vol 6, Issue 5, October/ November 1996, R Meakin and J Ward

'Unto the Breach – Doing Battle over Trustee Liability', *NGO Finance Magazine*, Vol 7, Issue 1, January/February 1997, J Claricoat and H Phillips

'VAT News', *The Tax Journal* 22 December 1997

Who Should We Treat? Law, Patients and the NHS C Newdick (Clarendon Press, 1995)

Working For Patients (HMSO, 1989)

INDEX

References are to paragraph numbers.